9401

Unsubmissive
Women

UNSUBMISSIVE WOMEN

Chinese Prostitutes
in Nineteenth-Century
San Francisco

by Benson Tong

University of Oklahoma Press : Norman and London

For those who made this possible:
my parents, Ai Ling and Yin Fah,
John and Irving,
and Gerald Thompson

Published with the assistance of
the National Endowment for the Humanities,
a federal agency which supports the study of such fields as
history, philosophy, literature, and language.

Tong, Benson, 1964–
    Unsubmissive women : Chinese prostitutes in nineteenth-century
San Francisco / by Benson Tong.
        p.   cm.
    Includes bibliographical references and index.
    ISBN 0-8061-2653-1 (alk. paper)
    1. Prostitutes—California—San Francisco—History—19th century.
2. Chinese—California—San   Francisco—History—19th   century.
I. Title.
HQ146.S4T66   1994
306.74′2′0979461—dc20   94-16168
                                                                        CIP

Text design by Cathy Carney Imboden.

The paper in this book meets
the guidelines for permanence and durability
of the Committee on Production Guidelines
for Book Longevity of the
Council on Library Resources, Inc. ∞

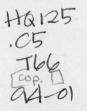

Intro
– Conditions in china
– Slave Trafficking
– Chinese Exclusion Act
Page Law
Arrival in America
Life in Chinatown
Violence
Conclusion

Contents

CONTENTS

Illustrations

ILLUSTRATIONS

Tables

Preface

The possibility of writing a book-length work on Chinese prostitutes in the western United States first crossed my mind in September 1989 after reading Lucie Cheng Hirata's "Free, Indentured, Enslaved: Chinese Prostitutes in Nineteenth-Century America" (1979). Hirata's well-researched article concentrates on the impact of Chinese prostitution on the economy and how different groups profited from hawking the sole commodity members of the demimonde possessed. This work, however, concentrates on the women themselves and deliberately avoids duplicating Hirata's approach. Furthermore, the focus here is on the years between 1849 and 1882, the first phase of the trafficking and vice trade. Following the passage of the Chinese Exclusion Act of 1882, the nature of the business and its modus operandi became more complex, and a second book would be required to adequately discuss those changes.

Like Hirata and most students of marginal groups, I faced the dilemma of writing a book on a group of women who had left few writings of their own. To compensate for the paucity of primary material, I relied on government publications, census schedules, newspapers, and records of missionary organizations to uncover the details of their existence. It should be noted that I have also used a few oral and written accounts of and by prostitutes who worked in the post-1882 years. That has allowed me to make some tentative comparisons of those prostitutes with their sisters who lived through the first phase of the trade.

The cross-country search for materials would have been impossible without the indispensable support of these friends: Joseph Mooney (*San Francisco Chronicle*), Robert Glenn Hughes (formerly Head Librarian of the Law Library, Lincoln University, San Francisco), Peter E. Hanff (Coordinator, Technical Services, the Bancroft Library, University of California, Berkeley), Irving Dawson (Professor of Political Science, University of Texas, Arlington), Dr. Dennis Tihansky (Flower Memorial Hospital, Fremont, Ohio), Gregory H. Brown (Librarian, Toledo-Lucas County Library), and Alvan Uhle of Ann Arbor, Michigan. Joe, Glenn, Irving, and Dennis hosted my visits to their cities; Peter and Greg secured obscure materials and provided much professional advice. All of them put up with the endless stories of research challenges and complaints of financial woes. I also appreciate the assistance rendered by Stan Carroll, librarian at the San Francisco History Room, San Francisco Public Library, who patiently searched the storage facility for materials that had been misplaced as a result of the 1989 earthquake. These many helping hands allowed for the canvassing of more materials than would have been possible for a researcher working alone. To all of them, I extend my heartfelt gratitude.

In Toledo, William J. Bigelow, Leslie Heaphy, Mary Keune, and Gerald Pierson offered the critical encouragement required to attempt this adventurous effort. Certain faculty members at the University of Toledo—Gerald Thompson, Charles N. Glaab, and William D. Hoover—deserve special mention for their scholarly guidance. Professors Glaab and Hoover made extensive comments on the original drafts and saved me from making glaring errors. In particular, I am indebted to my teacher, Professor Thompson, who painstakingly critiqued and edited an earlier version of the manuscript. He generously shared with me his skills and his experience as editor of The Historian. In a period of less than four months, I learned from him the meaning of academic discipline and, though slower, the complexity of simple writing.

Finally, many thanks to the staffs of the Bancroft Library; Asian-American Library; San Francisco Public Library; San Francisco Law Library at the City Hall; Society of California Pioneers; Wells Fargo Bank History Room; Hoover Institution Archives; Bridwell Library; Roberts Library; Library of Congress; National Archives; Presbyterian Historical Society; Rutherford B. Hayes Presidential Center; Bentley Library; and Carlson Library at the University of Toledo.

Introduction

I n the second half of the nineteenth-century,
America witnessed the arrival from China of
nearly 300,000 male sojourners, or *gum saan
haak* (Cantonese for travelers to Gold Mountain).*
This movement of people across the Pacific Ocean
constituted one of the many Chinese exoduses during that period to Southeast Asia, Latin America,
North America, the West Indies, and Africa — a mas-

*Most Chinese names appear in the Cantonese dialect, rather than the
Peking (Mandarin) dialect, because most emigrants originated from a
predominantly Cantonese-speaking region and thus were more familiar with those names. For names that do not have a Cantonese equivalent, transliteration follows the Wade-Giles system designed to achieve
Mandarin pronunciation.

sive migration of ten to thirteen million persons.[1] In the early years, those heading for the United States came in search of the supposed riches of *Gum Saan* (Cantonese for Gold Mountain, i.e., California). Quite a number, according to a local newspaper of the 1850s, were "enticed further by the golden romance which has filled the world."[2]

Bound by traditional customs not to plant their roots in the "devils'" country, many Chinese men left their wives and children in the villages of China. Though "separated by many mountains and vast seas" — to use a verse from an emigrant folk rhyme — these men were required to return to their homeland to fulfill filial obligations and maintain family ties. After all, Confucius once said, "While father and mother are alive, a good son does not wander far afield."[3]

While the men ranged across the American continent thousands of miles away from home, their wives stayed behind to maintain familial relationships. Chinese customs and family traditions dictated a woman's responsibility to her in-laws. As a daughter-in-law, a woman had to serve her husband's parents. Perhaps more important, in the event of the death of the elders, she was to act as her husband's substitute and perform the necessary burial and mourning rites.[4] In short, the long-term sojourning of the male members resulted in disjointed households.

Restrictive federal immigration laws further solidified the phenomenon of split-household families among the Chinese population in the United States. Women who aspired to join their husbands had to contend with the wall of legislation that blocked their entry.[5] Many failed to meet the stringent requirements of the immigration authorities.

Also, given the less than civil treatment and the lack of legal protection many sojourners had to endure, Chinese families had little inclination to leave familiar surroundings for distant, "barbarian" lands. In an 1852 letter to the governor of California, Chinese community leaders explained that "if the privileges of your laws are open . . . a better class will come . . . [and bring] their families with them."[6]

Equally prohibitive was the expense of maintaining a family in America. An early immigrant spoke of the predicament faced by many fellow countrymen: "You had to be either a merchant or a big gambler, have a lot of side money, to have a family here. A working man, an ordinary man, just can't."[7] Family development in Chinese America almost completely disappeared. Many men returned to China to marry and maintain the lineage. Typical of this was the story of one extended family in which the female members of three consecutive generations never stepped foot on the shores of America. Although the children came to America later, all were raised in China.[8]

Denied conjugal ties, many Chinese males idled away their leisure time and led the lives of homeless men. "Life didn't mean too much to us," one sojourner recalled bitterly.[9] Bereft of family life and female companionship, the men sought intimacy from prostitutes.

Most of the women who served these men were Chinese indentured workers. Their contemporaries stereotyped them as hapless victims of male exploitation. Viewed as passive victims thrown unwillingly into the subculture of an ethnic vice trade, all Chinese prostitutes were assumed to be unable to overcome the social and economic inertia attached to prostitution. Privation, followed by suicide or other untimely death, was seen as their lot.

The above images were derived from general nineteenth-century perceptions of Chinese women: "heathen," "enslaved," "passive." According to the lore, the typical Chinese woman was completely at the mercy of social forces beyond her control. In the minds of Euro-Americans of the Victorian period, the champions of middle-class respectability, Chinese women deserved pity and sympathy but not respect. These "public women"—women who were willing to associate with all men, not just one— occupied the lowest rung in the social hierarchy, both within the Chinese community and without. Valued in only financial terms, they were thought to have little control over their lives, make no decisions, and exist under the rule of their masters. Such notions, however, have dehumanized them. The stereotype that emerged has obscured their real lives and characters. In reality, they were actors in the chaotic world of prostitution.

Throughout the years from 1849 to 1882, a period that ended with the Chinese Exclusion Act, a number of segments in San Francisco society played an important part in shaping the lives of Chinese prostitutes. Chinese criminal organizations, better known as "fighting tongs," the federal, state, and local governments, and, to a lesser extent, San Franciscans of all ethnic origins proscribed Chinese prostitutes' daily routine and pushed them to the fringe of society.

Yet a significant number of these ethnic women refused to succumb to the socioeconomic forces that threatened to overwhelm them. They retained a grip on the choices available to them and attempted to remedy the misfortune of having been forced into prostitution. Though many failed to resist the pressures exerted on them by society, they retained the will to survive. Some even adapted to their new environment; others made use of available resources to change their lives for the better. A number of them eventually left the trade for the comforts and security of family life.

This book explores the lives of Chinese prostitutes in San Francisco as a case study of women who not only survived subjugation but also, in many cases, summoned the strength to change their fate. In many ways, this is a portrayal of the "powers of the weak"—the interaction of women's oppression and women's power.[10] The Chinese women pressed into commercialized sex in this cosmopolitan city of the American West were hardly passive victims of their fate. Rather, under circumscribed conditions, they opposed their oppression and, if the opportunity arose, left the sexual commerce for better fortunes.

Unsubmissive
Women

Chinese Prostitutes in the West, 1849–1882

As early as 1851, residents of San Francisco recognized a drastic imbalance of the sexes in the Chinese population arriving in California. San Francisco's *Daily Evening Picayune* of June 4, 1851, commented that "a great part of the Chinese immigration will become a permanent American population . . . if they would introduce a few more of their countrywomen."[1] A journalist of a popular periodical attributed the fact that many left their wives and children behind to the "social habits and national feelings" of the Chinese.[2] An examination of the 1852 California state census reveals only 19 Chinese females residing in the city as compared to 2,954 Chinese males, a ratio of 1:155. The sex

4

ratio for the non-Chinese population of San Francisco came closer to parity but still numbered only one female for every three males.[3] This general lack of familial patterns among early city dwellers reflected the frontier nature of the community.

In San Francisco, as in many thriving communities of the American West, such conditions set the stage for the growth of various recreational activities, including opium smoking, gambling, and prostitution.[4] Establishments offering such activities mushroomed everywhere in this urban center and quickly drew criticism from eastern writers. One author, E. S. Capron, condemned the "licentiousness" of this city and swore there was an "excess of immorality," that it "far exceed[ed] that to be found in other cities."[5] One female visitor from the eastern seaboard blamed the corruption of "naturally pure" Americans on foreigners, who, she said, seem to be "less stringent with regard to morality."[6]

Those who came under the scrutiny of the eastern establishment and educated pioneers included Chinese prostitutes newly transplanted to the disorderly houses of northern California. Large numbers of Chinese female prostitutes, better known to the Chinese in San Francisco as *baak haak chai* (one hundred men's wife), arrived in California in the period between 1850 and 1880.[7] European Americans in the Far West soon labeled them "bawd, broad, celestial females."[8]

For the first few years of the 1850s, the arrival of Chinese female prostitutes accompanied that of European and Anglo-American *filles de joie*. The latter, and a few of the former, were primarily entrepreneurs or aspiring entrepreneurs who flocked to San Francisco to take advantage of the dramatic demand for their services. The temporary and migratory nature of the population, a critical shortage of women for companionship, and the lack of conjugal life stood out as the main features of this male-dominated society.[9] Men "sang, danced, drank, and caroused all night," recalled one woman, "to drown the homesicknesses so often gnawing at their hearts."[10]

The prevailing cultural dictum on sexuality decreed that "true" women were "passionless." If respectable women did not enjoy sex, then the converse must be true about "bad" women or prostitutes. Ironically, prostitution flourished as a result of a cultural mindset that strongly condemned all improprieties.

As a consequence, opportunities existed for prostitutes to move both upward in the profession and outward into the wider society. Women were so scarce in the early days that when they "appeared in [the] streets, they were treated with the greatest respect and gallantry," according to one pioneer.[11] All women in frontier San Francisco enjoyed marked deference, and few male San Franciscans made a sharp distinction between "true women" and "bawdy denizens." A few self-righteous eastern matrons did not welcome into friendly association women who had undermined family values, which lay at the foundation of morality and civilization.[12] Since Victorian values of civility and mannerliness occupied a marginal position in the everyday life of most San Franciscans during the pioneer era, prostitutes encountered little overt prejudice or social disapproval, whether they were Anglo-Americans, Europeans, Mexicans, or Chinese. Some even managed to carve out a niche for themselves among the city's social elite.[13]

A few of the small number of Chinese female prostitutes in the early 1850s quickly learned to cope with their new environment. At least one prostitute, known only as Ah Toy, achieved a degree of success in business that rivaled the well-known vice enterprises of "Great Western" Sarah Bowman and Doña "La Tules" Gertrudis Barcelo. Bowman played many roles during her lifetime. She excelled as innkeeper, battlefield heroine, and camp follower of the American army during the Mexican War of 1846–48 but most of all, as procurer of prostitutes for soldiers and civilians. From the mid-1840s to the late 1860s, she enchanted many frontiersmen, who dubbed her "the greatest whore in the west."[14]

Less is known of Doña Gertrudis Barcelo. In the 1830s and 1840s, this Mexican woman ran a notorious gambling saloon in the trading town of Santa Fe. Later in her life, she invested in the Santa Fe trade, purchasing goods from the United States to the tune of $10,000. Then a nine-room house on 160 acres of land caught her fancy, and she promptly bought it. An astute woman, Barcelo wielded her charm and friendly disposition to influence the affairs of Santa Fe society. Her reputed intimate relationship with the Mexican governor, Manuel Armijo, allowed her to escape the many police raidings of gambling establishments.[15]

Just like Bowman and Barcelo, Ah Toy, who later prospered as a madam, succeeded by adapting to the changing conditions of her environment. Possibly the first Chinese prostitute in America, or "Flowery Flag Nation," she arrived in *Dai Fow* (San Francisco, or Big City) in late 1848 or early 1849. Unlike most Chinese prostitutes, she single-handedly operated establishments of commercialized vice and rebuffed attempts by male-dominated organizations such as the tongs to control her business or to extort "protection" money from her. Stories of her tenacity and determination to protect her interests appeared often in local newspapers, which sensationalized her repeated conflicts with Chinese tongs.[16]

Of course, Ah Toy did not fit the ideals of "true womanhood," as defined by Euro-Americans of the Victorian Era. Americans considered her neither pure nor pious nor domesticated. Nonetheless, as suggested by the historian Mary Murphy, not all madams and prostitutes diverged markedly from the nineteenth-century ideology of womanliness.[17] Like her domesticated counterparts, Ah Toy turned her sex to her advantage. For example, whenever she appeared in court either to protect her interests or to answer charges levied against her, she was suitably attired for specific cases in an attempt to draw attention and capture sympathy. On one occasion, she deliberately appeared in court with her hair disheveled, dress torn, and both eyes blackened to prove she had been attacked by a Caucasian man.[18]

Like many prostitutes of that era, she was a much romanticized and admired figure. A French visitor described her as that "strangely alluring" lady; a reporter for the *Alta California* spoke eloquently of her beauty, described her as "charming," and hinted that she provoked much admiration among her patrons. But beneath the romantic image drawn by a number of authors was the complicated life of a struggling working woman, a resident of a city undergoing chaotic growth.[19]

Ah Toy began her career as an independent prostitute operating from her humble residence, a small shanty on an alley off Clay Street, just above Kearny. In 1850, she expanded her business, employing two recently arrived Chinese prostitutes.[20] The

state census schedules for 1852 list Ah Toy together
with two other women, "Aloy" and "Asea," presumably her co-workers. At the beginning of 1851, San
Francisco had probably five or six independent Chinese prostitutes, but later in the year, authorities
deported two of them, which reduced the number of
Ah Toy's competitors. Within two or three years she
had garnered sufficient financial resources to move
to better quarters. The editor of a city directory for
1852 listed Ah Toy as the proprietor of not one but
two "boardinghouses" (frequently a euphemism for
brothels), one at No. 34 Pike Street and another
nearby, at No. 56 Pike Street.[21]

Her neighborhood, a densely populated middle-
class residential area already in flux, featured home-
owners, some of whom were skilled workers, government servants, and professionals. Within the next ten
years, many moved west as suburbanization intensified. Replacing the residential area would be a vice
zone concentrated along Dupont (present-day Grant
Avenue) and the cross streets between Dupont and
Stockton. The movement of Ah Toy's establishments represented part of the early stage of residential reconfiguration and specialization of land use,
particularly the segregation of businesses into clearly
defined zones, a pattern long practiced in American
cities.[22]

After moving into her houses, Ah Toy maintained control over her business operations for the
next two years despite the increasing involvement
of Chinese tongs in the trade. She even procured
prostitutes for other Chinese brothels, which caused
an outcry from some segments of the Euro-American
population. A local literary figure, Frank Soulé,
once wrote that "everybody knew that famous or

infamous character, who was alternately the laughing-stock and the plague of the place." Soulé also blamed Ah Toy for the immigration of several hundred Chinese prostitutes in 1852: "Her advices home seem to have encouraged the sex to visit so delightful a spot as San Francisco."[23]

It is not known how large a fortune she amassed from her entrepreneurship, although the *Alta California* once reported that a customer robbed her of a diamond "breastpin" (brooch) worth $300. There were reports that she was involved in running brothels in Sacramento and Stockton.[24] Certainly, she did not lack customers in a city where the sex ratio of both the Chinese and Euro-Americans was significantly skewed. Not until 1870 would the gap between the sexes begin to narrow for groups of European descent while that of the Chinese did not even out until the postwar years, following the 1943 repeal of the 1882 Chinese Exclusion Act.[25]

A. W. Loomis, a Presbyterian minister, claimed that in the early years of San Francisco, Chinese prostitutes served both Chinese and Euro-Americans. To some extent, Ah Toy profited from these conditions. One former judge and member of the state legislature, Elisha O. Crosby, wrote in his journal that Ah Toy "was quite select in her associates, was liberally patronized by the white men, and made a great amount of money."[26]

After 1854, the nature of the Chinese vice enterprise began to change. Increasingly, the trade gravitated into the hands of fighting tongs. The first such organization in San Francisco, the Kwang Tek Tong, emerged around 1852; two years later, the Hip Yee Tong made its appearance. Throughout the nineteenth century, there numbered probably no more than eight fighting tongs. Essentially, these structured, exclusive socioeconomic organizations struggled for political and economic power within the Chinese community.[27] Eventually, they monopolized commercialized vice establishments — gambling saloons, opium dens, and brothels.

Tongs should be differentiated from *hui-kuan*, benevolent clan and district associations somewhat akin to the German *Landsmannschaft*. A hui-kuan united people from the same region or district(s) and provided charitable and social services for compatriots. In theory, fighting tongs had scant affiliation with the politically oriented Chee Kung Tong or its Triad branches, organizations originally formed to spearhead an underground antigovernment movement in southern China. However, some tong members had been known to maintain concurrent membership in both hui-kuan and Triad lodges.[28]

In mid-1851, following a complaint made by two Chinese men, the first Committee of Vigilance (a group of San Franciscans who used extralegal action to combat the extreme general lawlessness of that year) deported two prostitutes, Ah Lo and Ah Hone. Since one of the two men who lodged the complaint, Yuen Sheng (better known as Norman As-sing), happened to be the organizer of a hui-kuan and leader of a protection ring, this deportation implied a possible conflict between free prostitutes and tongs.[29]

Tongs began importing women for prostitution sometime in late 1853 or early 1854. Statistics gathered from customshouse records by the historian Mary Coolidge show no arrivals of Chinese females in 1852 or 1853. But since the city government of San Francisco had closed a number of Chinese "houses of ill-fame" during the first quarter of 1854, immigration of Chinese prostitutes in large numbers in late 1853 might have taken place. Further, customs ledgers recorded 673 Chinese female arrivals in 1854. On April 20 of that year, the *Alta California* announced that a large number of Chinese women, probably prostitutes, had disembarked at the port a few days earlier. The newspaper also divulged that twenty to thirty of the women had moved into those brothels recently closed by city authorities.[30]

The arrival of new prostitutes controlled by male-dominated groups meant the beginning of the end of the period of laissez-faire, and it became increasingly rare for Chinese prostitutes to operate as free entrepreneurs. As early as 1851, Ah Toy's monopoly of the trade faced a challenge mounted by Yuen Sheng, the tong leader. Yuen Sheng struggled with Ah Toy for hegemony over Chinese prostitutes. The June 4, 1851, editorial of the *Daily Evening Picayune* gave some hints of the contest between Ah Toy and her competitors; her rivals "looked down upon and despised" her, while the rest of the Chinese community considered her "a sort of outsider."[31]

Accounts gleaned from local newspapers provide a composite picture of a working woman attempting, through the use of the American legal system, to protect her business from falling under male control. Ah Toy also had much compassion for her Asian "sisters of misery" working on Dupont Street. For example, in 1852, she appeared in court to defend a Chinese prostitute accused of attacking a countryman who had refused to pay for services rendered.[32]

In the years following the arrival of the first large consignment of trafficked women, Ah Toy proved unable to resist the encroachment of tongs into the business, or the measures taken by the police for social control. For her, the latter involved being charged with "disorderly conduct," a misdemeanor offense, and paying fines of up to $20 for each arrest and conviction. The frequent payments and mental and physical harassment, compounded by competition from tongs, eventually led to the breakup of her business. Sometime in 1857, she sold her house, packed her belongings, and sailed for China. But early in 1859, she returned to California. On March 20, 1859, the popular *California Police Gazette* pointed out that Ah Toy could not pay a $20 fine and was consequently remanded to the county prison, an indication of her diminished resources. In July, police arrested her for beating one of her coworkers; she was arrested again in September for running a brothel.[33] By the early years of the 1860s, Ah Toy no longer played a significant role in San Francisco prostitution. An organized trade led by tongs became the hallmark of Chinese prostitution after 1860 and would constitute the main feature that distinguished this Chinese vice from that of the Euro-Americans.

In the early 1850s, Chinese prostitutes showed up not only in San Francisco but also in other parts of California. Later, they moved into the hinterlands of the Far West, accompanying the eastward movement of Chinese men, albeit in much smaller numbers.

Chinese men maintained a ubiquitous presence in the American West during the major gold rushes of the latter half of the century. The influx of Chinese miners into a mineral district, according to Randall E. Rohe, often coincided with the exhaus-

tion of the rich surface placers but did not neces-
sarily correspond with a district's complete decline.
These workers moved from "mining locality to mining locality, fleeing from the kicks of one to the cuffs
of the other." The migratory nature of the Chinese
was well known; one long-time resident of Auburn,
Oregon, explained that "when the Chinese miners
had gleaned the last meager cleanup of dust from the
gulches, the story of Auburn was ended."[34]

A mining camp or town offered little to those
accustomed to the trappings of gentility. Edward
Gould Buffum, a disillusioned miner, advised readers who "are in good positions at home to remain
there." The primitive conditions notwithstanding,
Chinese miners did not abandon civilization. "The
Chinese camp was wonderfully clean," said J. D.
Borthwick, a white visitor. He noted "a great many
of them at their toilet, getting their head shaved, or
plaiting . . . pigtails, but most of them were at din-
ner."[35] Yet these sojourners missed family life. The
lonely Chinese man, who "forms no domestic ties,
and enjoys no social standing," resorted to prostitutes for companionship and sexual outlet.[36]

One western song probably explains best the
appearance of prostitutes in gold rush districts:
"The miners came in forty-nine / the whores in
fifty-one / and when they got together / they made a
native son."[37] Some non-Chinese prostitutes made
money, too, as evidenced by this poem: "Oh, the lust
for mountain gold dust / brought us lusty mountain
men; / who, through lust for mountain women /
quickly lost their gold again."[38] However, Chinese
public women, working under duress, saw little of
their earnings; most of it fell into the hands of
brothel owners and procurers. These business peo-

ple brought many of them to far-flung parts of the American West, to wherever the Chinese maintained a community, even if ephemeral.

One of the earliest dispersals of Chinese members of the demimonde occurred in 1852 when eighteen Chinese women arrived in Weaverville (a mining town in Trinity County) after sailing up the Sacramento River. Passenger lists for 1852 show fourteen Chinese females arriving at San Francisco during that year. At least some of these must have been part of the group of eighteen that went to Weaverville.[39]

Up until the late 1860s, most prostitutes operated in mining camps and boomtowns rather than in large cities because the transient male population of California emerged in those scattered spearheads of the frontier. Most Chinese male sojourners maintained split-household families; their wives and children remained in China while they struggled to survive in the increasingly rigid economic structure of the American West.[40] Chinese prostitutes followed their countrymen to the inhospitable subregions east of the Pacific Coast to offer social relations and intimacy to men who, in the search for conjugal ties, could not or would not cross racial lines.

The pattern of dispersal of Chinese women paralleled that of African-American prostitutes. During the nineteenth century, African Americans made up an insignificant proportion of the women who offered sexual services west of the Mississippi. Yet these few often set up their businesses in communities with a sizable population of black cowhands or black soldiers.[41] Racial separation caused both Chinese and African-American purveyors of sexual services to follow minority males to far-flung frontier settlements.

Chinese prostitutes on the California mining frontier represented 3 to 5 percent of the Chinese population in each of those settlements from the 1850s to the 1870s, slightly less than 1 percent of the total population. In a study of the federal census schedules for six selected California mining counties in 1860, David Dufault counted 360 Chinese prostitutes and 13,455 Chinese males. But by 1870, with the end of placer mining in California, the number of Chinese prostitutes had declined to approximately 232, and the number of Chinese males also dropped, to 8,585. A separate, statewide study shows that in 1870 the number of prostitutes stood at 2,157, which constituted 61 percent of Chinese women and 4.4 percent of the total Chinese population in the state.[42]

It seems that the demography of women paralleled that of men, with both being affected by the changing economic conditions of their region. Prostitutes, like miners and male providers of personal services, mirrored the fluctuations of the mining industry. Following the decline of the industry in the late 1860s and the completion of the Central Pacific Railroad in 1869, large numbers of Chinese males moved to cities such as San Francisco in search of employment. The female population of the Chinese entertainment world paralleled this shift in the demographic pattern; more prostitutes lived in San Francisco in 1870 than ten years earlier.

Chinese prostitutes in California commonly shared one trait — their youth. David Beesley found that the average age of Chinese prostitutes in Nevada County, California, in 1860 was twenty-four. In his study of six mining counties in California, Du-fault showed twenty-seven as the average age of Chinese females, including prostitutes.[43]

One young independent prostitute, Ling Loi, made enough money from the male population of Bodie, a trans-Sierra mining camp near the Nevada border, to draw the attention of a robber who knew of her financial status. She not only lost money but was also held for ransom for $2,000. The robber-turned-kidnapper, much to his disappointment, dis-covered that the Chinese population of Bodie re-fused to submit to his demands. Contemporaries claimed that the presence of two other Chinese prostitutes in that community tempered concern for Ling Loi's welfare. The kidnapper, resigned to the fact that he had lost, eventually released her.[44]

In the 1850s the mining frontier advanced east-ward and northward into the territories that would become Nevada and Oregon. But Chinese prosti-tutes did not follow apace. In the 1860s, however, an insignificant number moved from California into Oregon's southern counties. Oregon's census rec-ords of 1870 for three selected counties show eleven prostitutes, but ten years later none appears on the schedules. The arrival of Chinese prostitutes in Nevada, as in other parts of the American West, proceeded much slower than the almost instan-taneous rush of Chinese men. The first group of Chinese male laborers, numbering about fifty, reach Gold Canyon in 1856 and commenced work on a mining ditch. Although the building of the Virginia and Truckee and Central Pacific railroads lured some, throughout the 1860s the Chinese population in Nevada remained small.[45]

By the late 1860s, Chinese prostitutes had wended their way to the subregion. Census figures for 1860 revealed no Chinese women present in the territory of Nevada. Following the completion of the railroads, in the early 1870s, some discharged Chinese moved to the western hinterlands, gravitating to towns in search of employment. The eastward movement of the Chinese away from the West Coast picked up even more momentum as a consequence of mounting Euro-American hostility in coastal cities. As prostitutes trailed behind the eastward trickle of Chinese men across the Sierras, the Chinese population in Nevada by 1870 had climbed to 306 females and 2,840 males.[46]

One Chinese working woman who ended up in Nevada was a madam, known only to Nevadans as "Mary." Available fragmented evidence indicates that Mary had a successful career in segregated Virginia City's Chinatown during the heyday of the Comstock Lode.[47]

A shrewd entrepreneur, Mary moved into a building next to a popular Chinese saloon that served all racial groups. Patrons of the saloon often dropped by her business house to visit her or one of her charges. Sometime in mid-1866, Alfred Doten, a local newspaperman, jotted the following in his diary: "Went with Sam Glessner down to Chinatown — drank with her and smoke[d] opium with her . . . [and had a] long and interesting chat with her."[48] By moving into the entertainment district, Mary helped to further concentrate vice enterprises in well-defined areas of the city.

During the 1870s, the movement of Chinese males into Nevada jumped by 74 percent, reaching a peak by the end of that turbulent decade; thereafter, their numbers began to decline. But the percentage of Chinese female prostitutes between 1870 and 1880 plunged from 52 to 24 percent, and overall immigration of Chinese females into Nevada declined to almost nil.[49] The growth of the male population thus failed to stimulate a parallel expansion in Chinese prostitution. The spread of sexual commerce could have been impeded during the 1870s by Virginia City's antiprostitution campaign led by Protestant middle-class women. These genteel matrons from the East brought with them puritanical beliefs about the proper place of women in society. They sought, largely, to impose middle-class values on working-class and immigrant women who failed to conform to strict sexual norms. Their campaign resulted in the proscription of solicitation for sex outside designated red-light districts.[50]

In 1870, census takers counted 87 Chinese females living in Virginia City; of that number, 71 worked as prostitutes. Fifteen of the prostitutes were living with men of low socioeconomic status: gamblers, laundrymen, cooks, shoemakers, and laborers. None of the Chinese working women operated as independent entrepreneurs. The number of Chinese prostitutes in Virginia City peaked at 75 in 1875 and then dropped to 20 by 1880.[51]

The eastward movement of Chinese miners and laborers and the corresponding decline in the number of Chinese prostitutes may have been related to the downswing in the economic cycle that the country was experiencing. As the total number of Chinese females remained static at 306 during the 1870s and the number of prostitutes dropped during that period, it appears that some of them either married and left the trade or followed the movement of Chinese men and others to greener pastures. By

1880, more than half of the Chinese men on the Comstock Lode had left for other new bonanza camps, leaving Nevada with only 613 Chinese males and 20 Chinese prostitutes.[52] Similar to prostitutes in California, those in Nevada moved about according to the dictates of their owners, following the dispersion of their countrymen over the region.

In *Daughters of Joy, Sisters of Misery: Prostitutes in the American West, 1865–1890* (1985), Anne M. Butler explains that prostitution employed young women whose prime years were between the ages of fifteen and thirty. Using census schedules, Mary Lou Locke estimated that two-thirds of the prostitutes in San Francisco — all ethnic origins included — fell in the below-thirty age group. A study that examines the 1870 population schedules for Virginia City, Nevada, discovered that the median age of Chinese prostitutes was twenty-three. The average age of their white sisters was a little higher: twenty-seven.[53] The year 1870 marked the height of the city's prosperity following the discovery in 1859 of the treasures of the Comstock Lode. The average age of Chinese prostitutes a decade earlier, in 1860, was twenty-three in Nevada but rose to thirty-two by 1880, a sign of a decline in Chinese female prostitution in that state.[54]

As the mining frontier moved farther east in the early 1870s, Chinese female prostitutes joined — but in far lesser numbers — prostitutes of other ethnic backgrounds in the Rocky Mountain urban areas. For 1870, Butler identified three Chinese women among the 360 prostitutes of all nationalities dwelling in Denver. This could be the earliest group of Chinese prostitutes in Denver or possibly even in the territory of Colorado, as census information shows no Chinese population in 1860. In 1870, census takers counted seven Chinese persons in the state — six men and only one woman.[55] These official figures are probably low; Butler drew her statistics from a variety of sources in addition to the census.

It is possible that the small number of Chinese female prostitutes in the city of Denver was a result of growing anti-Chinese sentiments in the Far West. Entrepreneurs and their bordello workers shied away from subregions with tiny Chinese populations, possibly to avoid facing racial prejudice unprotected. J. P. C. Poulton, a well-known Denver journalist, labeled Chinese immigrants "unprincipled, bigoted, and superstitious people," reflecting Euro-American attitudes toward Chinese sojourners, prostitutes included.[56]

The explanation for the insignificant presence of Chinese prostitutes in Colorado lies in the minuscule number of Chinese men there until 1878, when the first large influx of Chinese males, estimated between 100 and 200, occurred. While Chinese men arrived too late for the halcyon days of placer mining, some opportunities for them still existed. The discovery of silver in Leadville in 1874 led to the "Great Boom" in Denver's history. A rapid growth of manufacturing quickly followed, creating new jobs for Chinese male immigrants, in contrast to the previous decade when mining stagnated and afforded only limited work for individuals bereft of skills or resources. Despite anti-Chinese riots in Denver throughout the 1870s, Chinese male immigrants continued to move into the state. The census for 1880 counted 593 men and 19 women, a dramatic increase from 1870.[57]

There is little evidence for determining the number of Chinese prostitutes in the other Rocky Mountain states. However, we know that at least a few of them worked in nineteenth-century Montana. Following the gold-mining boom in the mountain valleys of the northern Rockies during the early 1860s, Chinese miners and entrepreneurs poured into the newly created territory of Montana. By 1870, the Chinese represented approximately 10 percent of the territory's population. Out of a Chinese population of 1,949, the census lists 123 females. In 1880, only 80 were counted. Obviously some women had left Montana, probably following some of the transient male sojourners, as the total Chinese population had dropped to 1,765. The number of Chinese women would continue to shrink until the opening years of this century.[58]

The absence of women clearly induced prostitutes to push on to Montana. Although there was an absence of any extralegal organizations such as tongs to regulate the sexual trade — the first tong did not organize in Montana until 1917 — Chinese prostitutes reached the territory as early as 1870. Enumerators for a territory-level census in that year identified as prostitutes all 130 Chinese women in Deer Lodge County (where the greatest number of Chinese lived), as against 1,053 Chinese males of the same county.[59]

In Boise Basin, Idaho, some Chinese prostitutes populated the southern part of the territory following the transfer of claims from whites to Chinese miners after lucrative placer production had ended in the late 1860s. In 1870, for example, Silver City in the Owyhee Mountains of Idaho had perhaps fourteen Chinese prostitutes serving a total population of nearly four hundred Asian miners.[60] Chinese prostitutes and miners paid extra taxes in many towns. Yet these women managed to make a living as the mining industry figured prominently in Idaho's economy. The U.S. Census Office in 1870 classified nearly 43.8 percent of the population as "miners," more than half of them Chinese.[61]

One of the Chinese prostitutes who worked in a mining camp during the 1870s was Lalu Nathoy. Perhaps the most legendary Chinese prostitute outside San Francisco in the nineteenth century, she has been stereotyped by popular authors as a "harlot with a heart of gold" turned "gentle tamer."[62]

Born on September 11, 1853, Lalu Nathoy suffered severe privation as a child. She and her family barely survived, tilling a tiny plot of poor land. One year the crops failed badly, and during a raid on their village, outlaws forced them to give up what little they could harvest. To forestall further tragedy, her father sold her to one of the leaders of the outlaw band in exchange for seeds to plant another crop. Interviewed in 1921, she said, "They sell me [as a] slave girl. Old woman she smuggled me into Portland [probably from San Francisco]. I cost $2,500. . . . Old Chinese man he took me along to Warrens in a pack train." Thus, in 1872, at the age of thirteen, she had been sold to a Chinese saloon keeper in Warren, Idaho, who gave her the English name "Polly."[63]

Later she nursed a regular customer of the saloon who had sustained a serious gunshot wound. The grateful white man, Charlie Bemis, offered to marry her, and she accepted. She and her husband then ran a successful fifteen-acre homestead where they raised poultry and grew vegetables. After her husband was burned to death in a fire that razed her property, she rebuilt her business with the help of two friends, Charles Shepp and Peter Klinkhammer. Throughout her life, she provided succor to the sick and ailing in the community of Grangeville City.[64] Her life experiences set her apart from many Chinese prostitutes. Few married Euro-Americans or influenced directly the growth of the community they lived in but were excluded from. Lalu Nathoy's marriage perhaps allowed her to gain respectability in the eyes of Euro-American society.

South of the Rocky Mountains region, particularly in the territory that would become the state of Arizona, no Chinese women appeared before 1870. Until the late 1860s, only a negligible number of Chinese sojourners lived in the territory. The 1870 census, for example, lists 20 Chinese, all identified as males. The opening of Tombstone's silver mines and the building of a southern transcontinental railroad through Arizona territory in the years from 1878 to 1882 brought many Chinese male workers to this region. Chinese emigrants, escaping from prejudice in the coastal cities, considered Arizona a "safety valve." Compared to California, Arizona was less hostile toward the Chinese. Their relatively insignificant presence made them less of a social and economic threat to the Euro-American society. In 1880, census takers counted 1,601 Chinese males and 31 females.[65] One historian claimed that only 10 Chinese women resided in Arizona throughout the territorial period (until 1912), all of them having migrated to the territory to join their husbands. Perhaps he counted only spouses, as prostitutes made up the remainder of the female population.[66]

Evidence gathered from fire insurance maps and recently published secondary sources suggests

that, in all probability, at least a few Chinese prostitutes worked and lived in Arizona territory. Fire
insurance maps for Tombstone, Phoenix, and Tucson
provide few clues to the existence of Chinese brothels
or "boardinghouses" during the last quarter of the
nineteenth century. Yet Chinese families were hardly visible; in 1880, Tucson, pivotal to the region's
economy, became the settlement area for only 2
married Chinese women and 158 Chinese men.[67]

Since intermarriage between Chinese and His-
panics was not unheard of and existed as early as
1870, the demand for commercialized sex became
less urgent. One Chinese emigrant, Hi Wo, for example, married Emeteria Morena and apparently
adopted Western culture. All of his children bore
Spanish names and professed to be Catholics.[68] Of
course, those Chinese men who established cross-
cultural households found it unnecessary to return
to their native country for matrimony or to resort to
prostitutes. It seems unlikely, however, that Chinese prostitution never appeared in Tucson as businesses often associated with the vice, such as opium
dens and gambling houses, were prevalent.[69]

❧

Chinese prostitutes in the Far West led ambiguous
lives. On the one hand, they served a racially mixed
clientele; on the other, they led a segregated existence separate from the wider society. This pattern
was well established all over the Far West by the
turn of the century.[70]

Chinese workers in sexual commerce encountered Euro-American culture almost immediately
on arrival in the United States. In the early 1850s in
Sonora, California, one Chinese prostitute, always

"finely dressed in European style," "sat behind the bar of a Chinese store and served out drinks" to white patrons, most of whom were miners.[71] Clarence W. Kellogg, a retired U.S. Army major, visited a number of California mining camps in 1854 and gave an account of Chinese prostitutes in Tuolumne County. He described them as "the unwanted, poorest, and slave class, of the lowest valuation . . . dolled up as painted beauties and prostituted to all kinds of men (yellow and white alike) at a cheap price." In San Joaquin County, women visited work camps where Chinese laborers toiled on railroads or reclamation projects.[72]

Major Kellogg also noted that "under no circumstances were these women ever permitted to ply their trade except within the confines of Camp Chinatown [in Chinese Camp] where their domiciles were the crudest of shacks, but called 'Fancy Houses.'" His diary indicates that Chinese prostitutes resided in a segregated district. The segregation of Camp Chinatown, with its vice district, may have been an early attempt to establish a didactic culture in the larger community, one that advocated public conformity to Victorian values and the building of a uniformly shared public moral consciousness.[73]

Most writers of prescriptive literature in antebellum America urged single men to lead a virtuous — abstinent — life, while married ones were to engage in sex only within marriage and then solely for procreation. But some of these writers justified men's unchaste behavior on the grounds that males, as naturally bestial creatures, had insatiable sexual appetites. While conceding that prostitutes performed a function in the biological sphere, they found no place for them in the social realm. In any case, the outpouring of prescriptive sexual manuals and pamphlets implied that few nineteenth-century Americans led sexually repressed lives, a fact further demonstrated by the large numbers of brothels in American cities.[74]

It is also possible that nativistic feelings could have colored the perceptions of the mining community and challenged residents to exercise tighter control over Chinese prostitutes. Race relations had been tense in California ever since the passage of the discriminatory Foreign Miners' Tax (1852). Authorities collected this tax, three dollars per month, only from the Chinese population. Instead of placating white miners, it incited some mining districts to expel Chinese miners from their respective camps.[75] Like the mining camp riots, the efforts of Euro-Americans to limit the geographic mobility of prostitutes may have stemmed from hostility toward Chinese emigrants.

Whatever the motive, Chinese prostitutes in the Far West often found themselves isolated from the wider society, which further handicapped efforts to cope with their ebbing fortunes. To nineteenth-century observers, Chinese prostitutes did not fit the model of "true womanhood" because of their ethnicity and occupation, although prostitutes did in many cases bow to male authority.[76] The West failed to offer them a liberating and innovative environment, and most prostitutes led a marginal existence. They were ostracized by the greater part of the community they settled in. Upper-class Euro-Americans seemed to be the most critical of the degenerate influence supposedly exercised by prostitutes. The vision of the American West as the "earthly paradise" (jen-chien lo-t'u, a vast land rich in natural resources and agricultural products) was soon discredited, so far as Chinese prostitutes were concerned. The earthly paradise became "hell" (*ti yu*), and "good barbarians" turned into "Flowery Flag devils."[77]

Few Euro-Americans knew much of Chinese prostitutes' daily existence. Their lives were shrouded in mystery, and myths about them developed. One myth that circulated in San Francisco revolved around the claim that the vaginal opening of a Chinese woman was horizontal rather than vertical. The story first appeared in the 1850s and continued as part of San Francisco's folklore until the early 1880s. This titillating myth points out the chasm between the world of Chinese women and that of the larger society and the simultaneous fascination Americans had for Asian females. In contrast, some Americans praised their industriousness, offered compliments on their femininity, and admired their frailty.[78]

Of course, cries of disapproval drowned out the faint words of praise. Sexual advice books published during the middle of the century informed Americans that prostitution stemmed from immorality and contributed to it. A prostitute was a woman with "half [the sexual control] the woman gone." For example, Frank Soulé singled out Chinese women as "the filthiest and most abandoned of their sex."[79]

Victorian Americans considered prostitutes social deviants. The didactic morality of the day ordained that women had milder sexual needs than men. Prostitutes, of course, seemed to defy this "truism." While serving male sexuality on the frontier, Chinese women, far from being "passionless," were believed to exhibit qualities associated with male sexuality: grossness, animalism, and lechery. In the minds of the American public, Chinese males kept prostitutes for abhorrent sexual practices, part of the fearful "Chinaman" myth. Certainly in California fiction and poetry, Chinese prostitutes earned little respect and hardly measured up to the status of American women.[80]

Yet Victorian literature on the sexual depravity of Asian women failed to discourage some American males from patronizing Chinese brothels. After all, in the words of a western women's historian, "there is often a difference between what a culture tells us we ought to do and what we in fact do."[81] Advocates of Victorian respectability encountered indifference among some males; few men abandoned the doctrine of male sexual necessity that excused, perhaps even encouraged, indulgence in sexual intercourse. Supposedly, the virility and health of an unmarried male could only be sustained through contact with prostitutes.[82]

The Chinese male population also mirrored the ambivalent and contradictory attitudes of Euro-American society toward Chinese prostitutes. Until the first decade of the twentieth century, the issue of eliminating undesirable practices of women, including forced prostitution, received little attention from the Chinese community. Cantonese vernacular folk rhymes even celebrated the sexual exploitation of women. An anonymous male sojourner wrote the following:

> I never tire of the lust for women;
> At seventy, what do I care about destiny.
> Loose with my passion, wild with desire, just like
>   my younger days,

Brothels and whorehouses are places of my mad
indulgence.[83]

Another writer counseled his readers to "follow
[their] impulses" and "enjoy the company of a beautiful woman." But some writers saw prostitutes as
women who had lost their virtue and chastity. These
social critics implored the *loungei* (woman always
holding her legs up) to leave the trade, for "prostitution ruins the body most harmfully."[84]

On the whole, the Chinese community, compared to the non-Chinese population of America,
seemed less morally didactic about these "fallen"
women and their livelihood. Chinese America saw
prostitution as natural and inevitable in a virtually
all-male society. One elderly Chinese man who
lived in a small town in California at the turn of the
century claimed that "the Chinese people didn't
mind, . . . they didn't hide it. . . . I guess you could
say they condone it. . . . They just mind their own
business."[85] However, many frowned on affairs that
could interfere with the purpose of life in America:
to make a fortune and return to China as the de-
voted son of the family.[86]

❀

Chinese prostitutes were expected to adhere to both
Western and Chinese cultural standards even though
they enjoyed few opportunities available to the rest
of the society. Gender as well as racial discrimina-
tion in the labor market combined to restrict their
occupational opportunities. A lack of education further handicapped these women in their search for
better employment.

Regardless of their racial background, women's
choices for employment proved quite limited for

nearly thirty years after the discovery of gold in California. In 1858, the publisher of a widely circulated women's journal lamented, "There is no room for women [in the labor market]; the avenues where she may labor are few, and at best undesirable. . . . When we mention school-teaching and keeping boarders, we have covered the entire ground upon which woman may labor for her daily bread."[87]

Until 1870, most wage-earning women in California, 79.5 percent, were in professional and personal services. A decade later, two years before the passage of the Chinese Exclusion Act of 1882, women of all ethnic origins were still disproportionately represented in the service industry: nearly 65 percent were employed in this area.[88]

The California employment patterns for Chinese women duplicated those for non-Chinese women. Census takers counted 2,794 Chinese female workers in 1870; 77 percent apparently declared themselves as prostitutes, while the rest, 23 percent, listed their occupations as laundresses, miners, servants, seamstresses, cooks, or lodging house operators — all service-related occupations.[89]

The 1880 census shows 1,726 Chinese women in California with gainful employment, a marked drop from the previous decade. Forty-four percent were engaged in prostitution. Others, not unlike the pattern of the previous decade, could be found in this limited group of occupations, in descending order: seamstress, servant, laundress, cook, entertainer, laborer, miner, and lodging house operator. According to Hirata, racial hostility and the community structure shaped the roles that they eventually filled. However, limited opportunities for women in general — the result of sexism and patriarchy — played an equally important part.[90]

During the early stage in the development of the Far West, some Chinese prostitutes, given the relative fluidity of the emerging hierarchy within the Chinese community, operated as free independent entrepreneurs. However, it is difficult to ascertain the number of independent Chinese prostitutes living and working in California during the 1850s due to the lack of information and the scattered nature of available evidence. It is safe to infer that they made up a minority of the total number of Chinese prostitutes. The involvement of Chinese tongs in protection rackets as early as 1851, which by 1854 had rapidly expanded into importation of women for commercialized sex, doomed the continuation of free competition in this trade.

Chinese members of the demimonde seemed to have followed, although in smaller numbers, the gradual movement of Chinese male immigrants into the interior of the American West. Both men and women were responding to the economic development of the various subregions of the West. As each subregion underwent economic transformation, whether through mining of precious metals or building more extensive transportation networks, Chinese sojourners moved into the new area in search of economic opportunities.

Most Chinese prostitutes, however, differed from their countrymen in that they had limited control over their geographic mobility. Following the displacement of free competition by the centralized monopoly of the tongs, many Chinese prostitutes retained little independence in their lives. As they were brought farther east, they became widely dispersed, living and working in cities, boomtowns, and mining camps. Because of the isolation of the mining frontier, these pioneers suffered from social dislocation and extreme loneliness. Those in cities, like Ah Toy, were hardly better off, as they could never escape the physical and cultural separation of the Chinese population from the wider society.

Not all Chinese prostitutes could be called passive victims of male exploitation and white hostility. Deadwood, South Dakota, was the setting in 1876 for a series of remarkable events in which a prostitute, Chi-an, better known to her contemporaries as "China Doll," played a significant role. She earned a reputation as a shrewd, resilient woman who, despite being under the control of a pimp-owner, resisted his commands by providing poor services to her customers. She later died tragically when caught in the crossfire between two foes.[91]

Other evidence of women who had the strength to resist oppression is preserved in a series of telegrams supposedly sent by a few Chinese men from Downieville, California. One of these follows.

Downieville, Cal.
August 5, 1874

Fook Sing
Care Wing Wo Ching
Wadsworth, Nevada
Ah Tom write me Gan Que is at Auburn. You catch her go right away. Answer.

Tie Yuen

Gan Que, according to this and additional telegrams related to her, was a prostitute who escaped from Fook Sing with the help of How Ah Sing, possibly her lover. She and her companion constantly moved about for nearly two months to avoid Fook Sing and his assistants who were attempting to get her back.[92]

Leaving prostitution through marriage was not an aberrant course of action. Many Chinese prostitutes sought outward mobility through conjugal unions.

In the earlier years, the frontier held out for a few Chinese women and some Euro-American women the opportunity to control and profit from their own sexual commerce. However, once the social structure became more rigid and the population stabilized, the form prostitution took circumscribed their opportunities and their lives. Also, once families began to predominate in and around the frontier towns, the maintenance of traditional marital restrictions on sexual activity became an important part of community identity.[93] As the Victorian concept of respectability took hold in the minds of parents and concerned citizens, women who remained in prostitution ran the risk of being stigmatized as social deviants. For Chinese providers of sexual services, racial hostility further threatened to erode their will to survive. Of course, the way in which Chinese prostitutes reacted to their situation in America had been conditioned by their earlier personal experiences in China and by traditional cultural expectations.

Unwilling Travelers to Gum Saan

The movement of trafficked women to America in the nineteenth century, largely a consequence of events taking place in California, can also be traced to deep-seated problems that had existed in China since the early nineteenth century. By 1800, China, or *tien-hsia* (the empire), was undergoing rapid change and looking to a foreboding future. The ruling power, the Ch'ing dynasty (1644–1911), had passed its peak and commenced a slow decline. Numerous signs pointed to a dynastic cycle that had gone full circle: administrative inefficiency, widespread corruption, debasement of the military, a strained treasury, and the pressures of a rising population.[1]

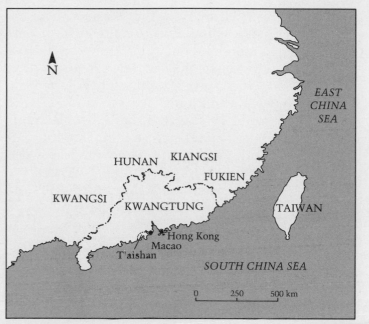

1. Kwangtung and the district of Toishan (T'aishan, according to the Wade-Giles transliteration).

In Kwangtung province (see map 1), home of at least 90 percent of the Chinese immigrants to America, the most fundamental indigenous change was the immense population increase that had been under way since the days of the Ming dynasty (1368–1644). This process accelerated in the early nineteenth century. China's population increased 47 percent between 1787 and 1850, from 292 million to 430 million. During the same period, Kwangtung showed a gain of 79.5 percent, as its population went up to 28,182 from a low of 16,014, making it one of the five fastest-growing provinces in China.[2]

The enormous population growth in southern China brought on an increasingly bitter struggle for land. Even the most marginal reclaimed lands became prized possessions because the total arable land for China increased only by 50 percent, failing to keep pace with the twofold increase in population since 1660. In Kwangtung, the population-land ratio far outstripped the national average. In 1817, the country averaged 2.19 *mou* (0.36 acre; 1 mou equals approximately 0.17 acre) per person, but for four major districts in Kwangtung it hovered between 1.02 mou (0.17 acre) and 2.45 mou (0.40 acre).[3]

The social implications of the shortage of land suitable for cultivation were further compounded by the effects of European economic imperialism following the first Opium War (1839–42). In the wake of the second Opium War (1856–60), European powers forced even more concessions from China. Consequently, an overabundance of cheap foreign goods flooded the domestic market, cornered most sales, and limited demand for products of the inefficient Chinese handicraft industries. A report submitted to the emperor in 1854 analyzed the economic crisis. "The rapid development of Hong Kong and Macao captured much trade from Canton. The heavy *likin*, an inland tax on all goods, only drove more trade out of Canton. Now Kwangtung [has been] undermined in its wealth."[4] Even though by 1870 trade by foreign powers at the port of Canton far exceeded that of the other five treaty ports, nonagricultural workers in Canton still suffered unemployment because many business interests had gravitated to northern ports.[5]

Many dispossessed male members of poor families were left unemployed. Wong Ah So, a Chinese woman later indentured for prostitution, recalled that her father, a sailor, also "*sometimes* [italics mine] . . . worked on the docks, for [they] were poor." On the average, semi- and unskilled jobs in the city paid fifteen to twenty cents a day, excluding board.[6]

Paralleling these problems created by foreign economic intrusions were a series of uprisings, including the T'aip'ing Rebellion (1850–64) and the Red Turban Revolt (1854–56), that caused widespread damage in the countryside. The Punti-Hakka feuds between 1853 and 1867, a local conflict that raged across the province of Kwangtung, further exacerbated the plight of poor families.[7] One male migrant recollected how the Hakkas, "good fighters," forced his family "to flee for safety." An anonymous female prostitute recalled how rebels captured her in a raid on her village. While "scores of the young men joined battle with the invaders and their heads rolled in the mud," she was abducted by the leader and later sold into prostitution.[8]

Natural calamities compounded the deteriorating conditions. It has been estimated that at least one major catastrophe occurred in the district of Toishan (Wade-Giles transliteration is T'aishan) for every three to four years during the period between 1832 and 1881. Located within the province of Kwangtung, Toishan would be the district of origin for more than 40 percent of first-generation Chinese Americans. Almost every year, Toishan and its neighboring subregions faced natural disasters—droughts, floods, snowfalls, typhoons, or crop failures due to insects or blight.[9] One of the floods in Kwangtung was so severe that, according to one official account, the "rivers and the sea and the streams, have joined in one sheet over the land for several hundred *li* [1 li equals 0.33 mile] and there is no outlet by which the waters may retire."[10] Most natural disasters resulted in famines. "Rose," later hoodwinked into prostitu-

tion, traveled to Hong Kong at the age of fourteen
following a series of famines in her village. She first
worked as an indentured servant but later moved to
San Francisco on the promise of marriage.[11]

Famines and natural disasters frequently struck
all classes of Chinese society; few escaped their
ravages. But the peasant family unit had an additional, onerous burden: it shouldered the heaviest
tax liability in the sociopolitical structure of the
village. Corruption sometimes worsened the financial strain on these families. William Hung, a Cantonese emigrant, asserted that "corruption by the
officials" was widespread; they always "collect more,
and then also make all kinds of trouble, make the
farmers have to pay more, and all that." Further,
according to the gazette of a district in Kwangtung,
the "generally remote, desolate, and sickly nature of
the region" handicapped peasants in their efforts to
overcome natural and human forces.[12]

The turmoil in the economy when set against a
backdrop of hostile environmental and climatic factors resulted in destitution and deprivation. The
U.S. consul in the city of Tientsin traversed the
country in 1877 and witnessed the tragedy. He reported seeing "many bodies of poor unfortunate victims of the famine who had drowned their suffering
and sorrow in rivers." A Nien chant recited in southern China relates how even "weeds from the ponds
were good food." A peasant, Ning Lao T'ai-t'ai, suffered privation, unable to survive on the little money
she received from selling her worldly possessions: "I
was so hungry one day that I took a brick, pounded it
to bits, and ate it. It made me feel better."[13]

Some peasant families survived because female
members became food gatherers, joined the labor

force, participated in communal living arrangements, or agreed to marry the son of a wealthy family who could offer a hefty bride-price. One Chinese female immigrant, "Mother Teng," recollected that she helped her family live through a famine by scrounging for grains of rice from harvested fields. Another woman, who yearned to leave the doleful times behind her, was more ambitious. Lin Yu-shih ignored traditions and left her family, traveling from Shanghai to Canton in search of employment. Unfortunately, she was later kidnapped and forced into prostitution. In some instances, women moved out of their parents' homes and set up all-female households with friends to help reduce expenses. The two sisters of a male emigrant, Huie Kin, "lived, with some other girls, in a house called the *Noi-ok*, near the edge of the village."[14]

Finally, families often married off their daughters as soon as possible to ease the financial burden and, more important, to earn the coveted bride-price. Lam Mei-ying, who lived in southeastern Kwangtung at the turn of the century, married the son of a respectable family in the next village who agreed to give her mother the equivalent of nearly 2,300 pounds of rice.[15]

Some families, however, simply could not function at below subsistence level. Living on the edge of subsistence, some families resorted to infanticide or abandonment. One local official noted that "the fields in the four directions were choked with weeds. Small families found it difficult to make a living and often drowned their girl babies because of the impossibility of looking after them."[16] The sociologists Arthur Wolf and Huang Chieh-shan studied some 1,478 families listed in household registers

and concluded that female infanticide rarely occurred, although they offered no evidence on the
question of abandonment. Yan Phou Lee, who studied in the United States during the early 1870s,
reassured Americans "that in proportion to the population and distribution of wealth infanticide is as
rare in China as it is in this country."[17]

Selling children for whom they could not provide seemed the preferred choice for many peasants.
Few parents openly consented to an outright sale of
their daughters into prostitution. Most believed that
they had sold their children as *mooi-tsai* (indentured domestic servants) or as young brides for
Chinese male sojourners in America. For parents,
such arrangements were pivotal to the survival of
the family. Left with meager food, Ho-tai and her
family sensed that "death was all around them," but
still, her mother refused to sell her. One night, while
Ho-tai's mother was away from home, her husband
sold Ho-tai for several silver pieces. Ho-tai later told
her mistress that as she and her purchaser sailed
down the canal, she caught glimpses of her anguished mother, "her dress open far below her throat,
her hair loose and flying, her eyes swollen and dry
from over-weeping, moaning pitifully, stumbling on
in the darkness, searching for the boat . . . but it was
gone."[18]

The emotional trauma of the sale for all parties
concerned was softened by the reassurance that
their children would not be thrown into a dishonor-
able profession and that their security would be
guaranteed by their adopted families. Most of these
exchanges involved young girls. Lilac Chen was
only six when she traveled to the United States, and
"Rose" was sixteen when she was sold.[19]

In the patrilineal, male-dominated Chinese family, daughters were sold more often and with less reluctance than sons. The teachings of Confucianism, which place far more value on sons than on daughters, help explain why some poverty-stricken families sold their daughters. The Chinese proverb, "A boy is born facing in; a girl is born facing out," encapsulates the general consensus on the low status of women in a patriarchal society.[20] Throughout her life, a woman had to submit to male authority — her father's, her husband's, and later, her son's. The lower expectations for female offspring, compared to those for males, are pointed out in a poem from the ancient classic *The Book of Songs* which begins, "Black bears and brown / mean men-children / snakes and serpents / mean girl-children." Boys, like the bear, are strong, while girls, like the snake, are lazy and good-for-nothing.[21]

Chinese traditional agrarian society considered female labor in the fields, compared to male labor, as marginal, although women in poor peasant families did their fair share of such work. An American traveler in 1875 saw a woman "drawing the plough through the field . . . while her husband followed holding the handle."[22] The married women of the rice regions of southern China and their young daughters had exclusive responsibility for domestic labor. Married women processed rice, tended to livestock, made and repaired clothes and shoes, and prepared the daily meals. Their daughters gathered wood and cut dry grass for fuel; they even cared for the vegetable gardens and fished in the nearby streams and small rivers.[23] Despite their crucial role in sustaining their families, women were considered dispensable.

The importance of the sale of daughters to fore-stall penury can be surmised from a report submitted by a Ch'ing dynasty official. On the average, wrote the official, one out of every ten families depended for their sustenance on a female child working as a prostitute.[24] One interviewee related the story of a fourteen-year-old girl who had to work as a prostitute "because the family was large and very poor and because the sons were all too young to work." After her entry into the trade, "the family lived very well, with new clothes and plenty to eat."[25] It has been suggested that a relatively high percentage of these women came from families with no male offspring, forcing them to serve as substitutes for sons. The Chinese were not the only ones to use daughters for economic gain. Impoverished rural Japanese families in the nineteenth century also survived on profits from the sale of their daughters.[26]

Few women sold into prostitution expressed resentment against their parents. When Lalu Nathoy first learned that her parents were planning to sell her, she rationalized that she had been sold so that "the family could live." Wong Ah So wrote to her mother that she did not blame her for her predicament. She understood that Chinese patriarchal bonds of mutual claims, responsibilities, obligations, and commitments obliged her to put her family's well-being ahead of her own.[27]

The wider Chinese society endorsed the sale of children; many considered it a pragmatic decision. In 1879, traders and other community leaders in Hong Kong petitioned the British governor of Hong Kong, I. Elliot, to allow this practice to continue so as to prevent infanticide. This plea came in response to measures taken by the colonial government to suppress the practice, including the imprisonment of those found guilty of trafficking in women for prostitution.[28]

The Ch'ing government also sanctioned the selling of daughters; the law intervened only if a girl had been purchased for marriage, concubinage, or domestic service but was used instead as a prostitute. But procurers had no trouble circumventing statutes governing fraud. Daughters bought as domestic servants, or *mooi-tsai*, sometimes would later be resold into prostitution. Those who became concubines could also be disposed of by their male companions as prostitutes. The Ch'ing government considered forced prostitution a minor crime that was difficult to control.[29]

Forced prostitution became even more covert when agents used luring techniques and kidnapping to procure females. Chinese women occasionally received fictitious offers of marriage. "Little Ah Yee" succumbed to the charms of a returnee from the Flowery Flag Nation. Supposedly financially secure and in easy circumstances, he promised to marry her in California. Upon arrival in San Francisco, however, he left his bride in the care of an elderly woman. Later, the woman took Ah Yee to a small room in a house on Spofford Alley. There the older woman revealed that she had bought her for prostitution for the sum of $4,800.[30]

More mature women found offers of employment. At the age of nineteen, Wong Ah So, enraptured with stories of a better life in *Gum Saan*, looked foward to finding bountiful riches in the "earthly paradise" of that time. Chun Ho gave the following account of the events leading up to her emigration.

When I was nineteen years old, the mistress No. 3 of
a noted procurer by the name of Gwan Lung, who
lives in San Francisco, went back to Canton, where
my mother happened to be living with me at that
time, and gave me glowing accounts of life in California. She painted that life so beautifully that I was
seized with an inclination to go there and try my
fortune.[31]

Some women fell into traps set by kidnappers.
Lee Sing, invited to see an American steamer anchored at the dock, accepted the offer. While en-
joying the tour inside the vessel, it set sail for San
Francisco. Kidnapping was also carried out against
daughters of wealthy merchants. Jean Ying, the
daughter of a well-to-do Chinese manufacturer in
Canton, went to visit friends who lived some distance from her home. On the way, thugs nabbed her
and quickly spirited her off to Hong Kong. The
captors kept her there for several weeks until a
purchaser agreed to take her to California.[32]

In general, the indifference of the Ch'ing government toward forced prostitution cleared the way for
procurement of potential prostitutes. Furthermore,
legal barriers to prevent general emigration often
went unenforced as early as the mid-eighteenth
century. One of these antiemigration laws stipulated, "Those who find excuses to sojourn abroad
and then clandestinely return home, if captured
shall be executed immediately."[33] Those who con-
templated making the journey probably harbored
the "fear of the mandarins finding them out; the fear
of persecution by the mandarins' runners." But as
early as 1839, the imperial commissioner based in
Kwangtung reported "unemployed paupers who . . .
accept employment abroad."[34]

Antiemigration laws became even less meaningful after 1866. In that year, the governor-general of Kwangtung and Kwangsi provinces legalized voluntary emigration at Canton, the port of embarkation for many travelers to Gold Mountain. A Chinese viceroy expressed the official attitude: "The Emperor's wealth is beyond computation; why should he care for those of his subjects who have left their home, or for the sands they have scrapped together?"[35]

Recruiters and their victims thus found it easy to proceed from the hinterlands of Kwangtung to Canton, Hong Kong, or another port to buy passage on foreign ships. In 1879, Chen Liang-shih traveled from the rural countryside east of Canton to Hong Kong accompanied by an aunt who offered her a job. According to Chen, no one raised any objections about two unchaperoned women traveling to the "foreign devils'" colony. In an 1879 letter to the U.S. State Department, Minister to China George F. Seward explained that any serious attempt to check effectively the flow of prostitutes to America required wider cooperation from Chinese authorities.[36]

Most treaty ports turned into havens for those engaged in the trafficking of women. Chinese employees of foreign traders often served as agents of brothel owners or tongs and thus functioned outside Chinese laws. The unequal treaties between China and Western powers allowed consuls to adjudicate cases involving their fellow countrymen. Though not originally intended to cover Chinese employees, the protection of extraterritoriality eventually embraced them.[37]

Aware of the loophole, the British government in Hong Kong passed two ordinances, one in 1845 and another in 1873, to prohibit the sale, purchase, or ownership of slaves. The February 25, 1879, editorial of the *China Press*, an English daily in the colony, claimed that although a law against female slavery had existed since the organization of Hong Kong as a colony in 1854, it had never been enforced vigorously. The colonial government itself admitted that it had failed to implement the law, resulting in the continuation of the trade for at least thirty years after 1850.[38]

American consuls in Hong Kong, often merchants themselves, were also culpable for aiding the trafficking. Corrupt consuls and their unqualified agents acted with impunity and made full use of their extraterritorial rights. Following the passage of the 1862 Act to Prohibit Coolie Trade, the American consul or his agent in Hong Kong had to examine each prospective emigrant to eliminate instances of involuntary travel. If a person was found to be emigrating voluntarily, a certificate of emigration to the United States would be issued. From 1862 to 1871, certification was treated in a perfunctory manner for vessels leaving for the United States. During that period, 3,834 females made the trip to the continental United States. A large number of these women must have been prostitutes, because as late as 1876 a letter from the Chinese Six Companies — the umbrella organization for benevolent organizations in San Francisco — to President U.S. Grant noted the presence of only "a few hundred Chinese families" in the country. Throughout the second half of the 1860s, the *Alta California* announced at intervals the arrival of female "prostitutes"; for example, on January 21, 1869, 240 of them disembarked at the port. David H. Bailey, the U.S. consul

(1871–77) for Hong Kong, blamed his predecessors for making the "whole proceeding . . . a complete farce."[39]

During Bailey's tenure as consul, two illiterate merchants, Capt. Thomas H. King and Peter Smith, aided Bailey in examining hopeful emigrants. The consul claimed that he was forced to engage these assistants because of the heavy workload. King and Smith would ask each potential passenger if he or she was a voluntary emigrant. If the applicant gave a positive reply, the agent would promptly issue the certificate. The lackadaisical attitude of these officials stemmed from a desire to pocket as much as possible of the twenty-five-cent examination fee, collected but never recorded until 1871. From 1871 to 1879, the records show that the total revenue derived from collecting this fee, an estimated $30,000, always balanced expenditures, with the major expense being the $400 a year paid to the agent for conducting the examinations.[40]

U.S. consuls and their agents, with the exception of Bailey, also failed to implement the provisions of the Page Law of 1875 and its regulatory measures designed to prevent the flow of Chinese prostitutes to America. Recommended by President Grant and passed unanimously by Congress, the law expressly forbade the importation of women into the United States for prostitution.[41] It stated that those found guilty of trafficking in women "shall be deemed guilty of a felony . . . [and] imprisoned not exceeding five years and pay a fine not exceeding five thousand dollars."[42]

One of the regulations of the law instructed female emigrants to sign a declaration swearing they had not entered "into a contract or agreement with any person or persons for a term of service within the United States for lewd or immoral purposes." The statement was to be countersigned by a trustworthy Chinese merchant and the woman's character and personal history investigated by a committee from the Tung Wah Hospital's board of directors. During the nineteenth century, this committee served as the intermediary for relations between the Ch'ing government and overseas Chinese commercial interests. Each female Chinese emigrant also had to submit three photographs, one of which the collector of customs in San Francisco was to receive and match with another copy on the embarkation papers.[43]

Unlike his successors, Bailey did implement these measures, which resulted in a 33 percent drop in female emigration for 1876. Frequent allegations in the Congress that the U.S. consul had been remiss in counteracting illegal immigration brought more vigilance.[44] Under pressure from his superiors, Bailey abandoned his earlier complicity in his staff's illegal activity. Although he had ignored his responsibilities previously, Bailey took stock of the situation and began stringently to control the emigration process. On December 9, 1875, the San Francisco *Evening Bulletin* announced that ten prostitutes had just been sent back to China. It further reported that Bailey promised "extra care will be taken to prevent further like emigration there." On October 29, 1877, San Francisco's *Morning Call* noted that "hardly a dozen Chinese women have come to the city from China for the last eighteen months." By 1877, the number of Chinese women arriving at the port of San Francisco had dropped by 80 percent.[45]

Bailey seemed enthusiastic in checking the trafficking. He did, however, endorse charging potential female emigrants an extra $15 per examination. The surcharge served as a guarantee that the applications would receive due consideration, but it was not prohibitive enough to stop altogether the movement of women out of China. Other steps to check the influx of prostitutes might have been hampered by the general disagreement of the Tung Wah Hospital committee over the details of the regulations.[46]

Bailey's replacement, H. Sheldon Loring (who served from 1877–79), maintained less vigilance on the traffic. A study of his correspondence for the second half of 1878 shows that he received no inquiries on female emigration and sent only three requests to the Tung Wah Hospital committee out of a total correspondence of forty-four letters. This period also witnessed a threefold increase in female emigration over the previous year. Minister Seward notified the State Department in early 1879 that the Page Law was "a dead letter."[47]

John S. Mosby, who took over in February 1879 until 1882, was more vigorous than Loring in curbing the flow of prostitutes to the United States. Praised by an American diplomat working in China as "an honest and efficient consul," the former Confederate cavalry officer was instrumental in causing a sharp plunge in the number of displaced females in 1880: it dropped to an all-time low of seventy.[48]

Mosby, however, admitted "that many mistakes [were] made regarding the permit [to emigrate] and who should receive it." One U.S. consul official working under Mosby conceded that, at times, the examination of applicants could be best characterized as brief and perfunctory. By late 1880, enforcement of the law was so slipslod that the State Department instructed commissioners (present in China to negotiate a new treaty) to persuade the Chinese government to take a more active role in restricting the traffic. The fact that the British colonial administration hesitated, for fear of preventing free emigration, to support the enforcement of the Page Law further doomed efforts to stop the illegal trade.[49]

In subsequent oral accounts, Chinese women who went to the United States after 1875 mentioned little about being interrogated extensively about their intentions. The absence of such accounts suggests a laxity in enforcing the rules.

Bailey claimed he subjected each female applicant to a barrage of questions supposedly designed to pressure women who were emigrating for "lewd and immoral purposes" to reveal their masquerade. Such questions included, "Do you go to the United States for the purpose of prostitution?" "What is to be your occupation there?" "Do you intend to live a virtuous life in the United States?"[50] For those who were subjected to this line of questioning, this was a fruitless exercise. Women unaware of their fate presented themselves as free emigrants, while those few who had no illusions had to deal, first, with a cultural gap that alienated them from the American agents and, second, with their oppressors who had invested a great deal in them.

Nearly all of these women discovered their sale, duping, or kidnapping just before or after they had set sail for America. All of them described their experiences as traumatic, and many did not passively accept their fate. Six-year-old Lilac Chen thought her father was taking her to visit her grandmother in

1893 but grew confused when her mother started to cry. Only later on board the steamer did she discover that her father had sold her to a procurer. Then she reacted violently and "kicked and screamed and screamed," she later recalled. The young girl refused to eat and insisted, to no avail, that she be brought home.[51]

Tsoi Yee, a prostitute at the age of fourteen in 1897, ended up in a Hong Kong brothel. Hardly a passive victim, she resisted efforts to put her to work, although she was under the control of the woman who managed the brothel. The manager physically abused her; she "was scolded and beaten, and beaten severely." Finally, the owner placed her on a steamer bound for San Francisco. She claimed the following: "I did not know when I started from China that I was going to be brought here until after I got aboard the boat." She tried to draw attention to her plight by crying and wailing, but the tactic proved fruitless.[52] Though both Lilac Chen and Tsoi Yee were brought to the United States long after the period we are concerned with here, their experiences were quite likely similar to those young women sold into prostitution in the earlier period.

In contrast, Chun Amoey and her three companions were successful in escaping from the trade. Kidnapped in 1873, they were taken in a cargo boat to an awaiting Pacific Mail steamer docked near the port of Canton. When the lighter finally moored near the steamer, they indicated an unwillingness to go on board. The procuring agent relented and permitted them to return to the mainland.[53]

From approximately 1849 to 1867, Chinese prostitutes primarily journeyed to California by sailing ships on voyages that took fifty-five to one hundred days or more. The average fare to California was a hefty $50. With the advent of the Pacific Mail Steamship Company's China line in 1867, steamships dominated the trans-Pacific route until after the turn of the century. Unlike sailing ships, which held departure until fully booked, steamers (including *The Great Republic, China, Japan, City of Peking,* and *City of Tokio*) offered a regular timetable and a speedy voyage. The length of time required to reach San Francisco shortened from months to weeks. The route to San Francisco from Hong Kong via Yokohama, for example, averaged thirty-three days.[54] Steamships also had greater passenger capacity, which made possible the emigration of large groups of prostitutes. For example, on January 21, 1869, the steamer *Japan* carried as many as 240 prostitutes in steerage, in addition to numerous male emigrants. By the early 1870s, the price for a steamship ticket had also decreased and finally stabilized at around $40. Later, competition from the new Occidental and Oriental Steamship Company, which began service in 1876, drove the price down to $15.[55]

There is some evidence that these steamship companies might have been directly involved in the trafficking of women. As early as 1870, labor guilds in San Francisco criticized the Pacific Mail Steamship Company for its involvement in the shipping of procured women. They alleged that Chinese employees and sailors working for American steamship companies had smuggled women into vessels bound for the United States. In 1871, Hong Kong consul David Bailey made the same allegation.[56] These allegations may have had substance: between 1876 and 1916, steamship companies employed an estimated 70,000 Chinese in various capacities. In the 1870s, the Occidental and Oriental Steamship Company attempted to evade the whole process of certifying foreign travel, a strategy that seemed to indicate they knew their ships carried illegal emigrants.[57]

According to Henry Hiram Ellis, a San Francisco police officer from 1857 to 1877, Chinese procurers and brothel agents smuggled a small number of these women out of China or Hong Kong by hiding them behind false partitions in ship cargo holds.[58] Presumably, these women had either failed to receive clearance from the authorities to emigrate or had been directed to avoid the process. The majority of female emigrants, however, were packed together in steerage, separated from male emigrants.[59]

Conditions in the steerage section were extremely uncomfortable. In 1855, a San Francisco weekly reported that emigrants suffered from the "debility and scorbutic afflictions caused by the small quantity and bad quality of their food on board ship [and] in connection with the absence of proper ventilation and cleanliness." As late as 1888, one local journalist commented that "it would be a strange sight to one not accustomed to it to see a framework of shelves, not eighteen inches apart, filled with Chinese." He then remarked that "if a few barrels of oil were poured into the steerage hold, its occupants would enjoy the distinction, so often objected to, of being literally 'packed like sardines.'"[60]

For these women, the voyage to America was physically and emotionally exhausting. During storms, they curled up in berths and wedged themselves into firm positions; during meals, food, utensils, and people bounced about in all directions.

Cooped up in the overcrowded hold, these women endured primitive accommodations and poor food; sometimes, even basic human functions proved impossible because of overcrowding.[61] They felt confused and bewildered; the only person they recognized, and hardly a source of comfort, was the female chaperone. One woman, Chen Liang-shih, said, "While in Hong Kong, and after going on board the vessel, no one made any inquiries of me and I saw no one that I know." Lin Yu-shih wept for days on discovering she had been kidnapped. A female passenger offered her solace.[62] Undoubtedly, the greatest cause for anguish was leaving family and homeland behind.

❀

Whether eventually lured into prostitution or kidnapped, women made what they considered early on to be wise, albeit unwilling, choices. Many left their extended family and ancestral village under the direst circumstances. Suffering in a country undergoing social turmoil, many looked for employment beyond their village while others accepted marriage offers from sojourners in America. Like others lured into prostitution, Wong Ah So reeled from shock on discovering she had been duped. Her bewilderment was evident when she asked her "husband," "What is a prostitute? Am I not your wife?" She then endured seven months in San Francisco before seeing an opportunity to free herself. More tragic were women who committed suicide by jumping off the steamers.[63]

Almost all Chinese prostitutes, unlike Caucasian Western women, traveled unwillingly to the American West. As their steamers sped across the vast Pacific Ocean, they must have pondered what lay ahead. For most, it was an uncertain future, a period in their lives that would be marked by their struggle to extricate themselves from the chaos of the trade.

Nineteenth-century China was a country on the brink of catastrophe. It tottered under a ruined economy, and its people suffered untold misery. As forces converged to push Chinese women out of the country, these victims of circumstance tried to resist. A few succeeded, but the vast majority failed.

three

Arrival in America

Most Chinese emigrants to America during the nineteenth century found the voyage across the Pacific long and trying. But for a woman indentured or enslaved for sexual commerce, it was an especially painful ordeal. Even before setting foot on the shores of San Francisco, a "one hundred men's wife" faced a peculiar challenge that few travelers to Gum Saan ever experienced. Her entry into America, unlike that of free emigrants, depended on her willingness to cooperate with her victimizers.

During the voyage, agents and chaperones instructed women to memorize suitable responses to questions that customs officers might ask. Chinese emigrants at the end of the nineteenth century depended on a similar strategy — "training papers" — for their entry into America, but Chinese females imported for prostitution were the first group to employ such a technique. Agents also taught them to declare their occupation as seamstress.[1]

Such a ruse was necessary as the provisions of the 1862 Act to Prohibit the Coolie Trade prohibited involuntary immigration. Further, one of the stipulations in the Burlingame Treaty between the United States and China, a treaty ratified by Congress in 1869, disallowed involuntary immigration, including that of women under duress. Following the tightening of regulations in the wake of the Page Law of 1875, prostitutes increasingly posed as wives, sisters, or daughters of sojourners already in America. Depending on their age, they were told to identify the female chaperone as their mother or sister. Sometimes male agents accompanying them posed as fathers or husbands.[2]

Almost all the women agreed to comply with the instructions. Lee Sing, for example, crossed the Pacific Ocean with two men and a woman. One of the men asked her to pose as his wife during the forthcoming immigration clearance process. Her owners, out of fear that she would not acquiesce, promised her that she was on the "way to the land which flowed with gold, where she could make big money," and that she "could soon return to China a rich woman."[3] Another woman related that her agent "coaxed [her] to be quiet, and told [her] that she would have a rich husband and a fine time in California." Both were warned that failure to follow instructions would result in incarceration in a "devil [American] prison." Since many of these women were illiterate and from deprived backgrounds, they had little knowledge of their rights. Furthermore, for most, confinement on board the ship discouraged any thoughts of resistance or escape.[4]

Unsuspecting female emigrants, ignorant of their impending exploitation, must have shared the emotions felt by male emigrants when they first set eyes on the land of their destiny. Huie Kin, a male gum saan haak who came to California in 1868, remembered that the "feeling that welled up in us was indescribable," "to be actually at the 'Golden Gate' of the land of our dreams!"[5] When Wong Ah So landed in San Francisco she was filled with excitement because her "husband" had brought her to "such a grand, free country, where everyone was rich and happy."[6]

But women who were conscious of their plight reacted differently. Most of them felt a keen sense of anxiety, hoping that they could do something to change their lives. A few of them, after judging that no options existed, acted in desperation and committed suicide just before the ship docked at the pier.[7]

On arrival in Dai Fow (San Francisco), Chinese women disembarked near the old Oriental Warehouse on First Street near the Embarcadero, the landing point of most Chinese immigrants of the nineteenth century.[8] A few of the would-be prostitutes ignored requests to descend the gangway. Chen Liang-shih and Lin Yu-shih, seventeen and eighteen years old, respectively, and both procured by the same agent, cried to draw attention, shouting loudly that they had been kidnapped. This induced their agent, Wen Kuan, to flee. City authorities subsequently sent them back to China. Lui Nee U and Chan Lee Lung, both in their early twenties,

were lured on board the steamer in Hong Kong with
the promise of employment in another coastal port.
Instead, they found themselves journeying to America. By the time their steamer reached San Francisco,
self-pity had become resolve to free themselves.
They also refused to go ashore. "[We] told people
loudly that we had been kidnapped, begged them to
save us and to obtain redress; whereupon, Ah Man,
on seeing that the affair had oozed out, decamped
forthwith."[9]

Women also attempted to avoid their fate as
prostitutes by seeking assistance from Chinese diplomatic officials posted to the United States. On
February 19, 1879, Ch'en Shu-t'ang, the Chinese
consul in California, stood at the docks overseeing
the arrival of steamers carrying new emigrants to
America. One steamer, *City of Tokio*, carried forty-
four female passengers in its steerage section. One
of these passengers, a kidnapped woman, saw the
consul and pleaded with him for assistance. He
subsequently took her into his custody. On another
occasion, Ch'en sent two women back to China
following their dramatic suicide attempts. However, the consul reported regretfully that the "number of prostitutes here [San Francisco] is by far too
great," and he needed a better system to control the
trafficking.[10]

Chinese officials serving the consulate in San
Francisco throughout the nineteenth century exercised little power over the Chinese community and
never figured as major players in the struggle for
community leadership. There were just too few of
them to muster enough clout to threaten local mer-
cantile interests bent on maintaining control over
illegal immigration. In any event, these officials
looked out more for the interests of the Ch'ing

dynasty than those of the Chinese-American community; their primary loyalty lay with the government.[11] As a consequence, they did little to restrain the flow of prostitutes to California.

After disembarking, immigration clearance took place at the Oriental Warehouse, a five-story brick building with a metallic roof. Lighting was provided by oil lanterns and small skylights covered with wire netting. Window openings, consisting of iron shutters, existed only on the first floor of the building. From 1867 to 1910, this gloomy building greeted Chinese arrivals until the clearance process moved to the infamous Angel Island in San Francisco Bay, not far from Alcatraz Island.[12]

The immigration examination involved a barrage of questions. One Chinese woman, "Miss Ah Fook," during court proceedings to determine the legality of her entry, expressed her bewilderment with the extensive interrogation. The drawn-out process stemmed from problems in distinguishing between legal and illegal immigration. Customs officials had considerable trouble simply identifying Chinese women. As all of them dressed alike, their appearance did not reveal whether they were prostitutes or respectable wives of merchants.[13]

Some women who emigrated to join their husbands became victims of an imperfect system. In 1870, the California state legislature passed a discriminatory law that expressly required each Chinese female who wished to land on the California shore to provide proof that she was "a person of correct habits and good character." A later amendment to the law empowered the state immigration commissioner to demand from the owner or consignee of any vessel a bond of $500 in gold for each female passenger found to be "a lewd or debauched woman." In 1874, the commissioner of immigration, acting on the state law, charged that twenty-two women out of the eighty-nine who had disembarked from the steamer *Japan* had come to America for "immoral purposes." The police consequently removed these Chinese women to the county jail where they were held for more than a month. Meanwhile, immigration authorities made plans to send them back to China.[14]

Evidence is fragmentary, but it seems that those responsible for bringing the women to America decided to challenge this arbitrary exercise of the state's police power. Ah Lung, a prominent businessman, applied for a writ of habeas corpus, alleging that the women had been illegally deprived of their liberty. All gained a subsequent release when, in the case of *In re Ah Fong* (1874), the Supreme Court ruled that the laws exceeded the state's police power and also violated both the Burlingame Treaty and the Fourteenth Amendment.[15] The court's decision put to rest any further attempts by the state to control on its own accord the emigration of both Chinese males and females. However, after 1874, California and the rest of the Far West switched strategy and began lobbying for a federal solution to the "Chinese Question."[16]

Evidence points to the fact that at least a few of these women had come to join their husbands. This partly accounts for their emotional outbursts at the district court proceedings to determine the legality of their emigration. According to an eyewitness, one defendant insisted she had been wrongly accused, whereupon "one of the women jumped to her feet and let out a most unearthly yell." Almost immediately, "the whole lot were jabbering and screaming at the top of their voices, and it was found impossible to quiet them until they were hustled from the Court-room."[17]

Earlier in the same year, police removed two recently arrived married women from their homes on the suspicion that they had been sold into prostitution. The Methodist Chinese Mission authorities later took the women under their protection. Their husbands applied for a writ of habeas corpus demanding the release of their wives. When the case came before the court, the judge ruled in favor of the plaintiffs.[18] While poorly defined immigration laws at times victimized legal emigrants, loopholes in the same laws allowed women headed for bordellos to slip into the country. Of the twenty-two women freed following the court's ruling on *In re Ah Fong*, a few were later discovered working in Chinatown brothels.[19]

In general, male and female emigrants, including prostitutes, who failed to pass the immigration inspection were detained in a grim-looking frame building adjacent to the old Oriental Warehouse. One semiautobiographical novel described it as "a windowless barrack with flimsy walls [with] several policemen [standing] at the entrance to the compound."[20] In 1900, Reverend Ira Condit, a missionary who worked for years in California, spoke out against the inhumane conditions of the detention center: "All [are] penned up, like a flock of sheep, in a wharf-shed, for many days, and often weeks, at their own expense, and are denied all communication with their own people." Many fell sick, while others cried in anguish. Finally, the authorities freed them after receiving confirmation of legal entry.[21]

Photographs of the women sent by the U.S. consul in Hong Kong were the only evidence used to ascertain the legality of female emigrants in the wake of the passage of the Page Law (1875). However, immigration laws covered only the entry of women for prostitution; what took place after these women passed the examination was a local matter. Both federal and state laws tried to weed out illegal female arrivals, but they afforded only limited protection to Chinese women.[22]

During immigration examinations, most prostitutes did little to thwart attempts by their agents to pass them off as bona fide immigrants. The simple fact that many of them went on to join their sisters of misery in Chinatown might indicate that they accepted the deception. Those believing the promises of marriage or employment viewed the process as the norm for all emigrants. Chun Ho used a fraudulent certificate of emigration to enter America at the age of nineteen. She felt little compunction about illegally entering the United States, having been misled into believing that coming to Gum Saan would earn her a fortune. On her arrival, she furnished pat answers to predicted questions, and enduring little harassment, she received final clearance.[23]

Another example would be the twenty-two Chinese women who arrived in 1874 on board the steamer *Japan*. Although all insisted they had come to join their husbands or fiancés, Chinese merchants uninvolved in the trafficking claimed these women had been imported for prostitution. Newspaper accounts seemed to indicate that at least a few of the women told the truth, but other women found that a different fate awaited them.[24]

In 1878, another group of some sixty women, mostly older, testified that they had emigrated of their own free will. They produced certificates of emigration issued by the U.S. consul in Hong Kong as proof, although contemporaries later saw them working in brothels. Two Chinese women, kidnapped in Hong Kong and brought to America in 1879, entered with certificates that attested to their free will and voluntary emigration.[25]

Even if these women sensed something amiss, they had no motivation to seek help. They belonged to a different cultural and legal environment and had been brought up to believe that all "foreign devils" were "barbarians"—a belief reinforced by their agents during the voyage to America. A police officer who dealt with a number of runaway prostitutes claimed that young women "are made to believe that the Americans who interest themselves in their behalf and try to free them from their horrid conditions, are themselves women dealers, who are seeking to reduce them to slavery."[26]

Tentative evidence shows that a number of women might have resisted being parties to the deception. One group of twenty-four imported for the sexual trade failed completely their processing examinations. As related by a Chinese consulate official, all of them answered to names different from those given in the certificates. Since many of them were illiterate and could not read the Chinese version of the certificate, this may have been a case of failure to remember instructions. Some of them may have deliberately made the error to escape prostitution. But apparently one of them stepped forward during the examination and admitted that she had not traveled voluntarily.[27] In some instances, women had no reason to act contrary to their owner's instructions because they were still oblivious to their true status. The question of who defied and who complied hinged on the circumstances surrounding their separation from the familiar landscape of their birthplace.

Often more mature women played a role in the smuggling of opium, one of the biggest Chinese import-export businesses of the nineteenth century. Opium importers frequently also engaged in the trafficking of women for the sexual trade. Aware of this, customs officials paid close attention to Chinese women disembarking at the port. Although importation of opium remained legal until 1909, it was listed as "special merchandise" on which the U.S. Bureau of Customs imposed a hefty 100 percent ad valorem duty. Agents for importers of opium often tried numerous ingenious methods to escape the tax. These included hiding the substance in countless places: eggshells, wooden tubs and buckets, trunks and cabinets with false bottoms and secret drawers, birds' nests, shoe soles, and even bamboo canes and fishing rods.[28]

Sometimes drug traffickers hid packages of the drug underneath the clothes of mature prostitutes. In one case, opium was found by male customs officers on most of the 350 women who arrived on the *Japan*. A Chinese male traveler explained the search: "There were about twenty women in our company; this man was taking such liberties with the clothing and persons of these women as made me turn away mine eyes and blush for shame." The search took place in full view of passengers in the steerage section. The involvement of members of the San Francisco Ladies Protection and Relief Society in the body searches beginning in 1871 terminated this humiliation. The examinations then took place in the privacy of a Pacific Mail Steamship Company office.[29]

It is not known how significant a role trafficked women played in the contraband of opium, although Chinese importers did attempt on one occasion to bring in $15,000 worth.[30] Documents of the San Francisco customs collector's office indicate that the lackadaisical attitude of certain customs officials toward their duties occasionally resulted in smuggling or undervaluing of the goods. Records seized from a tong in 1875 show business dealings in importation of opium and at least 170 women.[31]

Both the consignments prostitutes carried with them and their own bodies became the focus of numerous power struggles between fighting tongs and what became, in 1882, the Chinese Consolidated Benevolent Association of San Francisco (CCBA-SF). The latter, better known to contemporaries as the Chinese Six Companies, served as the umbrella organization for district associations in the city. Fighting tongs represented importers of women; these organizations warded off political groups bent on waging a war against vice enterprises. One letter a fighting tong sent to a member read, "When a ship arrives in port with prostitutes on board . . . go down and receive them. . . . Use all your ability for the good of the Commonwealth."[32]

Struggles between the Chinese Six Companies and the tongs on occasion took place on the docks as soon as the ships reached port. On February 23, 1869, the *Alta California*, under the headline "The Great Excitement," reported the events of the previous day at the Oriental Warehouse. Since early morning, swarms of Chinese male onlookers had gathered at dockside waiting anxiously for the arrival of a ship. When the *Japan*, carrying 390 Chinese female passengers, finally tied up, a group of men, possibly tong members, rowed over to the ship, presumably with the intention of seizing the "cargo." The attempt ended in failure as the Chinese Six Companies had made arrangements for their protection.[33]

Contrary to what might be expected, tongs frequently resorted to the legal system with the help of Caucasian attorneys. Owners would rely on writs of habeas corpus to secure the women. The CCBA-SF also used the courts under the professed aim of thwarting the traffic. By and large, the CCBA-SF was locked in a bitter struggle with fighting tongs for hegemony over the Chinese community.[34]

During the 1850s, the Chinese Six Companies occasionally requested city authorities to "enact vigorous laws, by which these brothels and gambling places may be broken up."[35] As early as 1854, the organization committed itself to directly help break up the traffic because members had economic and family interests to protect. In that year, the benevolent associations signed a petition requesting city authorities to suppress Chinese brothels.[36]

As the anti-Chinese movement slowly gathered momentum in the 1850s – it would reach its peak in the 1870s – the Chinese Six Companies became more compelled to adopt measures to improve the image of the Chinese community. At least once, Chinese leaders released to newspapers a telegram they sent to the Tung Wah Hospital committee in Hong Kong which carried a plea "to inform the Chinese that they must not come. . . . [There will be] danger to life and property if they do." Through the use of newspapers and broadsides, the Chinese leadership also made sure that whites knew about their offer of free passage to any prostitute who desired to return to China.[37]

Overall, Chinese community leaders struck few blows at the brute forces behind the unlawful trade. Interviewed in the 1920s, a Chinese female informer, who had been a young girl at the end of the nineteenth century, struck at the heart of the problem when she said, "All kinds of people get mixed up in it. . . . I don't believe they will ever get rid of that until they get a generation that couldn't stand for that sort of thing, and respectable people couldn't get mixed up in it."[38] In the early decades of the twentieth century, progressive second-generation Chinese-Americans — banding together as sociopolitical groups such as the Chinese Society of English Education, the Chinese Students' Alliance, and the Chinese Native Sons — would convince the Chinese-American community that prostitution was a sign of decadence and should be rooted out. Until then, the attitude of most Chinese emigrants, males and females alike, was indifference.[39]

Exploited by both the tongs and the CCBA-SF, prostitutes attempted to adjust to the new conditions. Many elected to stay with those who brought them to the United States since they lacked the means to go back to China and had not received any assistance from the benevolent associations. The Chinese Six Companies nevertheless did succeed in sending a limited number of groups back to China in 1863, 1864, 1867, 1868, 1869, 1870, 1874, and 1876. In most cases, sources reveal little information on the women's reactions to these efforts to return them home, but there is no reason to suspect that they objected to the offer. In 1867, an undetermined number of women admitted to Chinese community leaders immediately on arrival that they were illegal emigrants. The Chinese Six Companies promptly arranged to send them home.[40]

During the frontier days of San Francisco, particularly in the 1850s, Chinese prostitutes who remained in the city were openly sold on the docks, with bidding being carried out in full view of the spectators, who frequently included police officers. As Victorian values gradually permeated the general moral consciousness, the chorus of disapproval swelled. Euro-American society objected to these blatant displays of moral transgression, and the site of the auctions moved to the vicinity of present-day Chinatown.[41] Sometime after 1860, prostitutes were immediately brought to Chinatown following their arrival in Gum Saan. On December 11, 1871, the *Alta California* gave the following account: "Seven or eight cars of the Omnibus line were reserved for the transportation of the women to the Chinese quarter . . . under the guardianship of policemen."[42]

In constant danger of being kidnapped by competing groups, most of the women also had to put up with physical and verbal abuse from a hostile white society. It was not unheard of for Chinese newcomers to be pelted with bricks thrown by white hoodlums. The violence perpetrated against Chinese emigrants grew so intense that in 1876 the Chinese Six Companies singled it out as one of the factors dissuading male emigrants from bringing their families with them.[43] Chinese women targeted for the entertainment world had to endure the harassment not only of Euro-Americans but also of their countrymen. One observer in 1874 described how a group of recent female arrivals were "jeered and 'hi-hied' by the crowd of common Chinamen waiting outside the gates."[44] A few women, such as Wong Ah So and "Rose," evaded the humiliation because they came as part of a family and thus managed to slip unobtrusively into the country.[45]

For Chinese women, the fear and anxiety engendered by the general animosity and the unpredictability of their future increased on arrival at the "Queen's Room," the place where they would be sold. The location of the auction changed over time, corresponding to the downward spiral in the status of prostitutes. In 1871, the sale was held in the Chinese traditional theater on Dupont Street, a major thoroughfare in San Francisco. In the next ten years, prostitutes, relegated to the periphery of both the Chinese community and Euro-American society, gradually concentrated along alleys and by-streets. By 1880, the sale took place in the basement of a "Joss House" (Chinese temple) fronting St. Louis Alley, where prostitutes plied their trade.[46]

Most Chinese women found the sale demeaning. The San Francisco Chronicle claimed that these women "were stripped and paraded onto a platform where prospective buyers could inspect and bid." In 1871, the Alta California reported that they "were assorted, marked over and sent" to buyers. A purchaser usually paid $40 for protective service rendered by tongs, over and above the asking price for each woman.[47]

During the auction, a few merchants and tradesmen might buy a woman to be a secondary wife or concubine. A reporter of a local newspaper claimed that "the fresh and pretty females who came from the interior are used to fill special orders from wealthy merchants and prosperous tradesmen."[48] The fate of such women depended on the social status of their husbands. One unnamed secondary wife, married to an herbalist, led an arduous life. Back in China, her husband's first wife played the role of a matriarch overseeing family properties. In contrast, the younger wife raised a number of children, ran the household, and worked long hours in the family shop.[49]

Certainly, Chinese men benefited from the domestic labor performed by their companions. Secondary wives or concubines were not always treated as drudges. They sometimes led a fairly comfortable life and usually enjoyed a status higher than that of a prostitute. Cohabitation with a Chinese sojourner provided access to a standard of living otherwise closed because of the restricted labor market. In his notes, the Presbyterian minister A. W. Loomis observed, "[They are] not concubines in the Turkish sense but in the old patriarchal sense—the child born of them by Chinese law and usage are perfectly legitimate. These families live in the upper stories and rooms in the rear of the stores, . . . crowded but cozy and comfortably furnished."[50]

Wealthy Chinese families bought young girls for domestic service, while proprietors of brothels purchased the remainder. Some of those purchased for brothels were sent off as far north as British Columbia.[51] It is possible that entrepreneurs engaged in legitimate businesses were also a party to the exploitation of women, as hinted by the following document.[52]

BILL OF SALE
Loo Woo to Loo Chee

Rice, six mats at $2	$ 12
Shrimps, 50 lbs., at 10¢	5
Girl	250
Salt Fish, 60 lbs., at 10¢	6
	273

In time, women sold into prostitution learned of their value to brothel proprietors and used that knowledge to improve their lives. During a period of ten years, Wong Ah Sing worked for four different owners. When sold at the age of ten, she fetched only $20, but ten years later, her master received $750. As she grew older, she became wiser. She refused to cohabit with the owner and insisted that he bring her to the inner city closer to the Chinese community where available female companionship offered relief from the humdrum routine. Her owner, Lee Chuen, acquiesced to her demand. However, he ignored her pleas for money to seek medical treatment.[53] In another case, an unidentified married woman in her thirties, sold in 1873, fetched merely $105, although the price included her son. As a prostitute past her prime, she feared possible ill-treatment at the hands of her master when she failed to draw customers. She decided to escape and sought protection from the local police authorities. She was finally remanded to China.[54]

Chinese prostitutes usually signed a bill of sale, which also served as an agreement between the purchaser and the victim herself. For the buyer, the agreement offered protection from future legal entanglement. Few prostitutes could read the terms of service in the contract, although most acknowledged receiving a lump sum of money from the purchaser. Possibly, their parents had received this sum during the earlier transaction. Yut Kum's agreement stipulated that her owner expected her to work for four years without receiving any wages.[55]

In general, most prostitutes had to labor for a fixed number of years. However, these women could end up serving extended contracts because their owners penalized them by increasing the length of their service if they fell ill, even due to menstruation and pregnancy. Women also faced the same penalty if they left the sexual trade before completing the required term. The contract issued for Ah Ho provided for a penalty if she ran away before the end of the four-year working period. The penalty of a longer service term seems to indicate that attempts to escape from owners were common occurrences.[56] Finally, just like commodities, these women were considered transferable. Loi Yau's agreement stipulated that she would work for someone else if her current master decided to return to China.[57]

Although many women could not read their contracts, most understood their situation. Apparently, only a few succeeded in escaping from the place of auction before their sale. Perhaps the unfamiliar surroundings weighed against their chances of a successful escape. In 1870, on arrival in San Francisco, ten Chinese women fled to the Methodist Chinese Mission for protection. (Its rescue home, the Mission House, was not yet in full operation, so the women were directed to the general mission.) They eventually made their way back to their homeland.[58] On August 12, 1873, four escaped from a house designated as the auction site. Each of them decamped with $155, the amount they had received from the manager of the brothel. Nothing was ever heard of their fate.[59] The life of one woman, Ah Tsun, is clearer. Sold apparently as a mooi-tsai at the age of sixteen, she fled to the Presbyterian rescue home — officially known as the Chinese Mission Home — when she discovered her mistress was shortly going to transfer her to a brothel owner. She stayed at the rescue home for a few years before she finally married a Chinese immigrant.[60]

To these new arrivals, the city and its people seemed a puzzle. In fact, a few even resisted attempts by police officers to take them into protective custody. During a police raid on the Queen's Room on August 12, 1873, four Chinese women insisted on remaining with their owner, although the police informed them of their rights. Two other women, being minors, were forcibly removed to the Mission House of the Methodist Church and ended up in the homes of benevolent Chinese families.[61]

Although new residents of brothels confronted unmitigated oppression, they were not without the spirit of resistance. One girl of sixteen refused to submit to the demands of her owner. He starved her for days on end, whipped her, and even threatened to kill her. But she still could not be coerced. A few weeks passed. Then she heard about the Presbyterian Chinese Mission Home and with the help of some friends, took flight for the sanctuary.[62]

At times, however, freedom proved exceedingly elusive despite the aid of beloved ones. In an open letter, Chen Ha begged his fellow sojourners to help him rescue his sister, Ah Shau, from a life of infamy. He shared the tale of his sister being "constantly subjected to distressing persecutions to compel her to yield to dishonor." Yet, he continued, "firmly she resists, and continually suffers trials and scourging with anguish." Chen Ha finally secured enough money and brought the case to court. Unfortunately, Ah Shau saw her hopes dashed; the court ruled in favor of the defendant, and she was returned to the custody of her owner.[63]

For women who stayed with their owners, albeit unwillingly, life took a different path. Unless sold to brothel owners in remote areas of the Far West, most women were brought to the Chinese ghetto. Moving along narrow alleys, they saw the wooden buildings wedged in between earlier brick structures.[64] Finally, they arrived at the brothel houses, many of which featured a number of compartments to be inhabited by the women. "A room is divided into several compartments, by gay colored chintz or cambric partitions," according to one account.[65] Most of the quarters were sparsely furnished, perhaps a few rickety chairs, small boxes, and hard bunks of shelves covered with matting against the wall. A few brothels appeared to be more comfortable and in some cases, even elegant. "Rich drapery of gorgeous colors falls in graceful folds from the arch of chamber alcoves; the carpets are soft and pretty, the furniture quite costly," wrote a visitor to one such establishment.[66]

Often dressed in plain cotton, these brothel residents plied their trade in the evening.[67] During the daytime, prostitutes worked in sweatshops. They sewed shirts, undergarments, and shoes. Their unpaid labor fulfilled subcontracts negotiated by the brothel owners with major manufacturers — an economic relationship known as the putting-out system. As nonskilled workers, they joined many other Chinese in the industrial development of San Francisco. By 1872, both Chinese males and females made up nearly half of the labor force in the city's four major industries—boots and shoes, woolens, cigars and tobacco, and sewing.[68]

❀

The experience of Chinese prostitutes on their arrival in America differed. While most suffered a harrowing voyage, an unbearable test of human endurance, it would be wrong to argue that all women became disenchanted with the Flowery Flag nation image while on board ship, or even on arrival in California. Some women did not discover what was expected of them until much later. Wong Ah So's idyllic portrait of America was shattered only two weeks after she arrived in San Francisco. "Rose" knew nothing of what her owners had in mind for her until a month after her arrival. The period of false security lasted longer for Chun Ho. According to her story, she lived with a family for two months following her arrival in San Francisco. At the end of that period, her employer lured her into prostitution.[69]

Some of the women understood their fate and took it on themselves to change their lives after landing in America. But most of the young girls, those below the age of fifteen, did nothing to resist exploitation because they were powerless. They were too young to assess their situation and choose an available option. One such young girl, Tsoi Yee, came to America at the age of fourteen. During her childhood years in China, she had never wandered beyond the perimeters of her village. Suddenly plucked from that environment and transported halfway around the world, she landed in a foreign country with no family to fall back on for support. Her reaction was predictable; she suffered emotional anguish and in frustration, threw tantrums.[70]

Only a small number of women escaped on arrival at the auction site. In 1869, the police arrested twenty-eight importers of Chinese prostitutes, but the newspaper reported no cases of runaways from the auction locale throughout that entire year. For the period 1870 to 1873, the *San Francisco Chronicle* reported, on the average, only two cases of runaways per year.[71]

The period after arrival for most Chinese women was a time of harsh adjustment to a new environment in which cultures—Chinese and Euro-American—were in collision with one another. Later on, prostitutes found themselves on the receiving end of anti-Chinese rhetoric. Some women resisted the exploitation, but others accepted it, though reluctantly. Those still bound to the ties of Confucianism apparently accepted prostitution fatalistically. Wong Ah So, for example, described her condition as "very tragic" but with resignation, said it was "just my fate."[72]

Following their arrival, prostitutes struggled to adapt to a rapid succession of events. Various groups and individuals—tongs, the Chinese Six Companies, policemen, and businessmen, particularly brothel owners—used them for financial gain. Many yielded to these covert and overt pressures; some even committed suicide. Others resisted by adopting measures that would release them from sexual exploitation. Some triumphed and rejoined the wider society. A number of them, however, failed to break free.

An 1881 sketch of U.S. Customs officers searching Chinese immigrants for smuggled opium. After 1871, women were examined in a separate facility away from public view. From *Harper's Weekly*, January 7, 1882. Courtesy Rutherford B. Hayes Presidential Center, Fremont, Ohio.

A "one hundred men's wife" dressed in traditional clothing. Courtesy Society of California Pioneers.

Officials of the Chinese Consolidated Benevolent Association of San Francisco, who provided much of the community leadership during the nineteenth century. Courtesy Society of California Pioneers.

Bartlett Alley, infamous for brothels and opium dens. Courtesy
Society of California Pioneers.

A Chinese prostitute outside her domicile. Courtesy Society of California Pioneers.

Young woman brought to the United States to work as a domestic servant, or *mooi-tsai*. Courtesy Society of California Pioneers.

Chinese prostitutes soliciting customers. Note the decrepit buildings that served as both places of business and residences. Courtesy San Francisco History Room, San Francisco Public Library.

Chinese women in a predominantly white business district. This is an unusual occurrence as Chinese women were rarely seen outside Chinatown. Courtesy San Francisco History Room, San Francisco Public Library.

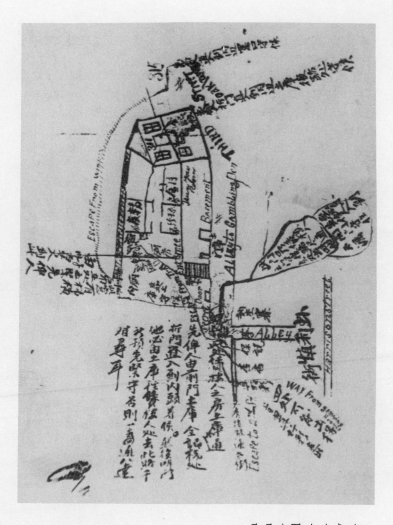

Diagram of the location of a brothel drawn by a young man based on information two residents had provided. The police apparently used this to rescue the women. Courtesy Society of California Pioneers.

The corner of Sacramento Street and Dupont Street (present-day Grant Avenue) at the turn of the century. By then, few prostitutes lived along these busy thoroughfares. Courtesy Society of California Pioneers.

Ella May Clemmons and her husband, Wong Sun Yue. The two met when she was working as a missionary in Chinatown, San Francisco. Their marriage, a rare interracial union at that time, lasted at least ten years. Courtesy Society of California Pioneers.

The Methodist rescue home on Washington Street. Courtesy San Francisco History Room, San Francisco Public Library.

A mock wedding presented as an evening entertainment at a mission rescue home. Courtesy Society of California Pioneers.

A cartoon in the *San Francisco Illustrated WASP* (June 26, 1880) mocking intercultural marriages. The children have been given grotesque features. Courtesy Bancroft Library, University of California, Berkeley.

Adjusting to Life
in Chinatown

Whe Chinese prostitutes finally became part of the business, they found their daily existence drastically altered. They had to adjust to an alien environment and to the constant pressure exerted by both the Chinese community and white society. Their predicament was representative of that experienced by those who are poor, female, and nonwhite in urban America: economic exploitation, poverty, and cultural domination. As the years dragged on, Chinese women who were members of the demimonde were increasingly pushed to the periphery of society. Some found it impossible to cope with the emotional stress, while others remained steadfast in their resolve to join mainstream society.[1]

The census schedules for the city of San Francisco of 1860 yielded 583 prostitutes (table 1). This figure was computed by eliminating from a total Chinese female population of 681 those women engaged in the following occupations: laundrywoman (17); gardener (5); domestic servant (1); fisherwoman (1) (see table 2). In addition, those aged twelve and below—a total of thirty-six—seemed unlikely to be prostitutes because of their youth. Finally, another thirty-eight women lived in households with at least one Chinese male present; possibly many of these women considered themselves housewives. Single women living alone or with other females and not holding down any job in all probability provided commercialized sex. The nearly six hundred women involved in this line of work made up 85.6 percent of the Chinese female population or 96 percent of Chinese women employed in a money-earning capacity.

The high percentage of Chinese women involved in prostitution in 1860 falls within the bounds of earlier historical studies. Prior to June 1860, the

TABLE 1

Number and Percentage of Chinese Prostitutes Relative to the Chinese Female Population in San Francisco, 1860–1880

	Number of Prostitutes	Total Population	Percentage
1860	583	681	85.6
1870	1,565	2,499	62.6
1880	305	1,742	17.5

SOURCE: U.S. Bureau of the Census, Eighth Census of the United States (1860), *Population Schedules, San Francisco*, M-683, reel 67–68; Ninth Census of the United States (1870), *Population Schedules, San Francisco*, M-593, reel 79–85; Tenth Census of the United States (1880), *Population Schedules, San Francisco*, T-9, reel 72–79.

TABLE 2
Occupations of Chinese Women in San Francisco, 1860–1880

	1860		1870		1880	
	Number	Percentage	Number	Percentage	Number	Percentage
Prostitute	583	96	1,565	92.3	305	52.9
Domestic servant	1	0.2	69	4.1	129	22.3
Seamstress	–	–	18	1.1	64	11.1
Factory worker	–	–	20	1.2	44	7.6
Cook	–	–	3	0.1	12	2.0
Laundress	17	2.8	1	0.1	1	0.2
Laborer	–	–	11	0.6	5	0.9
Gardener	5	0.8	–	–	–	–
Fisherwoman	1	0.2	1	0.1	2	0.4
Actress	–	–	6	0.3	2	0.4
Schoolteacher	–	–	–	–	4	0.7
Merchant	–	–	–	–	4	0.7
Butcher	–	–	–	–	2	0.4
Nurse	–	–	1	0.1	2	0.4
Carpenter	–	–	–	–	–	–
Total	607	100.0	1,695	100.0	576	100.0

SOURCE: U.S. Bureau of the Census, Eighth Census of the United States (1860), *Population Schedules, San Francisco,* M-683, reel 67–68; Ninth Census of the United States (1870), *Population Schedules, San Francisco,* M-593, reel 79–85; Tenth Census of the United States (1880), *Population Schedules, San Francisco,* T-9, reel 72–79.

month when the census began, some 1,900 Chinese women had arrived at the port of San Francisco since 1854 and had dispersed all over California. Chinese-American historian Sucheng Chan, who examined selected surviving California schedules of population censuses excluding those of San Francisco, concluded that virtually all the Chinese women in northern rural California in the year 1860 were prostitutes, constituting 3 to 7 percent of the Chinese population in each of the examined counties.[2]

In the city and county of San Francisco, the number of Chinese women working as providers of sexual services increased nearly threefold during the 1860s. This increase stemmed from the large influx of trafficked women during the 1860s, the decade with the highest number of female arrivals and the lowest number of women returning to the Middle Kingdom. The growth of the female population was part of the expansion of the city's Chinese community during that decade. A cutback in mining activities resulted in an exodus to the metropolis in search of a livelihood. Even available seasonal or temporary employment in agriculture and railroad construction failed to stem the flow of sojourners to San Francisco from inland California. The number of settled residents in the city's mutable Chinese community tripled between 1860 and 1870, from less than 3,000 to over 12,000 and from less than 8 percent to over 24 percent of the state's Chinese population.[3] The arrival of new urbanites led to boom times for the vice industry. From the late 1860s onward, opium dens, gambling establishments, and, of course, houses of prostitution blossomed in Chinatown.

Census takers in 1870 — told for the first time to describe as accurately as possible the occupations of all inhabitants — identified approximately 72 percent of the Chinese female population as prostitutes. They recorded 1,807 prostitutes in a total Chinese female population of 2,499. Some 242 persons might have been mistakenly listed as prostitutes as the conditions in which they lived suggest they had conjugal ties and established family units with their husbands. Some shared a dwelling with only one man, and many of these households had children. Seventy-one of those placed in the prostitution category resided in households with men whose occupation was specifically listed as "laborer." This means that in all probability, the city housed 1,565 Chinese prostitutes, that is, about 63 percent of the Chinese female population (table 1).

Compared to the number of non-Chinese public women — 469, including Mexican-Americans and African-Americans, for a citywide non-Chinese female population of 63,291 — Chinese women were represented heavily in this occupation (table 3). The actual figure could have been a little higher because the census as a whole suffered from extremely poor field procedures, resulting in many undercounts.[4] The preponderance of Chinese public women among the female population in the 1870s extended beyond the San Francisco Bay area. One Chinese official who visited California in 1876 estimated there were 6,000 Chinese women living in the United States and deemed between 80 and 90 percent of them "daughters of joy."[5]

In 1870 a smaller percentage of the Chinese female population was engaged in prostitution than had been ten years before. It is obvious from the data

TABLE 3
Prostitutes and Female Population in San Francisco, 1870–1880

	Chinese			Non-Chinese		
	Prosti-tutes	Female	Percent-age	Prosti-tutes	Female	Percent-age
1870	1,565	2,499	62.6	469	63,291	0.74
1880	305	1,742	17.5	265	99,609	0.27

SOURCE: U.S. Bureau of the Census, Eighth Census of the United States (1860), *Population Schedules, San Francisco,* M-683, reel 67–68; Ninth Census of the United States (1870), *Population Schedules, San Francisco,* M-593, reel 79–85; Tenth Census of the United States (1880), *Population Schedules, San Francisco,* T-9, reel 72–79.

that since 1860, Chinese women in San Francisco had moved into a wider variety of jobs — mostly occupations also engaged in by Chinese men — though many still worked as prostitutes.[6] Women employed in fields outside prostitution included 79 in personal and professional services, of which 69 worked as domestic servants, 6 as actresses, 3 as cooks, and 1 as a laundress. Census takers also listed 11 laborers, 1 carpenter, and 1 fisherwoman. The rest of them, 38 persons, labored in industries, particularly in shoe factories and the sewing trades (table 2). This gives a total of 130 women, or only 7.7 percent of Chinese female wage-earners, who worked outside prostitution.

There is a possibility that the increased number of women in nonprostitution jobs indicates that women were leaving the trade. But immigration records refute this assumption. The decade of the 1860s witnessed the arrival of almost 3,500 females, the largest number for any ten-year period in the nineteenth century.[7] Although prostitutes made up the majority, it is likely that some were married women traveling across the Pacific to join their husbands, especially since the number of women listed as "keeping house" increased tenfold after 1860. Hence a large number of the Chinese women in other occupations in all likelihood were new immigrants. This interpretation is further supported by the explosion in the Chinese female population in 1869 and 1870, comprising roughly 60 percent of female immigration in the second decade of Chinese arrivals. What becomes evident is that by 1870, Chinese women, both in San Francisco and neighboring counties, had made very limited progress in moving away from the sexual trade.

Of the remaining 804 Chinese women in San Francisco, most earned no wages. Women who were not identified by occupation and those identified as "at home" fell into this category. As many as 448 of the women, or close to 56 percent of the unemployed, listed themselves as housewives who managed households. The rest stayed at home — most female children were in this category — with their families.

Prostitution continued to be the main occupation for female wage-earners in 1880, although an overall decline had become evident since the last census. Disregarding women listed as "keeping house," "housewife," or "at home," and those not identified by census takers, 683 women from a total female population of 1,742 were gainfully employed. Of this female workforce, census takers recorded 412 women, or 60.3 percent of the workforce, as prostitutes. One hundred seven of them, however, appeared on the schedules as married. Since Chinese culture did not condone married women working as prostitutes, it is safe to say that census takers very likely mistakenly identified those 107 persons. Deducting that figure from the total number of women listed as "prostitute" leaves an estimated 305 women, or 52.9 percent of the workforce, active in sexual commerce (table 2). This figure appears reasonable. In 1879, the *Morning Call* claimed that between 300 and 400 Chinese women were working in inner city brothels.[8] Compared to the 265 non-Chinese in a total female population of 99,609 persons, the Chinese by far constituted the majority in the trade (table 3).

Approximately 1,260 Chinese women, or 80.5 percent, engaged in sexual commerce in 1870 had either left the business or moved out of the city by 1880. Obviously, the interval between the two censuses witnessed the continuing steady decline in the percentage of Chinese women working as prostitutes relative to the overall female population. The number of such working women climbed back a little in the late 1880s. In 1887, the California Bureau of Labor reported 567 prostitutes inhabiting the city together with 87 children.[9]

A small number of the Chinese women who left the vice trade might have gravitated to a limited number of new fields, although spread out thinly in those occupations. Domestic service emerged in the late 1870s as the sector that employed the largest number of nonprostitutes. Tabulation of the census schedules of 1880 yielded 129 women working as domestic servants, paralleling the movement of a disproportionate number of Chinese males into the service sector. Forty-four of the women labored as factory hands, many employed in the tobacco industry. Another sixty-four worked as "tailoress" or "seamstress" and labored in the shoe and tailoring trades (table 2). "In the trimming and finishing [of shoes and clothing]," commented a Presbyterian minister who ran a mission in the Chinese quarters, "occupation is afforded to many of the Chinese women."[10]

The movement of women into the manufacturing industries followed the increasing involvement of Chinese males in such enterprises, as manufacturing gradually displaced the service sector in importance in San Francisco. Both Chinese women and Chinese men held mainly semi- or nonskilled jobs, facing sweatshop conditions and receiving low pay. During the nineteenth century, Chinese women and men alike found limited economic opportunities in a racially segmented economy.[11] For some women, it was necessity that forced a move into the workplace. Census schedules sometimes show women and children living in domiciles without any males present. Some of these mothers held jobs other than prostitution. Possibly abandoned by their domestic partners and left to fend for themselves, these wage-earning women overcame, aside from the barrier of prejudice, the sanctions of Chinese culture against women in the workplace.[12]

The concentration of Chinese women in a narrow number of occupations and their overrepresentation in prostitution suggest the workings of a labor market in which not only racial but also gender stratification relegated ethnic women to the bottom of the job market. Both the 1870 and 1880 censuses provide invaluable information on the distribution of sexes in various occupations.

In 1870, women of all racial origins in California formed a mere 5.8 percent of the workforce, although women aged ten and above, considered physically able to work, constituted 34 percent of the state's general population. Ten years later, women in California had gained little ground. Scarcely 7.5 percent of the total labor force was composed of women, although those aged ten and above made up 37.6 percent of the state's population.[13]

On the surface, Chinese women who held wage-earning jobs seemed economically better off than their countrywomen in commercialized vice. But often they were not adequately rewarded for their toil. Nearly all of them can be found living in households in which at least one man, frequently more, held the same job, perhaps suggesting participation in family-run businesses. Chinese women did not control the finances of the ventures; they were not given a voice in a matter deemed to be a male prerogative. Women engaged in prostitution had limited choices if they chose to leave the trade, and for many, marriage proved the only option available.

Those who remained prostitutes—and many did—faced a bleak life; they could not shake off grinding poverty rooted in their powerless position in the vice enterprise. This conclusion becomes obvious after studying information in two specific columns—"value of personal estate" and "value of real estate"—included in the 1860 and 1870, but not in the 1880, census schedules. In 1860, none of the Chinese prostitutes owned any real estate. Only 6 among 583 owned personal assets of any worth. All, except one, possessed a personal estate valued at less than $300. All six were in their late twenties, possibly free prostitutes who had worked for some time. While it seems that almost all of them held negligible amounts of property, this cannot be taken

at face value because most of the people in Chinatown left those columns blank.

Comparing Chinese prostitutes to non-Chinese
prostitutes is one way of drawing a better picture of
the former group's economic standing. In 1870, forty-eight non-Chinese working women owned property ranging in value from a low of $100 to a high of
$17,500. The average was $1,315. In the same year,
three Chinese women revealed as "keeping brothels" held assets worth less than $600. None of the
other Chinese prostitutes gave information on their
personal wealth. It is fair to surmise that Chinese
public women fared worse than their white sisters.
In one study of the 1870 census of Virginia City,
Nevada, it was found that none of the seventy-one
Chinese prostitutes held any property. Yet twenty-
four of the sixty-three Euro-American prostitutes
had acquired some form of property, with the most
well-to-do owning assets totaling $5,000. Among
the twenty-four women, $31,900 had been amassed.
Interestingly enough, these white prostitutes were
far better off economically than any of the "respectable" women.[14]

One quantitative historian used the NPH (number of people per household) index to study the
status of various occupational groups within the
Chinese community. His index, which rests on the
assumption that the smaller the number of persons
in a household, the higher the status of the head of
that household, was applied to a random sample of
residents in Chinatown. The results show that in a
list of fifteen principal occupations, prostitutes came
out ahead of just three others — gambler, shoemaker,
and cigar maker — in the socioeconomic structure of
the Chinese community. Within the community, a

one hundred men's wife occupied a marginal position.[15]

Many Chinese prostitutes had little economic power as a result of the nature of their relationship with their owner or manager. Just like those in China, these women had given away, albeit unwillingly, their economic rights.[16] Indentured for sexual commerce, few had control over the monetary returns of their work. One sociologist has estimated that in the nineteenth century, on the average, a prostitute earned about $850 per year.[17] In the early decades of the twentieth century, a Chinese prostitute by the name of "Rose" made $7,000 for her owner during the first twenty-two months of her residence in San Francisco.[18] Since the average purchase price of a woman was approximately $530 in the late nineteenth-century and the cost of maintaining a woman at subsistence level was a trifling $96 per year, an owner obviously pocketed a more than comfortable profit within the space of just a few years.[19]

Typically, a prostitute turned over all her earnings to the owner or brothel proprietor. Cum Choy alleged that her owner made her hand in all payments to him. In contrast, Ah Woo, aged twenty-two, retained a portion of her earnings. There must have been a significant number of women like Ah Woo who maintained limited control over their finances, for a number paid special policemen (employed by Chinese citizens) surcharges of fifty cents a week.[20] Few women, however, enjoyed the enviable position of "Selina," an independent Chinese prostitute popular in the early 1880s. Already a working woman in her early twenties, she rose quickly in the hierarchy of her trade, leaving behind the days of being a crib prostitute and becoming a genteel courtesan. Her services much in demand, she boldly charged twice the usual amount. Her earnings afforded her a leisurely life.[21]

The poverty faced by most of these women caused additional hardship during periods of debility. When struck down by ailments induced by drug abuse, the infirmities of old age, or physical disorders, including venereal diseases, few had the means to seek medical treatment. Undoubtedly, most Chinese emigrants avoided Caucasian doctors because of the language barrier, higher fees, and unfamiliar medications and methods. Those unencumbered by such problems discovered that health authorities, reflecting the anti-Chinese mood of the nineteenth century, often shut them out from medical facilities. Physicians in San Francisco lobbied to ban Chinese prostitutes from the City and County Hospital. Nonetheless, a few Chinese emigrants did gain admission to hospitals.[22]

Joan B. Trauner, a medical historian, calculated that during the years 1870–97 less than 0.1 percent of the patients in the San Francisco City and County Hospital were of Chinese origin. Census schedules for 1870 and 1880 prove more illuminating. For both of these years, census takers listed patients found in the hospital. The records indicate that none of the Chinese patients in that institution identified themselves as prostitutes. However, some of the white female patients professed to be prostitutes. Unlike Euro-American public women, the Chinese found themselves also banned from the San Francisco Female Hospital.[23]

Not until 1900 could Chinese women turn to some sort of nursing facility; in that year, under the sponsorship of the Chinese Six Companies, the Tung Wah Dispensary opened at Sacramento Street. Actually a far cry from the Western hospitals of the times, this "deathhouse" continued to operate for the next quarter century.

The year 1925 marked a new era in medical rehabilitation for the ethnic community. The opening of the Chinese Hospital in that year heralded the end of a long period of neglect.[24] Until then, Chinese women sought compassion elsewhere. Unfortunately, little around them offered much hope. Owners of Chinese women refused to provide nursing care when they could no longer work. Accounts of the treatment these women endured at the hands of their owners abounded in popular writings of the nineteenth century. A typical piece read, "and when — from whatever cause — no longer able to serve the purposes of bringing money to their masters or mistresses, they are flung aside to die miserably in any corner, without any alleviation of their sufferings."[25]

The stereotype, however, misrepresented the women's efforts to find medical care. A few prostitutes who had the means sought medical help provided by herbalists and pharmacies in the classic tradition of Chinese medicine. There was no lack of Chinese traditional physicians; signboards outside their practices boasted about their efficacy in curing diseases of all sorts. But the poor found the cost prohibitive. Most prostitutes, who had little money, could not afford the remedies prescribed.[26] Tragically, Chinese prostitutes in grave health faced death alone.

Some slightly more fortunate women found their way to so-called hospitals established by clan associations, facilities consisting of little more than a few tiny rooms furnished with straw mats.[27] A visitor to one such "hospital" recounted how he and a police officer went through a "low" door into a room, dimly "lighted by a China nut-oil lamp." They found, "stretched on the floor of this damp, foul-smelling den . . . four female figures, . . . victims of the most fearful . . . loathsome disease."[28] Because of the prostitutes' tarnished image and insignificant position in the community, clan and district associations offtered only token assistance. For some, suicide became the quick solution to their despair. When death came, Chinese prostitutes' remains, unlike those of most Chinese emigrants, were seldom sent back to China.[29]

The marginal existence of Chinese prostitutes also manifested in social status. Over a period of twenty years, their social standing in the society eroded. This is reflected in the changing spatial distribution of prostitution.

During the 1850s, Chinese prostitutes lived in two different vice zones: most were within a zone of Ward Four and a few were scattered in a smaller zone of Ward Ten (which until 1856 was part of Ward Eight) (map 2 and 3). In 1852, Ah Toy and a handful of Chinese prostitutes moved from north of Clay Street to Pike Street in Ward Four closer to Sacramento Street or T'ang Yen Gai (Chinese Men's Street), the core of the Chinese ghetto.[30] By then, Pike Street had been transformed into one part of the general zone of prostitution in San Francisco.

When the first sizable group of Chinese prostitutes arrived in 1854, they dispersed all over Ward Four — Chinatown — living in brothels clustered along major thoroughfares such as Dupont Street (present-day Grant Avenue), Pike Street (Waverly Place),

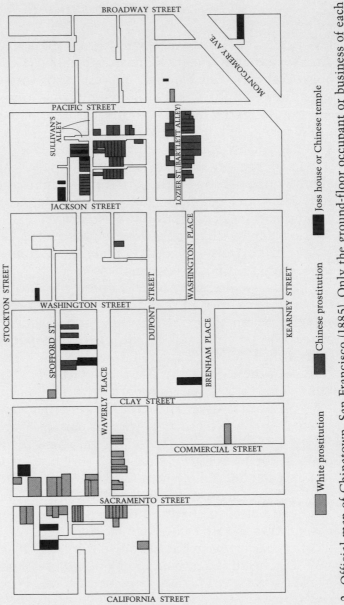

2. Official map of Chinatown, San Francisco (1885). Only the ground-floor occupant or business of each building is shown. Prepared by the San Francisco Board of Supervisors.

■ Joss house or Chinese temple

■ Chinese prostitution

■ White prostitution

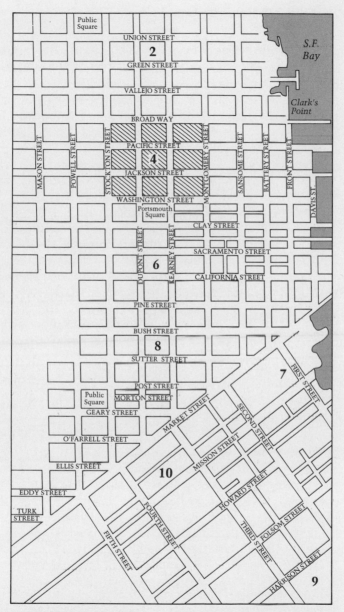

3. San Francisco, 1860, showing ward numbers and the Barbary Coast (cross-hatched area), the primary zone of prostitution during the nineteenth century.

and portions of Pacific Street. A few must have lived
on Jackson Street as newspapers in 1859 covered a
number of acts of violence committed against Chinese prostitutes on that thoroughfare. Brothels along
Pacific and Jackson lay just outside the Chinese
immigrants' neighborhood, which was concentrated
in a section bounded by Stockton on the west, Kearny on the east, and Sacramento and Clay on the
south and north, respectively.[31] The locale implies
that these women served both whites and Chinese.
Most Chinese prostitutes, concentrated by residence
and occupation in an area less than half a mile from
Dupont Street, operated within a primary zone of
prostitution. In the 1850s, both Chinese and non-
Chinese worked along these streets, especially Dupont and Pacific, and the cross streets — Pike Street
included — between Dupont and Stockton. Even in
San Francicso's early years, the physical and spatial
patterns of prostitution (both Chinese and non-
Chinese) showed the beginnings of the tenderloin
district of saloons and brothels, an area radiating
from the center of Chinatown.

The majority of prostitutes of all ethnic origins
congregated in one specific area by the late 1850s,
segregated from other commercial enterprises by
specialization of land use. Since men worked downtown and lived in the suburbs, Dupont Street and
the thoroughfares around it became access routes to
the downtown business district. Because men could
conveniently reach that vice district from either
work or home, a large cluster of brothels sprang up
in that area.[32] Unlike New York City, the general
shortage of women in San Francisco encouraged the
domination of prostitution over streetwalking. This
was especially true for Chinese women. Streetwalk-

ing, alien to Chinese culture and unnecessary because of the skewed Chinese sex ratio, never became part of the modus operandi in the nineteenth century.[33]

A few Chinese public women worked along Fifth Street south of Market Street in Ward Ten, an area where non-Chinese prostitutes also operated. This secondary zone of prostitution, located south of the central business district centered on Market, was anchored in a residential district.[34]

In 1854, some white citizens and Chinese benevolent associations proposed to the city leaders that Chinese prostitutes be removed from the "more inhabited line of streets."[35] Equally vocal were middle-class Protestant women. These proselytizers for family and community complained about "being thrown into proximity with this district, whose inhabitants were entrenched upon the access routes to downtown."[36] City authorities, in response to the uproar, commissioned an investigating committee, which also recommended "immediate expulsion" or "removal outside the more inhabited line of streets." The committee went further, however; it urged that such action be taken against all Chinese persons, not just prostitutes.[37]

As it turned out, only prostitutes, and not the whole Chinese population, were singled out for legislative action. The 1854 City Ordinance 546, "To Suppress Houses of Ill-Fame within the City Limits," outlawed prostitution in the city by women of all races. It is not known why all women were targeted; perhaps this was an early expression of resentment against prostitution in general. As explained by the chief of police, the police largely reflecting Euro-American society's attitude, aimed to suppress "outrages to public decency," not so much the enterprise itself.[38] Protecting polite society dominated the mindset of the police. They even went so far as to log arrests of prostitutes under the guise of breaking laws against vagrancy, misdemeanors, or indecent exposure.[39]

In an age of corruption, however, the law was enforced only against Chinese and Mexican prostitutes, causing the *California Police Gazette* to comment sarcastically that the officers "do not pitch into white females who pursue the same course" because "their pleasures and interests would be interfered with!" Presumably, some, like so many poorly trained officers in American cities of the nineteenth century, took bribes from white prostitutes and acted against specific ethnic groups to satisfy the public clamor for speedy action. Thus police authorities shifted part of the blame for threatening the ideology of civilized morality to Chinese "denizens" of the vice district.[40]

But the 1854 ordinance did little to reduce the Chinese prostitutes' visibility. Nor did it placate Victorian arbiters of virtue and values. Late in 1854, the court convicted a few Chinese madams for keeping brothel houses and slapped on each a staggering fine of $1,000. Then the judge advised the harried women to consider "the alternative of removing outside certain limits which the court would hereafter prescribe."[41]

Efforts to isolate prostitutes in a confined geographic area were somewhat successful. Census schedules for 1860 gave no hint that Chinese prostitutes still lived south of Market Street, although a number of non-Chinese prostitutes, particularly Irish women, lived together in households without male residents. This area also served as the residential neighborhood for the homeless and single men of the city, many of whom patronized these purveyors of sexual services.[42]

By 1860, all or nearly all Chinese prostitutes had left this vice zone for the area north of Market Street. In 1859, the *California Police Gazette* noted that residents complained about the "disgrace" in the Fifth Street neigborhood. They also urged municipal authorities to take measures to follow the dictates of white middle-class society.[43] The authorities duly responded, and prostitutes stayed for only a short time in that residential neighborhood.

By the summer of 1859, the constant struggle with the authorities had forced the few Chinese women outside the primary vice district or those beyond the perimeters of Chinatown to change their residences. From the early years of the 1860s onward, almost all Chinese prostitutes and those of other ethnic origins lived between Stockton and Montgomery streets, north of Sacramento. Over the next few decades this area, north of the central business district, developed into a well-defined, fixed primary zone of prostitution—a functionally segregated red-light district, an identity that endured until the end of the century. According to Neil Larry Shumsky, such districts in America "helped [to] establish the boundaries of proper behavior" and served as the means of "controlling the lower and working classes," including prostitutes and others in commercialized vice.[44]

City authorities in the nineteenth century expected Chinese prostitutes to share the burden of upholding common standards of respectability in inner-city districts, and this could be accomplished only by removing them from thoroughfares.[45] Consequently, to avoid further arrests, many Chinese prostitutes relocated from their former residences along public streets, where white prostitutes worked, to alleys and by-streets such as Washington, Starr, Spofford, Bartlett, and Sullivan.[46]

Once Chinese prostitutes settled down into their new residences, often decrepit dwellings, the process of being relegated to the bottom of the social hierarchy accelerated.[47] While most Chinese prostitutes from the early 1860s onward worked in brothels that opened onto alleys and by-streets, non-Chinese prostitutes, particularly whites, continued to operate from brothels along major streets, a result of selective law enforcement. Enumerators working on the 1880 census—the first to ask for specific addresses from respondents—listed the residences of most non-Chinese prostitutes as Broadway, Waverly Place, Sacramento, Stockton, and Morton, none of which were occupied by Chinese prostitutes.

The physical and spatial patterns of prostitution on the Chinatown map of 1885 commissioned for the board of supervisors and the Sanborn fire insurance maps for 1887 confirmed this racial segregation within the trade. Both sets of maps show that white bordellos clustered at the south end of the perimeters of Chinatown, as opposed to those of the Chinese, located on the north end.[48] Of course, racial separation in prostitution was hardly limited to San Francisco alone. In Virginia City, Nevada, Chinese prostitutes resided in a segregated neighborhood and had no professional or social relationship with white prostitutes. Isolation from mainstream society also afflicted the lives of African-American women. Black prostitutes formed a distinctive subgroup in San Francisco and huddled together in a separate section of the tenderloin district, living in "cribs" located along narrow alleys.[49]

Judging from the Pacific Union Express Company's directory of principal Chinese merchants of San Francisco for 1868 and 1869, Wells Fargo Chinese business directories for 1873 and 1876, and also the Chinese classified business section in a general city directory, Chinese prostitutes were excluded from the higher levels of the Chinese social structure.[50] The directories indicate that nearly all Chinese legal establishments and business houses, save for some sweatshops and small manufacturers, opened into public streets. In contrast, prostitutes, shunned by the Chinese community and pushed to the physical as well as social fringe of society, led separate lives.

A few prostitutes, however, continued to maintain their residences along Jackson, Dupont, and Pacific streets. As expected, the police occasionally raided these brothels, with the rate of arrests peaking in the mid-1860s. City leaders, by then fed up with the impasse, passed a stringent law against owners and prostitutes. But as it turned out, the latter, not the former, bore the brunt of the crackdowns on vice.[51]

The harassment abated somewhat in the early 1870s but stepped up in the second half of that decade. Annual reports of the chief of police did not break down arrests according to race, but records show that more women — white, yellow, and black — were charged with either "keeping house of ill fame," being an "inmate of house of ill fame," or "solicit[ing] for house of ill fame" during the second half of that decade than the first. From a low of twenty-nine for the year ending June 30, 1870, the number of arrests steadily climbed to 357 for the year 1874–75 and then doubled within the next four years. In 1880, the number of arrests, inexplicably, dropped to nil.[52]

Municipal reports often singled out Chinese women for additional comment. For example, in the 1875 report, the chief of police reassured his readers that "the Chinese inhabitants have not been allowed to keep brothels on the main thoroughfares of the city, and the streets on which the street railroads run have been kept free from the contamination."[53] By 1880, close to 85 percent of the Chinese prostitutes lived in the overcrowded, cramped residences that dotted the narrow, ten- to fifteen-foot-wide alleys. The new pattern points to the fact that city authorities had been successful in driving the women out of major thoroughfares.[54]

City authorities expected Chinese prostitutes to remove themselves from mainstream society and also abide by municipal ordinances. In the early 1860s, authorities tried to force Chinese brothel owners to erect and maintain screens near the mouths of the alleys and by-streets to "hide the vice and degradation of those localities from the view of the women and children." However, this measure failed to placate the affront to civilized morality. Under public pressure, the city leaders mandated in 1869 that the doors of all brothels must be shut. Few establishments seem to have abided by this ordinance, because in 1878 another ordinance was passed that required prostitutes to work from behind closed doors; solicitation, however, was permitted through a wicket-covered opening.[55]

The underlying aim of these ordinances was to hide prostitution from public view. Those who threw their support behind such measures sought to protect the family, the base unit of the community. Parents, insistent that their children adhere to traditional moral values and behavior patterns, considered prostitutes bad role models for the young. Yet some men accepted prostitution as a necessary service for transient, single males, and some even brazenly patronized these working women themselves. Chinese prostitutes were part of the perpetuation of a double standard of sexual behavior practiced by the American middle class, in which men's sexual appetites were assumed to require the sexual services prostitutes provided.[56]

During times when authorities concluded that Chinese prostitutes had failed to abide by the law and had offended the moral sensibilities of the larger society, police officers would raid the brothels and lock up women in the county prison. This pattern occurred in towns and cities throughout the Far West. These arrests symbolically reaffirmed that prostitutes operated outside the community's moral boundaries.[57]

But why did Chinese prostitutes suffered more police raids than the whites, given the general lack of judicial concern with sexual commerce in the West? It is easy to assume that the increased arrests for prostitution in years when anti-Chinese activities peaked proves that the police made those roundups to maintain the support of nativistic city voters.[58] This explanation, however, fails to take into consideration historical change over time.

The higher rate of criminal prosecution and apprehension of Chinese women did stem in part from their ethnic and sexual ascription. As women of "disreputable" backgrounds, society saw them as failing in its consensual standards of feminine behavior. As members of a "heathen" civilization, they allegedly contaminated the West and contributed to its moral decay.

Anti-Chinese feelings accounted in part for the higher number of arrests of Chinese prostitutes relative to that of whites. This was especially evident in the late 1860s following the passage in 1866 of a board of supervisors' "Order to Remove Chinese Women of Ill-Fame from Certain Limits in the City." Later, the attorney for the board of supervisors persuaded the board to strike "Chinese" from the final wording, but this hardly changed the intent of the statute: Chinese working women remained the object of the crackdown. In the same year, the California legislature, responding to its San Francisco citizens' outrage, passed the "Act for the Suppression of Chinese Houses of Ill Fame," which prompted the police in San Francisco to take steps to shut down Chinese brothels. A few months later, the cleanup abated; the Chinese women and their owners agreed to occupy "only certain buildings and localities under restrictions imposed by the Board of Health and Police Commissioners," according to one newspaper.[59]

Yet earlier, in 1862, three-fourths of the Chinese convictions had fallen on prostitutes, despite this being a quiet year for anti-Chinese sentiments. That San Francisco had more Chinese than non-Chinese prostitutes by the end of the 1860s (a disparity that was exaggerated by newspapers and rumors) also explains why more of the prostitutes who were arrested were Chinese. In fact, judging from internal police records, the argument that Chinese prostitutes were particularly targeted does not hold for some years during the 1870s. From a total of 624 arrests of Chinese offenders listed in a police ledger during a period of forty-two months in the mid-1870s, none were for prostitution. All other forms of criminal activities were listed, even visiting a gambling house.[60] Keeping in mind that this was the height of the anti-Chinese movement, it would be fair to infer that arrests of prostitutes sometimes sprang from causes other than racism.

Since the vast majority of Chinese prostitutes possessed little power to threaten the commonweal of the dominant society and had been removed from white neighborhoods by the early 1870s, the rationale for harassment of them disappeared. Yet prostitutes — white, yellow, or black — still drew the attention of the police. However, in 1880, 547 persons were arrested for pimping but none for prostitution.[61] Because prostitution fell under the category of "victimless" offenses, the decision to take action against prostitutes rested with the police. Officer Alfred Clarke, testifying in 1876 before the congressional committee investigating Chinese immigration, conceded that "there is a big number of Chinese prostitutes and gamblers, but it varies a good deal in proportion to the energy of the police in prosecuting them or breaking them up."[62] Clearly, the motivation of police officers or police departments must be taken into account in explaining the ebb and flow in the arrest rate.

As in many nineteenth-century American cities, corruption plagued the San Francisco police force. Some officers, especially those assigned to the Chinese quarters, exploited the circumstances surrounding the lives of prostitutes to reap monetary gains from them and the brothel owners. Owners, many of whom had concurrent membership in tongs and the Chinese Six Companies, provided the funds to maintain a police squad in the Chinese neighborhood.[63] One brothel operator, Fong Ching, made the most of this tacit cooperation. Popularly known as "Little Pete," Fong Ching periodically passed information on Chinatown vice rackets to law enforcement authorities. Following the arrests of the wrongdoers, he would take over their establishments and reopen them under police protection.[64] In addition to receiving paychecks contributed by Chinese businessmen, many officers also accepted bribes from the same source. To make matters worse, officers assigned to Chinatown often influenced other colleagues to cooperate with them.

The numerical strength of Chinese prostitutes encouraged police officers to make Chinese prostitution a target for prosecution at a level just sufficient to demand kickbacks. This explains the capriciousness in enforcing the law. In 1872, for example, the *San Francisco Chronicle* reported the arrest of only one Chinese prostitute, but in the subsequent year, the police arrested forty-eight.[65] The perfunctory manner in which some officers carried out their antivice duties — an attitude that permeated the police forces of many eastern cities — made even the chief of police, Patrick Crowley, lament that legal redress, helpful in the struggle against "the avarice of keepers," failed to reach Chinese "disorderly women."[66]

The legal system of nineteenth-century America extended little protection to Chinese prostitutes. As Butler has pointed out, enforcement officials did nothing significant to reverse the fundamentally poor conditions of prostitutes in the American West.

The nature of their relationship with police officers reinforced their low status. Violence and brutality defined this interaction. When arrested, these women often resisted. For example, an unnamed one hundred men's wife, dressed in the latest fashion of Caucasian women, was soliciting customers on a Saturday evening. An officer of the law, Edward Ward, spotted her. He tried to arrest her, but she resisted. She screamed and refused to be led away, whereupon the officer kicked her. Later the court imposed a fine on Ward for assaulting her but also found her guilty of a misdemeanor.[67]

The occasional entanglement with law enforcement authorities followed a standard pattern. After the arrest, prostitutes appeared in the police court to face judgment. Because of the lack of qualified interpreters or proper counsel, few received a fair hearing. The general inadmissibility of Chinese testimony left them even more defenseless.[68] Frequently, newspapers gave accounts of public women who failed to appear in court and thus forfeited their bail. "The usual offense, the usual bail," an editor commented drily, "and the usual result: bail forfeited."[69]

In the 1860s, those found guilty paid a fine ranging from $5 to $10, an amount equal to that paid by non-Chinese prostitutues. As anti-Chinese agitation intensified in the 1870s, the typical fine imposed on Chinese members of the demimonde fluctuated between $15 and $20 but remained steady at $5 for the non-Chinese. The law provided for a maximum of $100.[70] These fines, similar to those imposed in many western settlements, brought sizable revenues into municipal coffers and operated as a mechanism to control social outsiders, including prostitutes. The release of prostitutes was contingent on payment of the fine. Those ignored by owners and unable to scrape together the monies to pay the fine ended up behind prison bars for as brief as twenty-four hours and as long as three months. The harassment intensified somewhat in the 1870s; each year police arrested an increasing number of Chinese prostitutes. However, the number of arrests dramatically tapered off in the 1880s.[71]

The concentration of Chinese prostitutes in increasing numbers within a clearly defined prostitution zone in the 1870s, paralleling the situation of many eastern cities, facilitated police efforts to make arrests. Law enforcement obviously responded to growing hostility against the Chinese within Euro-American society. However, the concomitant legal and extralegal relationship that existed between brothel owners (often tong members) and police officers tempered the victimization suffered by prostitutes at the hands of the city authorities. Most enforcement officials maintained a permissive attitude toward prostitution. When regular, professional police officers replaced special constables in Chinatown in 1878, the number of raids increased for a short time, and authorities incarcerated more brothel residents.[72]

The Chinese community was less antagonistic toward prostitutes, but no more sympathetic or helpful. Chinse society considered prostitutes "polluted" and "unclean"—in the physical, moral, and spiritual senses—because they engaged in frequent sexual intercourse.[73] Educated Chinese male emigrants wrote folk rhymes condemning them. These songs remonstrated the one hundred men's wife to leave the "shameful" profession by getting married. One rhyme begins with the following lines: "A word of advice for you, dear *peipa* girl: / Best to find a good man and get hitched to him." Another rhyme relates the tale of a high-class prostitute who got rid of "the infamous label and becomes his [young man's] second wife."[74]

Although evidence is incomplete, one incident in 1868 seemed to demonstrate the aversion and antipathy toward a loungei, or a "woman always holding up her legs." The decision of a new Chinese theater to allocate a portion of the dress circle for unaccompanied women, including prostitutes, gave rise to a vehement protest from a Chinese laundry workers' association. A couple of nights after the official opening, enraged laundrymen gathered in large numbers in front of the theater and jeered at every female patron. The police soon arrived. A scuffle broke out, and some were hauled to the station on charges of using obscene language and possession of firearms. The next day, a smaller crowd milled around the establishment. The flames of passion burned out, and the afternoon passed quietly.[75]

Of course, the condescending attitude toward prostitutes did not permeate all levels of the Chinese community; most working-class males saw prostitutes as providers of a necessary service to the largely bachelor community. Chinese male sojourners, unperturbed by the prescriptive advice offered by Chinese folk wisdom, considered the presence of prostitutes unavoidable. "The Chinese people don't resent them; they know that it's a service, . . . a needed service," explained one Chinese immigrant.[76] At best, the attitude of the Chinese community appeared indifferent and resigned to the situation. A few lucky women left the trade with the aid of relatives. After 1879, a negligible number of them returned to the mainstream of society through the mediation of the Chinese consulate. In truth, prostitutes could harbor slender hope of receiving help from their own community.[77]

Various individuals and groups — brothel owners, members of the police force, American moralists, and even the general Chinese population — created emotional stress for prostitutes. No doubt, missionaries and sympathetic travelers from the East recognized the unjust treatment accorded to these women. Methodist missionary and longtime friend of the Chinese, A. W. Loomis, bewildered by the undue attention paid to Chinese prostitutes, reminded the public that "the solicitation and indecent exposure of fallen women of other nationalities is far more disgusting than anything seen in the Chinese quarters."[78] Caroline Dalls, in California on vacation in 1880, made a more pointed argument: "So long as the men of San Francisco are unwilling to close their own houses of assignation . . . they have no power, either human or divine, to close those of the Chinese."[79] Unfortunately, the voices of the defenders of the Chinese were no match for those of the exclusionists.

Few prostitutes ventured into wider society to seek employment given the conditions outside the Chinese ghetto. Successful in fleeing from her owner, Tsoi Yee spent some time in the Presbyterian rescue home and then left to work as a domestic servant in a white household. She subsequently returned to the home because she "did not feel safe elsewhere." She feared not only her owner's attempts to regain her but also the alien environment.[80] Her long isolation in a brothel ever since arriving in the

United States kept her uninformed of her surroundings and left her apprehensive of the outside world.

Many prostitutes never had the chance to step into the cultural mainstream. For those who found the deprivation and debasement intolerable, moving into a conjugal relationship became the obvious choice. But before they could contemplate what they might do besides prostitution, they had to figure out how to overcome the violence and mayhem surrounding their lives.

Violence and Public Women

Nineteenth-century non-Chinese Americans envisioned Chinese prostitutes as daily victims of violence rooted in the frenzied atmosphere of city life. Euro-Americans blamed much of the violence on Chinese male immigrants. One California senator said that Chinese women "are treated worse than dogs" and "are held in a most revolting condition of slavery."[1] The hardship of prostitutes' lives seemed to be another example of the violent heritage of the American West.

The current state of historiography on violence in the American West, however, has in the last two or three decades gravitated to the thesis that the West, as a frontier or region, was no more violent than, say, the East or South. Yet western violence remains a complex subject. Particularly, its precise definition and meaning continues to elude academics.

Scholars have studied western violence in many different settings such as mining camps, boomtowns, and cities. In these places, violence involved types highly romanticized: cowboys, gamblers, lawmen, and gunfighters. Some, like W. Eugene Hollon, include racial conflicts within their paradigm. For all of them, "violence is the history and organization of power," to borrow the words of Richard Maxwell Brown. Such a framework obviously excludes the so-called gentle tamers, the disenfranchised and passive western women. Thus, hardly any western historian, with the exception of Roger D. McGarth, has looked at violence committed against or by females. The regendering of western history, a process that began nearly twenty years ago, has yet to include the topic of violence. Hence many authors have provided an incomplete picture of violence and lawlessness in the American West.[2]

In *Gunfighters, Highwaymen and Vigilantes: Violence on the Frontier* (1984), McGarth looked at acts of disobedience related to women in Bodie, California, during the late 1870s and early 1880s. He concluded that prostitutes of all racial origins, despite being a minority group within the female population, accounted for most of the brute force and lawlessness committed by or directed at women in that small frontier town.[3]

But the subject of violence and women gains an added perspective when it is examined in relation to Chinese women. Because the majority of Chinese women in America during the nineteenth century were prostitutes, most of them shared similar life experiences and faced essentially the same conditions. Their low status made them fair game for abuse by men who denied them any personal dignity. Antiforeign prejudices held by Euro-American society created further disorder in their lives. Such lines of argument lead to the contention that violence dominated the lives of Chinese prostitutes. After all, unlike white immigrants, businessmen, or workers in tightly knit communities, these women stood outside any constituent group. In large cities like San Francisco, power was widely dispersed, but it did not extend to prostitutes — especially Chinese prostitutes. They were denied the political means to extricate themselves from the tangled web of prostitution.[4]

But such an analysis somewhat dehumanizes these women by seeing them as only passive participants in their own lives. An examination of how violence affected these prostitutes throws new light on the role of women in violence and, more important, shows that not all of these women fit the stereotype of hapless victims of societal and male exploitation. It is also possible that violence — and its impact on women — in a city could be significantly different from that in a small frontier town like Bodie, the setting of McGarth's study.

❦

During the nineteenth century, Euro-American society was clearly hostile toward Chinese prostitutes. This attitude hinged on the racist premise that Chinese women constituted a depraved class and that their degeneracy originated from their physiognomy. This was believed also of African-American women. One nineteenth-century writer asserted that their "whole physiognomy indicates but a slight removal from the African race."[5] Just like black women, Chinese females supposedly could erode the superiority of the Caucasian race if allowed to mingle with the white population.

While the racial argument explains in part the widespread animosity, Caucasians also advanced other specific allegations against Chinese prostitutes. Adopting a defensive psychology, Californians felt that the flow of prostitutes to their shores threatened an established way of life; many agreed that the United States had become "the great seat of [the Chinese] slave trade," "the dumping ground of their criminals."[6]

Chinese public women not only corrupted proper sexual conduct in the face of a perceived gradual breakdown in nineteenth-century morality but also threatened the physical survival of Anglo-Saxon civilization. In an age of confused medical knowledge, physicians diagnosed "deviant" behavior as a symptom of mental retardation, an effect of hereditary disabilities. According to medical theories, venereal diseases had much to do with these disabilities. Prostitutes, already weakened by earlier attacks, were indeed vulnerable to more venereal infections, aside from being susceptible to common disorders.[7]

Medical textbooks warned that syphilis resulted from a vitiated ovum (or sperm) and could be passed on to offspring. Such medical information slowly reached the public. One editor of a popular medical journal aimed at women claimed that Chinese prostitutes, bearers of "a poisonous virus" who were "brought to this country to pander to the passions of our youth," had "corrupt[ed] the purest blood of the civilized world."[8] The medical argument against

Chinese women soon spread to other levels of society. In 1868, business interests in California wrote a joint letter to the state legislature. The signatories claimed that the presence of large numbers of Chinese "denizens" constituted "a source of pollution to the large rising generation of young men" and warned, "the dreadful effects of which will be transmitted to future generations."[9] Quickly, a prostitute acquired the image of being immoral, foreign, feebleminded, nymphomaniacal — and the principal source of venereal contagion.[10]

Most San Francisco newspapers related the concordant public opinion on this subject. The *San Francisco Chronicle* rebutted the argument that Chinese people helped to revitalize the economy by pointing out that it "was not just a question of money; it is a question of life and money." An editorial in the *California Police Gazette* in 1869 blamed Chinese prostitutes — and to a lesser extent, their white sisters — for spreading syphilis. Mortality statistics for the years 1866 to 1873 compiled in an annual report of the board of health show that syphilis accounted for 1 to 11 percent of the deaths among the Chinese during that period. Overall, syphilis was not a major cause of death for the Chinese, and the small number of cases each year did not lead to an outbreak of epidemics in subsequent years (table 4).[11]

The fact that Euro-American society censured Chinese prostitutes in Chinatown for their "sanitary evils" drew attention to what was perceived as the syphilitic menace posed by these women. According to the miasmatic theory of disease popular until the late 1870s, epidemic outbreaks could be traced to the state of the atmosphere or poor sani-

TABLE 4

Chinese Mortality in San Francisco Caused by Syphilis for
Each Fiscal Year (July 1–June 30), 1866–1873

Year	Syphilis	Total Deaths (all causes)	Percent
1866/67	18	161	11.2
1867/68	7	171	4.1
1868/69	2	226	0.9
1869/70	10	220	4.6
1870/71	16	295	5.4
1871/72	15	359	4.2
1872/73	6	405	1.5

SOURCE: San Francisco (Calif.) Board of Supervisors, *Municipal Report*, 1872–73, 340.

tary conditions. Health officials and medical experts singled out Chinatown as a primary source of atmospheric pollution within San Francisco. Labeled a "moral purgatory" by one officer, Chinatown, claimed another, emitted "foul and disgusting vapors." Leaky pipes, burst drains, messy homes, and garbage everywhere in Chinatown—all were used to explain the general hygienic threat plaguing the city.[12]

In spite of the hysterical outcries, city leaders made no allocations for sanitary services. This state of affairs in the ethnic enclave continued throughout the 1860s and 1870s. In a special 1871 health report, sanitarians touched little on the allegations of careless garbage disposal or faulty construction of privy vaults and drains. They found only bad ventilation due to overcrowded conditions, even as they blasted the Chinese as the "lowest class of degraded bestiality."[13]

The poor socioeconomic status of most Chinese emigrants and the necessity of staying close within the boundaries of Chinatown, primarily to avoid violent confrontations with white society, caused residential overcrowding. Housing was at a premium; like it or not, the sojourners had to brook cramped quarters.[14] James B. Angell, presidential appointee to head a commission to China in 1880, passed through San Francisco and wrote in his diary that "nothing was noted which called for special criticism" about the sanitary conditions in Chinatown. On a visit to a Chinese brothel, Myriam F. Leslie observed, "Every room we entered was exceedingly clean and the inmates looked remarkably neat and tidy."[15] Few whites ever ventured into the living quarters of these women, and thus prostitutes were lumped together with their fellow countrywomen; all were charged with committing "sanitary evils."

Medical theories against Chinese prostitutes gained credence because they blended into the cultural argument. Some California politicians, in a struggle to capture the support of their constituents during the turbulent decade of the 1870s, exploited the fear already ingrained in the hearts and minds of Californians. Politicians introduced bills in the Congress aimed specifically at Chinese women, claiming that immorality was a greater problem among the Chinese than among other Californians.

In the eyes of white society, the degradation of these women reflected the general inferiority of Chinese culture. Prostitutes had supposedly inherited immoral characteristics; this explanation justified in part Anglo-Saxon superiority in the racial hierarchy of Victorian America during an era when Social Darwinism held sway. A few religious figures, both Catholics and Protestants, cast aspersions on these women, perhaps blaming them for the lack of missionary success among the Chinese male population.[16] Even the bulwark of pro-Chinese forces, Rev. Otis Gibson, shared the widely held prejudices of his times and labeled them "a bad class of women."[17] The image that prostitutes were "bad women" converged in an English-Chinese phrase book compiled for the use of Chinese sojourners. The only two sentences about Chinese women in that three hundred-page guide read, "She is a good-for-nothing huzzy" and "female occupation."[18]

Influenced by the outpouring of demagogic propaganda, the presidential leadership of the 1870s joined the chorus of disapproval. President Grant denounced Chinese prostitutes, calling them a "disgrace [to] the communities where [they] settled." His successor, Rutherford B. Hayes, implied that Chinese prostitutes and their compatriots threatened American Republicanism when he interpreted Chinese immigration as an invasion. Like his predecessor, he favored "any suitable measures to discourage the Chinese from coming to our shores."[19]

The dominant society's animosity toward Chinese members of the demimonde was unleashed during occasional racial conflicts between Chinese and Euro-Americans. During the 1870s, Chinese prostitutes were often the targets of this sinophobic violence. During the second half of the decade, the anti-Chinese movement gathered momentum in California and galvanized communities to drive away Chinese settlers within their midst. In 1876, in Antioch, northwest of Oakland, some young men allegedly contracted a venereal disease after patronizing a Chinese brothel. Subsequently, enraged citizens led by the parents of those boys banded together and forced residents of Chinese brothels to leave the town. Placed on board a riverboat cruising down the Sacramento River, they left for Stockton on the way to San Francisco. But they returned to Antioch the same day, much to the consternation of the townspeople. That evening, at around eight o'clock, a fire broke out in one of the Chinese brothels and quickly spread to other parts of the neighborhood. In Congress, a senator claimed that arsonists had fanned the embers of smoldering hatred.[20]

Sometimes, the intolerance expressed against prostitutes was less direct and less violent. In Humboldt County in 1885, a mob ran the Chinese out of the city of Eureka. While the death of a city councilman who was hit by a stray bullet during a fight between two Chinese men spurred this incident, the roots of the conflict dated back to the early 1880s. The arrival of prostitutes and the habit of opium smoking among Chinese males alarmed the citizens of Eureka. In their eyes, the Chinese constituted a menace to public safety. However, the subsequent expulsion — quiet and somber — injured none of the Chinese. The crowd witnessing the orderly removal also kept their hands to themselves.[21]

Violence also erupted in Southern California. On October 24, 1871, in what was called Nigger Alley, an ethnic neighborhood of Los Angeles, a mob attacked and murdered nineteen Chinese males. This outrage, ironically, developed from a conflict within the Chinese community that had little to do with whites. Ya Hit, a baak haak chai under the protection of prominent tong leader Sam Yuen, had run away but somehow ended up with Yo Hing, the rival of her former owner. On a fraudulent charge of thievery made by Sam Yuen, Ya Hit was arrested and offered bail. Sam Yuen promptly paid the bail and made off with her. Far from giving up, Yo Hing moved fast to reclaim his property. Ya Hit's whereabouts were discovered, and Yo Hing somehow got her to accept his marriage proposal. A showdown between the two competing parties seemed inevitable.

On October 23, two gunmen in the employ of Sam Yuen ambushed Yo Hing in Nigger Alley and shot him. Police officers rushed in and arrested all. Released on bail pending a court hearing, the warring factions returned to Chinatown. At sunset the next day, violence between the parties erupted again. A police officer was shot during the confusion and died shortly after.

At this point, enraged white citizens in the vicinity went after the Chinese "thugs." The mob, armed to the hilt, chased them to a building. An exchange of shots leading nowhere, the rioters charged in and killed a number of Chinese. Other besieged Chinese in the building found no escape. Throwing restraint to the wind, the rioters hanged fifteen and mutilated the bodies of four others killed during the melee. The source indicates that less than three of the dead had been involved in the fray that led to the pitched battle; the rest lost their lives simply because of their racial identity. As for Ya Hit, the woman at the center of the furor, little is known of her fate.[22]

In San Francisco, the most serious conflict involving prostitutes took place on July 24, 1877. Coming in the wake of inflammatory speeches made during anticoolie meetings held by the Democratic party, a widespread riot occurred that night. Several hundred men rampaged through the city attacking any Chinese persons in sight. Rioters looted laundry houses and set several on fire. Chinese men wandering on the streets were struck, and Chinese prostitutes were dragged from their houses and physically abused by large gangs of men. The violence continued for three days.[23]

Essentially sporadic outbursts of antiforeign prejudices, these incidents rocked the Chinese communities. Together with the waves of violence that erupted after the passage of the Chinese Exclusion Act in 1882, the Chinese were subjected to considerable anguish. During the nineteenth century and beyond, eloquent voices decrying injustice were heard in Cantonese folk rhymes. One wrote, "Since coming to the frontier land, / I have taken all kinds of abuse from the barbarians." And another, "Savages rob and loot with frequent violence. / I ask Heaven: Why is there hatred against the yellow race?"[24]

On a daily basis, the Chinese did not face violence akin to that of the 1877 San Francisco riot, or even on the scale of the Humboldt expulsion. Chinese prostitutes, for example, encountered considerably less anti-Chinese physical violence than did other Chinese immigrants. On the streets of San Francisco, white hoodlums sometimes physically abused Chinese women but not only those working as prostitutes. Both contemporaries and the press recounted just as many stories of nonprostitutes being attacked.

Local newspapers had routinely reported cases of violence committed against Chinese women ever since they began landing on the shores of San Francisco Bay. On February 27, 1859, a drunken black man, David G. Brown, forced his way into a Chinese brothel and verbally abused the residents. The few women in the brothel shouted for help. Before the police arrived, Brown had assaulted and possibly slapped one of the women. A clear-cut case, the judge fined him $20 after hearing the testimony of the victims.[25] These Chinese women could testify against him because the law on the inadmissibility of Chinese testimony protected only white defendants.

A few months later, police arrested Alexander McLane, a white, on a misdemeanor charge. According to one local newspaper report, he had vandalized some brothels on Jackson Street. He had kicked doors and smashed the windows of those residences, terrifying the women there. Charges against him were later dropped since no Caucasian witness stepped forward for the prosecution and the Chinese could not testify against him. The California Supreme Court in *People v. Hall* (1854) had ruled that a state criminal statute on the exclusion of testimony from blacks and Indians in courts included the Chinese since all came from the same ethnic stock. This landmark ruling guided the exercise of jurisprudence until 1873, whereupon section 16 of the Civil Rights Act of 1870—the right to testify in court—went into operation, thus removing one Chinese legal disability.[26]

But the 1870 act made little headway in rolling back the avalanche of anti-Chinese legislation. California began to pass, in the words of two legal historians, "laws that were neutral on their face but that by their terms operated effectively only on the Chinese or that could be enforced selectively against the Chinese." A typical enactment was the so-called queue ordinance of 1876. This San Francisco city ordinance mandated prison authorities to crop the hair of every prisoner to within one inch of the scalp; this, in effect, forced Chinese sojourners to pay fines in lieu of losing their queues and imprisonment.[27] Racist ordinances, of course, came in the wake of the public's vindictive mood.

On March 30, 1879, a massive fire, possibly the work of racist arsonists, broke out in Chinatown. At one spot on Dupont Street, "a crowd of loafers and thieves and roughs amused themselves by throwing a Chinese woman down in the mud," wrote one reporter. Then the ruffians dragged the woman "backward and forward by the hair for some moments."[28] Examples of such cases of violence against women discouraged Chinese wives from venturing out alone. Already vulnerable, those with bound feet felt even more compelled to remain at home since they would be unable to run away if attacked.[29]

Sometimes women rescued from prostitution and placed in mission homes were also targets of racial animosity. On one occasion, a group of these women went out for a walk accompanied by female missionaries. Shortly after, they were set upon by a gang of men and boys who pelted their bodies with small stones. They manhandled the women, tore at their clothing, and yanked off their earrings. Missionaries also reported how one white boy held a brush well soaked in black paint and "bravely [came] up to" an ex-prostitute "from behind, drew the brush across her face and slunk away, [while] other white men stood by laughing and applauding."[30]

These incidents clearly show that Chinese women were subjected to some abuse by a hostile society during the 1860s and 1870s. As Richard Wade has pointed out, violence against new immigrants has been a major theme in the history of urban unrest. It seemed that Chinese prostitutes fitted into the common pattern of small groups who were assaulted by older, more established ones.

But cases of violence against Chinese public women were few and far between, even though the foreign-born in the nineteenth century, according to one recent study, were disproportionately arrested.[31] During 1872 and 1873, a period that witnessed the passage of a number of discriminatory ordinances aimed exclusively at the Chinese, only three instances of racially motivated cases of assault and battery by Caucasian men against Chinese prostitutes appeared before the police court. Most of these outrages received scant attention from local newpapers, indicating that none of them were deemed serious enough to warrant extensive coverage. The insignificant number of cases of racial injustice in 1872 and 1873 has also made these two years suitable for drawing a fairly representative sample of nonracial violence of all types.

During the first ten months of 1872, police made no arrests for any crimes of assault, rape, or murder on the basis of color. Then on November 20, 1872, Lora Marks, in a stupor after imbibing a large amount of liquor, staggered across an alley just as a Chinese prostitute strolled by. When Marks saw her, he began to utter racial profanities. Then he stumbled toward her and swung his right arm at her. She cried for help and tried to ward off the blows. A police officer probably came to her rescue as Marks was arraigned on charges of disorderly conduct, using vulgar language, and assault and battery. Convicted, he spent 110 days in the county prison in lieu of paying a hefty fine.[32]

The only other case of racial violence against Chinese prostitutes in 1872 occurred on December 29. An undisclosed number of ruffians assaulted a prostitute, but no further information is available on this case. In 1873, there was only one case of unprovoked violence in spite of the fact that two discriminatory ordinances were passed during the course of that year. William McHenry, a middle-aged man, accosted a prostitute on her way to purchase some necessities. Apparently the attack was severe enough to warrant a fine of $200.[33]

If most Chinese prostitutes suffered few racist, unprovoked violent incidents in the world outside the brothel, the same cannot be said about physical abuse that took place within their business surroundings. Because brothels advertised openly the nature of their businesses (with names such as "White Sparrow" and "Young Willow" written on red slips of paper and posted on the facade of the establishments), criminals could easily identify easy targets for certain forms of premeditated violence such as racial abuse, theft, robbery, and kidnapping.[34] In pluralistic societies, violence has often figured in the struggle for power.

Much of the violence directed against prostitutes stemmed from their tenuous relationships with owners and customers. This is not surprising as these relationships were essentially marketplace transactions or commercial exchanged. Violence was used, with varying results, by owners, customers, and prostitutes, all of whom sought to gain economic leverage.[35]

Prostitutes, whites and Chinese alike, suffered beatings at the hands of customers. Much of the violence directed against prostitutes erupted when a man thought he had purchased more than a woman was willing to give. On these occasions, prostitutes found themselves on the defensive. The nature of their work—alone when entertaining customers—made them easy targets for an individual with a violent temperament.[36]

One day in 1872, one unnamed prostitute living on Dupont Street, near Pine, had a little "unpleasantness" with a "full-fledged hoodlum," a white man, at around two o'clock in the morning. Presumably unhappy with the service offered, he started to quarrel with the woman, then grabbed and wrestled her down. She broke free and dashed out onto the street. He followed, and the struggle continued. Finally, the "hoodlum" retreated, and she chased after her assailant, throwing glass tumblers at his departing figure. One of these struck the driver of a passing night cart and inflicted an ugly gash on his head.[37]

On another occasion, one disgruntled white customer argued with a Chinese man, presumably the proprietor of the brothel, over the quality of the service provided, in light of the fee charged. He got into a scuffle with the proprietor, broke free, and then struck a prostitute. The conflict ended when the brothel owner stabbed the customer in the back; the latter survived the assault. As for the prostitute, she received her revenge when she testified against the customer.[38] Since this case was heard in 1872, it is possible that the prostitute was allowed to testify under section 16 of the Civil Rights Act of 1870, although the provisions of the act were not to become effective until 1873. Possibly, either the schedule escaped the attention of the presiding judge or the case simply followed procedures already adopted in other cases. After all, the grand jury in San Francisco on December 10, 1870, had returned an indictment against the sheriff of a California county in a case in which the victim, Ah Koo, testified for the prosecution.[39]

Prostitutes also faced violence from dissatisfied Chinese patrons. One client, Ah Song, had a heated debate with some residents of a brothel. A fracas ensued, and Ah Song managed to lay his hands on a knife. One of the prostitutes then took him on in individual combat. The encounter turned bloody when Ah Song stabbed her in the abdomen. The injured prostitute died from the wound, and the county prosecutor arraigned Ah Song on the charge of manslaughter.[40]

Equally heinous was the crime committed by Ah Look, an actor performing with a Chinese theatrical company. He had fallen in love with a prostitute and had then become jealous when she entertained other customers. Rebuffed in his attempts to win her, he confronted the woman and threw acid at her. The victim sustained burns on her head, face, and hands. Her assailant paid the price for this atrocity when the court found him guilty of assault and battery.[41]

The abuse prostitutes suffered was not limited to that inflicted by clients. Pimps or brothel owners, the center of male authority and power in the establishment, used force to coerce compliance with their wishes, particularly to make reluctant new prostitutes accept their fates or to compel women to work harder and bring in more money. A prostitute recalled that "they beat [her] time after time, and threatened to kill [her] if [she] did not behave right."[42] Mistreatment of women working in brothels was not unknown to white society as missionary writers gave extensive coverage to the subject to demonstrate the barbaric nature of this exploitation.[43] American newspapers also ran stories about the abuse going on in these brothels but almost always in a sensational, often pejorative, vein. Typical headlines were "Confessions of a Chinese Slave Dealer," "Her Back Was Burnt with Irons," "Why Chinese Woman Suddenly Disappears," and "Chinese Girl Flees to the Mission from Inhuman Owner."[44] Seeking to add a lurid element, many of these accounts distorted reality; consequently, historians have perpetuated the errors.

First, some of the women who were abused were domestic servants, not prostitutes. One historian cited the case of how the owners of a "prostitute" often beat her with wooden clubs and once even threatened her with a pistol. In fact, this woman worked as a servant for five years, from the time she was twelve years old until her rescue at the age of seventeen.[45] The plight of another mooi-tsai, or domestic servant, was equally heartrending. The male head of the household for which she worked "pulled her pigtail, pinched her on the arms, ears, mouths, and cheeks, and also struck her with stovewood," all because she had refused to speak respectfully to a guest of the family.[46]

A few Chinese prostitutes did suffer physical abuse at the hands of their owners. The rate of incidence was probably higher than that for white prostitutes because of the controlled circumstances in which these Chinese women found themselves. However, white women captured and sold into forced prostitution also had to brook intimidation and brutality. One historian has estimated that women in slavery during the Progressive Era made up about

10 percent of the white prostitutes' population.[47] Indeed, it was a difference in degree rather than kind when the two groups are compared.[48] For both Chinese and white prostitutes, as for "respectable" women, the number of cases of violence in a private or domestic setting could have been higher than the reported figures.[49]

Most cases of violence committed by Chinese brothel owners in the nineteenth century involved adolescents who could not defend themselves. The single reported case of women being attacked bodily during these two years involved three young females, all below the age of eighteen. In their sworn statements to the police, they claimed that "unless [they] made so much money nightly, [they were] whipped and tormented."[50] Various factors precipitated the physical abuse, the most frequent being that the prostitute failed to earn enough money. Research into present-day prostitution indicates that violence can be triggered by violation of prostitution rules, departure or threatened departure from the profession, or simply a woman's disrespectful attitude toward the owner. Perhaps this pattern of cause and effect was also true in nineteenth-century prostitution.[51]

Violence more often visited crib prostitutes and streetwalkers, regardless of their ethnicity, than higher-class prostitutes or brothel residents. The squalor of the surroundings, compounded by the large number of customers they served daily, left these unfortunates exposed to undesirable elements within the neighborhood.

Since most Chinese prostitutes occupied the lower rungs of the profession's hierarchy, they would be expected to suffer turmoil in their daily existence. But from early 1872 until the end of 1873, a total of only eight Chinese public women were reported to have suffered abuse at the hands of either customers, pimps, or owners. Except for one case, in which the brothel resident's face was badly scarred, none of them resulted in permanent physical injury. Owners and pimps exercised some restraint because their charges were valuable properties. Customers rarely inflicted serious harm on providers of sexual services as they were anxious to avoid publicity about their visits, particularly if they had a wife and family. The value owners and customers placed on prostitutes' services allowed them to retain some measure of control over their own lives even as they gave their oppressors the illusion of total submission.[52]

Women controlled what took place in their cribs and in their beds. When a client became a nuisance or blind drunk, prostitutes — Chinese and white alike — stole anything they could lay their hands on. One demanding monte dealer left the Shingle House, a popular brothel, less one precious diamond breast pin worth $600. Obviously, he had been the victim of a lightfingered "disorderly" woman.[53] Similar to Euro-Americans, Chinese prostitutes apparently pilfered to retain some personal power. As many of the women were dispossessed and most of their earnings fell into the hands of their owners, stealing from clients was a chance to cling to what must have seemed the last vestiges of economic control over their lives.[54]

Men robbed by prostitutes rarely filed a legal complaint for fear of adverse publicity. This probably explains why from 1872 to 1873, only one case of robbery by women was reported in the *San Fran-*

cisco Chronicle, although isolated cases of robbery by prostitutes in other years had been reported in the newspaper. In 1869, though charged with robbery, a lack of evidence allowed Yah Hee to go free, for example. In another account, early in the morning of August 20, 1872, an unnamed Chinese woman drugged one of her clients and stole $40 and a diamond ring. A day later, police found her hiding in a friend's house and placed her under arrest.[55]

In contrast, these two years witnessed more cases of men robbing prostitutes or burglarizing their dwellings. Newspapers occasionally reported instances of "women of ill-fame" who became victims of "unscrupulous scoundrels." One white woman who lived in a boardinghouse on Dupont Street was robbed of $500 and a considerable amount of jewelry by a man who had recently rented the room next door. He apparently broke into her room when she stepped out for breakfast. The victim had to cancel plans to leave the profession and return to Germany.[56]

In five separate reported incidents, all in 1872, Chinese prostitutes lost small amounts of property. In three of the cases, youngsters accosted women on the streets and snatched the gold pins that adorned their hair. Since many of these women lived in households with just one male present or none at all, burglars considered them easy targets. On most occasions, they struck during the early morning hours because the residences turned into business houses during the day. In one case, police charged Ah Wan with petty larceny. He had broken into the residence of Ah Hoo well before daylight and stolen some apparel and a clock. Just as he was ready to leave, Ah Hoo woke up and called for help. The last reported case — the only one in 1873 — was also burglary. See Ah Hock forced entry into the house of Sin You and got away with an umbrella, three pairs of pants, a number of Chinese musical instruments, and two dollars in coins.[57] These thefts show how little the women owned. None of the encounters caused bodily harm.

When we look beyond 1872 and 1873, cases of robbery or stealing from Chinese prostitutes prove just as infrequent. One case, however, almost ended in tragedy for a prostitute. A customer, Chin Keong, stayed the night in Ah Chu's residence on Sullivan's Alley. Sometime around midnight, he attempted to strip her arms of a couple of gold bracelets. Startled from her slumber, Ah Chu pushed him aside. Thrown from the bed, he snatched a knife and in the struggle, stabbed her in the breast. Luckily, she survived the wound.[58]

Property crimes were common in Chinese America, and the violence Chinese prostitutes encountered was often perpetrated by their compatriots. A three-year tabulation of arrest records of the Chinese kept by the San Francisco police department from 1875 to 1878 indicates that property crimes — petty larceny, grand larceny, burglary, housebreaking, and robbery — constituted 94.2 percent of the violations reported.[59] During a single year, 1880, property crimes constituted 67.2 percent of all offenses committed by the Chinese.[60] In neighboring Oakland, it has been demonstrated that the Chinese committed more burglaries and thefts than any other types of felonies. In contrast, street robbery and homicide were rare occurrences in most American Chinatowns. A heavily unequal distribution of material wealth in cities encouraged the growth of property crimes, especially during times of recession.[61]

One historian, Frank Prassel, argues that in the American West violence of all types may have been more closely related to the developing urban environment than the former existence of a frontier.[62] This probably explains the total absence of property crimes against women in Bodie. According to Mc-Garth, men's deference to "respectable" women accounted for the lack of robberies and rapes committed against females. But the absence of property crimes against all women in Bodie may have stemmed simply from a numerically insignificant number of females. Furthermore, Bodie, a frontier town with a malleable socioeconomic structure, afforded social and geographic mobility to most segments of the society. In San Francisco, however, a more rigid power structure pushed some to commit robberies against both "good" and "bad" women of all ethnic backgrounds.[63]

In addition to being robbery victims, several Chinese prostitutes suffered rape at the hands of Chinese men. The tremendously skewed sex ratio in the Chinese population probably contributed to the rapes. In 1872 alone, three cases of rape were brought before the police court, although two of them ended in acquittals because of a lack of concrete evidence. No cases were recorded in 1873. Hardly any details are available on the three 1872 cases.[64] Presumably, police authorities wanted to maintain the anonymity of victims. Although 9,523 Chinese males lived in San Francisco in 1870, few prostitutes, estimated for the same year at 1,565, became the prey of thieves.[65]

With the exception of rape and one case of

assault, none of the violent encounters had an enduring physical effect on the women. They suffered light external injuries and lost some property. However, the threat of violence was a psychological burden for these female victims. As Ruth Rosen has suggested in *The Lost Sisterhood: Prostitution in America, 1900–1918* (1982), prostitutes gradually developed self-hatred and guilt, blaming themselves for their own condition. The demoralization of personality and character prevented some women from attempting to escape prostitution.[66]

These sporadic and unrelated cases of brute force made up only a small amount of the violence that took place on a daily basis in San Francisco. Kidnapping and extortion were more serious affairs and far more common. Sometimes, brothel agents carried away Chinese women, prostitutes or otherwise, to other parts of the American West. More commonly, abducted women stayed within California's borders. Their predators feared breaking the federal law on kidnapping that applied to instances of victims crossing the state line. Those individuals who had seized women for prostitution but who remained within the state with their victims usually faced a lesser charge, such as assault and battery, which carried a fine, brief imprisonment, or both.[67]

In California fiction, the Chinese fondness for "slave girls" placed white women living in San Francisco in jeopardy of kidnapping.[68] Frank Norris, in his short story "The Third Circle," cautioned his female readers about the sinister elements that lurked in Chinese establishments. One of his white characters, accompanied by her fiancé, is kidnapped in broad daylight from a Chinese restaurant.[69]

In a panic whipped up by popular literature, Americans believed the kidnapping of women ran rampant along the Western Coast and even threatened to appear in the East. According to Jacob Riis's *How the Other Half Lives* (1890), Euro-American women, especially Irish women, married to Chinese men and living in New York's Chinatown were "hapless victims of [Chinese] passion."[70] A short story published in 1893 in a popular magazine warned white women not to go alone into Chinese laundries; to do so was to risk kidnapping, drugging, and sexual abuse.[71] These Chinese captivity narratives probably inspired one film producer, D. W. Griffith, to make *The Fatal Hour* (1908)—a film that traded on the fear of Chinese vice, the terror of Chinese hatchet men armed with cleavers and shotguns. In the *Fatal Hour*, the Chinese villain Pong Lee, with the help of a white man by the name of Hendricks, pounces on unsuspecting young white girls and bundles them off to faraway dens of sin and vileness.[72]

In reality, the kidnapping of women, with white and Chinese, occurred very rarely. Only seven cases— all involving Chinese women—were reported in 1872, and two of these involved prostitutes. In 1873, only one case—a completely botched attempt—was reported, and it involved a married Chinese woman. When kidnapping did take place, the victims (prostitutes or otherwise) generally attempted to escape or draw attention to their circumstances. They rarely used deadly weapons because they lacked access to them. Women also concluded that fighting their oppressors, given their superior strength, was pointless. Instead, many sought legal help during their confinement.

Some kidnapping cases involved complicated legal entanglements. Often, with the aid of corrupt sheriffs and constables, tongs brought charges of robbery or petty larceny against their victims. The tong would then tender bail to gain possession of the women. Sometimes the plan backfired when the victim refused to be intimidated or cajoled. Such a woman usually had tried to resist the kidnapping or had run away after being captured.[73] In six of the eight cases of kidnapping in 1872 and 1873, women resisted in some form or another.

One unnamed prostitute found herself in a violent confrontation with a group of men who had resolved to take her from her residence in Bartlett Alley. She rejected their efforts to get her to come outside. The kidnappers then tried force, using stones, hatchets, and knives to break into the house. The windows were smashed and the facade of the building considerably damaged, but the female victim was uninjured. Police arrested those who failed to escape the scene of the crime.[74]

In another case, Taem Ah Cheong kidnapped Ling Kuy, the concubine of an old man. When told that she would be sold into prostitution and taken to the interior of California, she quietly escaped and eventually returned to the old man. Ah Cheong followed her, forced his way into her home, and then sneaked up from behind and stabbed her. Ling Kuy died four days later from wounds about her hips.[75]

Some women, both prostitutes and nonprostitutes, depended on the judicial process for legal redress against their kidnappers. The fear of an organized tong reprisal and the language barrier, not to mention unfamiliarity with the procedures, could have discouraged quite a few from speaking the truth when hauled before a court on a trumped-up charge of petty larceny or prostitution.[76] However, a few, sensing that some good could result from truth, overcame the fear of possible adverse consequences resulting from their damaging testimony. The wrath of their owners and the tongs loomed large in their minds, but those who chose to testify pinned their hopes on the workings of the judicial and enforcement systems, their imperfections notwithstanding. In five separate cases during those two years (1872 and 1873), victims testified on behalf of the prosecution. They brought to light the duplicity and fraudulent nature of their kidnapping, particularly the false charges kidnappers levied against them. Because kidnappers typically received light punishments—just a fine or a short jail sentence— prostitutes, to avoid any further entanglements with their oppressors, pleaded for police protection and frequently requested help to return to China.[77]

When cases of kidnapping in other years are examined, the same pattern of behavior emerges. One woman refused to leave the courtroom after testifying against her kidnappers. She claimed that they were prepared to take her away and sell her on her release from confinement. The judge allowed the woman to remain in the city prison until a relative or friend appeared to escort her home, or until arrangements had been made for her return to China.[78]

In a subtle way, women exercised power for a brief moment when they became the focus of bitter struggles between individuals who desired economic or emotional control over them. Owners, in particular, exacerbated the disputes when they called on their tong affiliates for assistance. Most of the

time it was men who were the victims of the violence. They often suffered physical injuries and
even death in their attempts to wrest control of
women from each another. Sometimes, these disputes seemed to arise from jealousy between two
suitors competing for the hand of a young prostitute.[79]

Disputes over Chinese women were not an
everyday event, however. During 1872–73, the *San
Francisco Chronicle* recorded only one case of fighting over a woman. This particular event on Sullivan's Alley turned into a bloodbath; "knives and
cleaves [*sic*] were freely used," said the newspaper,
and one man sustained serious wounds. "The left
side of [his] ear was nearly severed; the left arm at
the elbow was pierced to the bone and the fingers of
his left hand were almost severed from the palm,"
according to the report. Presumably, the other com-
batants had somehow avoided injury, judging from
the absence of additional information.[80]

Reports of extortion of prostitutes appeared in
the press more often than kidnappings and fights,
although even these reports were not frequent. Police made eight arrests for extortion in 1873 but
none in 1872. It is possible that many cases of such
intimidation escaped the attention of the authorities as some members of the force were on the take
from the extortionists. Moreover, the burden of re-
porting such crimes rested with victims, namely,
the prostitutes themselves. Given the fact that few
knew anything about American law enforcement, it
is not surprising that only a handful of extortion
attempts came to the knowledge of the authorities.
No physical violence against anyone resulted from
this crime, and when isolated cases in subsequent

years are examined, the same pattern of few extortions and little violence emerges.[81]

Instances of suicide related to prostitution are more difficult to trace. Because suicide was considered a victimless offense, it drew little attention from the police. Nevertheless, suicide, although self-inflicted violence, constituted one of the two most serious forms of violence common among prostitutes (the other being rape). In China, suicide was a socially acceptable solution to a variety of problems.[82] In San Francisco, prostitutes also resorted to drastic means when life seemed an endless series of despondent moments. Chun Fah, a woman in her early twenties, is an example. According to her lover, Chun Fah received distressing news of the death of a close relative in China, and she rapidly sank into low spirits. For the next few days, she kept to herself, ignoring everyone and everything around her. On the night before she took her life, she cried and talked to her companion about her loss and expressed a desire to return to China. The next morning, the lover found Chun Fah dead from an overdose of laudanum.[83]

As only one suicide was reported during the course of 1872 and 1873, an in-depth analysis necessitated looking at cases in other years. In later decades, newspapers capitalized on suicide stories to help increase their circulation. According to these accounts, almost all Chinese women used some form of opium, which seemed to be the method of choice for female suicide.[84] Most prostitutes had easy access to opium because at that time anyone could obtain a license to sell it on the payment of a small fee. The board of supervisors moved exceedingly slowly in restricting the possession of opium to licensed druggists and in requiring a physician's prescription to obtain it.[85] Of course, suicide was not unique to Chinese prostitutes. White prostitutes, too, resorted to drug overdoses or, less frequently, shooting themselves to escape from prostitution.[86]

Finally, Chinese prostitutes, just like their white sisters, at times expressed their hostilities and resentments by unleashing their fury on each another. In many instances, these fights arose from trivial causes. When "Miss Kong" caught "Miss Sing" cheating at a game of dominoes, the former threw a handful of dominoes at her to "remind her of the maxim 'honesty is the best policy,'" the *San Francisco Chronicle* gleefully reported. Hauled before the police court, "Miss Kong" pleaded guilty and had to pay a fine of $10.[87] These fights probably reflected the insecurity prostitutes felt as a result of their limited opportunities for outward mobility into society. One unnamed prostitute assaulted a colleague so badly that the judge refused to release her on bail until four Chinese merchants submitted guarantee bonds on her behalf. In defense, the assailant claimed that the victim had stolen some of her clothes.[88]

Acts of violence against the Chinese that were rooted in racial tensions grew from the general xenophobia of white Americans, who also resented new immigrants from southern and eastern Europe. Local medical officers called Chinatown "a pesthole, a breeding place of smallpox, cholera, and leprosy." The ghettos of other ethnic groups withstood similar slurs.[89] For the Chinese, the situation was compounded by a classic cultural misunderstanding: the majority of white Americans were ignorant of Chinese culture and their ignorance produced fear and prejudice.

The Chinese female subculture as transplanted to America puzzled Euro-American society. Segregation from the male population in public places like Chinese theaters, self-confinement within residences, and donning traditional attire comprised aspects of their daily existence that made them objects of curiosity, ridicule, and derision.[90] One writer described the "moon-faced children" attired in the "most bizarre and brilliant colors" and likened them to "wax dolls or decorated idols."[91] Prostitutes' clothing especially came in for deprecating remarks. "Usually dressed in dingy blue sacks with huge sleeves," these "women . . . without beauty or grace," scoffed one female observer, "all wore the mechanical smile which seems part of the national character."[92] Even their "paint," claimed one author, invited ridicule: their faces showed "bright vermillion in one blotch, beginning with the chin, covering the eyebrows, and reaching back to the ear."[93]

Intolerance and racial prejudice aside, certain local conditions also gave rise to violence rooted in economic distress. One urban historian has suggested that red-light districts of the latter half of the nineteenth century attracted criminals and marginal characters. This, in turn, made it easy for the police to maintain urban public order as they "always knew where to find them [criminals]."[94] But San Francisco's Chinatown fought an uphill battle against crime, crippled by lax enforcement of the law, at least until 1879 when regular police constables began patrolling the neighborhood. Both the lack of sufficient police officers and, perhaps more important, the compromising attitude of the officers assigned to Chinatown undermined efforts to maintain public order.[95] As a result, prostitutes came to play a part in relieving the social pressures of urban living, particularly for dispossessed, poverty-stricken individuals.

Many of these scuffles left no serious physical injuries on prostitutes. When these did occur, they were a result of verbal disagreements over certain contractual obligations, written or otherwise, between the one hundred men's wife and customers or between the prostitute and the owner. Except in isolated cases, most prostitutes suffered only light physical harm at the hands of customers and owners, although psychological effects on self-esteem and self-worth must have lingered.

In terms of their number, cases of violence against and by Chinese prostitutes seem to be few given their significant presence in San Francisco during the early 1870s (see table 5). The minuscule number of racially motivated cases of violence against Chinese prostitutes is particularly striking. This phenomenon arose from a consensus that these

TABLE 5
Violence Against and by Chinese Prostitutes, 1872–1873

Types of Violence	Number
Racial attacks	3
Physical abuse	8
Robbery by men	5
Robbery by women	1
Rape	3
Kidnapping	2
Extortion	8
Suicide	1
Fights with women	2

SOURCE: Compiled from *San Francisco Chronicle*, 1872–73.

women must be excused for their involvement in commercialized sex because they had been forced into it by culture and circumstance. Various politicians sympathetic to them highlighted their plight in Congress. One member of the House of Representatives pointed out that these women were "bought and sold like chattels."[96] The trafficking of Chinese women was "cruel and unfair," according to one senator, and in the opinion of Edwin R. Meade, congressman from New York, these women should not be considered immoral.[97] Most newspapers in San Francisco, while condemning the negative impact of the brothels, excused the women themselves. One newspaper expressed bewilderment over police harassment of prostitutes and asked, "Do they not know that these poor serfs are obliged to do as they do?"[98] Even the Workingmen's Party, an aggressively anti-Chinese organization, exonerated the women for "plying their miserable vocation" because they were "slaves" and had been sold to the proprietors of bordellos or to rich merchants.[99]

Brothel prostitution provided some protection against organized crime and unpredictable assaults. Prostitutes faced the threat of violence from a variety of sources, but few actually saw it on a regular basis. Though the anonymity of city life was not extended to prostitutes, they learned to ward off potential dangers. One simple way was to avoid contact with the wider society. Voluntary confinement thus became the choice for many women. In the long run, however, this voluntary separation served to widen the imaginary gap between Chinese Americans, especially Chinese prostitutes, and the mainstream culture.

Leaving the Trade

During the 1870s, a large number of Chinese prostitutes left the trade and very likely entered into matrimony. While the number of prostitutes in San Francisco in 1870 stood at 1,565, within a decade there were only 305.[1] This dramatic decline stemmed largely from the movement of many of them into conjugal relationships, mainly with Chinese sojourners. The lack of rigid Chinese cultural barriers against acceptance of a former prostitute as a conjugal partner, particularly as secondary wife, worked to the advantage of these women. However, many had to find a way to overcome restrictions imposed by their owners. For these women, social agencies played a key role in tipping the balance between their vulnerability to intimidation and the opportunity to leave prostitution.

In 1870, some 448 women lived in households that had at least one male whose occupation was not one of the following: "keeper of brothel house," "Chinese keeper of brothel," or "keeps house of ill-fame." Children also lived in many of these households. These women, who constituted close to 18 percent of the Chinese female population, had obviously established family units with Chinese men. Ten years later, census takers (instructed for the first time to identify relationships between members of a household) identified 914, or 52.5 percent, in a Chinese female population of 1,742 as married women. These data confirm that within a period of ten years, many had established family units.

The steady rise in the aggregate number of married women during these ten years — 1870 to 1880 — partly resulted from Chinese wives migrating to California, which thereby swelled the female population of San Francisco. Yet from 1871 to 1875, the entry of Chinese women into the United States had entered a period of gradual decline, and yearly figures never climbed back to the level of the pre-1870 immigration rush period. In fact, the number of female arrivals between 1876 and 1882 dropped from the previous seven-year period by 68 percent.[2] While a modest percentage of the married women may have been new arrivals, a sizable number of them must have come from the ranks of former prostitutes who had edged into mainstream life.

A close look at one particular ward illuminates some of these demographic shifts. In 1870, in Ward Six, one of the areas in which the Chinese predominated, census takers listed 76 Chinese women as "keeping house," or housewives. Within the span of ten years, the number of housewives tripled, to 222. For the same period, the number of working prostitutes plunged from 209 to 39. This precipitous drop cannot be accounted for by movement out of the ward because the number of female residents increased to 626 in 1880 from 417 in 1870.

Perhaps the drop in the aggregate number of prostitutes stemmed from their large-scale exile in 1876 to the interior of California. Constant police raids and arrests in that year apparently forced about a thousand of them to seek new homes. But this argument, based on the testimony of one police officer, Michael A. Smith, demands refinement. Smith, who patrolled Ward Four (the principal Chinese business and residential zone), claimed in late 1876 that, following raids in the early months of that year, a great many women had "gone to the country, or mountains, as they [Chinese] say." Their departure, he guessed, left San Francisco with slightly over four hundred prostitutes.[3]

In contrast to Smith's statement, the chief of police reports for the years 1875–76 and 1876–77 appeared strangely silent on these raids. Statistics of monthly arrests for vice related to prostitution such as "keeping house of ill-fame," "visitor to house of ill-fame," and "soliciting for ill-fame" show that these crimes continued to be a constant negligible percentage of all arrests made during the two years before 1877.[4] One newspaper report in 1878, however, gave a rough estimate of some 500 to 600 Chinese prostitutes still living within the city limits.[5] Obviously some women had left during those ten years as frequent harassment led to the closure of their establishments and their expulsion. But contrary to Smith's claim, the process unfolded gradually.

The changing median age of prostitutes provides additional evidence that many women married during the course of those ten years. Close to 74 percent of those engaged in commercialized sex in 1870 gave their ages as between sixteen and twenty-five, the average age being twenty-two. Ten years later, the average rose to twenty-six. Also, fewer women fell in the age bracket sixteen to twenty-five, with only 60 percent below the age of twenty-five. The drop in the average age, which took place in the context of a roughly 80 percent decline in the total number of prostitutes, can be explained by the exodus by 1880 of older prostitutes from the profession into either other occupations or marriage.

Indeed, as Butler has pointed out, prostitution generally employed young women, and the prime years were between the ages of fifteen and thirty. After thirty, prostitutes had to look for other employment.[6] Both Chinese and Euro-American prostitutes faced loss of their occupation with the passage of time and the loss of beauty or youth. During the 1870s, the average age of Chinese working women (both prostitutes and non-prostitutes) also changed. From an average of twenty-six in 1870, it rose ten years later to thirty-one. This increase occurred while the city's total Chinese female population declined by 30 percent. Thus the increase resulted from the movement of prostitutes — the majority of the Chinese female population in 1870 — into new fields from 1870 to 1880.

In most occupations, employers offered women, regardless of their ethnic backgrounds, lower wages in comparison to men performing the same type of job. A woman who held the position of a domestic servant earned $20 to $30 a week.[7] By comparison, a man working for a family as a general helper earned $30 to $40.[8] Most Chinese women served as workers in service or manufacturing industries, particularly as laundresses and unskilled factory hands.

In San Francisco's manufacturing sector of the 1870s, Chinese women joined their male compatriots to make up nearly 50 percent of the labor force in the four key industries of the city—tobacco and cigars, woolens, boots and shoes, and sewing. Ironically, Chinese men and women became integrated into the larger economy even as whites rejected them as full members of the San Francisco community.[9]

Those who toiled in sweatshops, just like women of European descent of the time, concentrated on textile production. These women "sew[ed] button holes and buttons on white shirts designed for the Caucasian trade," according to one journalist, "for which labor they received from 35 cents to 30 cents per dozen." A few of them stitched slippers at the rate of 30 cents per dozen.[10] According to Loomis, women "[were] also, to some extent employed in certain branches of the tobacco business."[11] Some women rolled cigars to support their families when their husbands abandoned them for the fabled riches of the western interior.[12]

Although few relished the grinding work in these sweatshops, factory employment seemed to offer an opportunity for prostitutes to leave the profession. However, most of the women listed as factory workers and laundresses had married and set up family households. In many instances, they worked for either their husbands or close relatives in family-run enterprises. Few public women made a direct transition from indentured prostitution to hired help. Thus, the question remains as to how these women left the trade.

Unlike white society, which believed that members of the demimonde were not respectabe and were wholly unacceptable as wives, for the most part the Chinese did not attach the same stigma to prostitution. Of course, prostitutes in China were not the equals of chaste women, who remained the preferred conjugal partners.[13] Yet far from being considered "fallen women," prostitutes were seen as daughters who obeyed the wishes of the family. Though less than an honorable profession for Chinese women, those who could get out of prostitution usually were accepted into working-class society. Among the Chinese gentry, a baak haak chai could occupy the position of a secondary wife or concubine.[14]

Literary works encouraged the admission of prostitutes into Chinese society. Writers of Cantonese folk rhymes urged "peipa girls" to give up their trade and find a husband. The last two lines of one rhyme reads, "The domestic life may lack the luster of the gay quarters / But it's far better than living in a green mansion [brothel] as a hundred men's wife!" Another folk rhyme gives this bit of advice: "Get out of this business while there's still time to reach paradise / the gaiety of pleasure houses in the past, where is it now? / You want respect, don't you?"[15]

Rev. Otis Gibson, testifying before a congressional committee in 1879, claimed that in the preceding five or six years cases were "increasing rapidly where Chinamen take these women and live with them as their wives."[16] Chinese prostitutes probably had more social mobility than their white sisters, although marriage, for both groups, became the most common route out of prostitution. For Chinese public women, marriage offered privacy, domesticity, and permanence.[17]

Much has been said about the onerous burden of the gender system on Chinese women. Scholars have argued that the traditional system of patriarchal control dictated the subordination of young wives within extended families. One academician even went as far as to claim that "the full weight of the gender system of traditional China descended on young women" following their marriage.[18]

In reality, though faced with cultural constraints, women often carved a place for themselves within their husbands' families and adapted to whatever unfavorable circumstances they found. No doubt, the bride-price — money and gifts presented by the groom to his bride's family — symbolized the transfer of rights over the bride from parents to husband and in-laws. But here a trade-off took place: in accepting the woman as a new member of the family, the groom's lineage was committed to supporting her for the rest of her life.[19] Further, young brides who had bound feet and were skilled in feminine accomplishments received deference from their new family.[20]

While the Chinese patriarchal and patrilineal society demanded submissiveness to husbands and in general to society, women's status steadily improved as they grew older.[21] Though young women lacked all rights of property ownership and management or formal, independent decision-making authority, they did not consider themselves marginal members in the family system. Moreover, in the words of one feminist scholar, "they rely heavily on

developing and manipulating informal interperson-
al relationships and emotional ties to gain influence
over their lives and to partially overcome the imposed handicaps of male-dominated authority structures."[22] Later in life, many achieved significant
social status as mothers and mothers-in-law. The
principle of reverence for the aged worked in their
favor. In short, a young wife's status "improves at
the birth of a son, and climaxes when she becomes a
dowager with adult sons."[23]

Young wives who married into families of means
were expected to serve their in-laws and, to a lesser
extent, their female relatives. Unsatisfied mothers-
in-law and relatives at times created discord in
extended families, often the result of competition
with young wives for the loyalty and affection of
their husbands.[24] Chinese lore has it that husbands
often took the side of their wives' enemies. Out-
matched, these women kept their patience until
they had graduated to motherhood.

Unlike women who joined wealthy joint or
extended families, those who married into peasant
families sometimes enjoyed a more psychologically
comfortable position.[25] In peasant families, frequently smaller in size, the lack of competing female
relatives often placed young brides at the center of
their husbands' attention. Women in China who
joined poor peasant households sometimes gained
the respect of the elders for their roles as domestic
artisans and field hands. They carried wood, gathered fuel, spun thread and weaved cloth, tilled the
land, prepared meals, raised the children, and still
found time to practice ancestral rites and customs.[26]
Their role in the family economy became crucial in
the second half of the nineteenth century in the

wake of the large-scale migration of Chinese males. One witness noted, "Because all young men in this community left home for overseas, four fields were abandoned. . . . The women, therefore, were compelled to come out of their seclusion and tilled lands for their subsistence."[27]

The phrase that most parents attached to their daughters, "goods on which one loses," hinted that they were of little value to their natal families.[28] Yet they served important purposes in their peasant husbands' families. These women also ran less of a risk of having to cope with other mature women in the household compared to those placed in rich, extended families. Therefore, they might have had far greater power.[29] The husband-wife relationship in peasant households was usually stronger than that in joint households and the value of a wife more obvious.

Chinese society did cast limitations on peasant women, however. The hierarchical and patriarchal society in China kept itself stable, permanent, and eternal by proscribing work for women outside the home, lest they sow disorder and confusion throughout the empire.[30] In situation-centered Chinese society, a woman valued what her peers thought and said about her. Ning Lao T'ai-t'ai, a peasant woman in China, refused to seek work despite having to endure starvation, even with death lurking around the corner. "If a woman went out to service, the neighbors all laughed," she explained. She later broke conventions when, in a fit of rage, she left her husband following the sale of their older daughter, an exchange she had resisted all along. Even then, she realized the price she must pay; she could never bring herself to return to her husband's family since the "women of her family had never 'come out' before."[31]

Chinese women understood and accepted their subordination in the broad hierarchical kinship system. Wong Ah So assured her mother that she harbored no resentment against her for selling her. When she wrote, "It seems to be just my fate," she indicated that she recognized her submission to elders within the context of filial piety. She further told her mother that "earning money by living this life of prostitution" fulfilled in part the "requirements of complete filial piety."[32]

Few Chinese women—and this was certainly true in the case of illiterates—recognized an oppressive gender system in their culture. The seeds of modern Chinese feminism would not be sown until the turn of the century. An offshoot of the Reform Movement of 1898, modern feminism formed part of the larger struggle to modernize China and defend it against Western imperialism. Wide acceptance of Chinese feminism, however, did not take root immediately in the public consciousness; in fact, feminist concerns did not become part of the national political agenda for years—certainly not until after the Communists wrested control of the country in 1949.[33] Though women lacked equality with men in social and political life, Chinese females of the nineteenth century in general did not demand it. Married life, which revolved around a far from rigid value system, gave women a sense of fulfillment and a degree of happiness. Marriage served as the only passage to security, respect, and power.[34]

In the United States, the skewed sex ratio of the Chinese offered economic opportunities for prostitutes who could find a way to profit from it, as did the extreme sexual imbalance in the nineteenth-century and early twentieth-century Japanese immigrant population. Few women came to America in the initial phase of Japanese immigration; American customs statistics record 30,077 Japanese arrivals between 1861 and 1900, of whom only 1,195 were females. This gives a sex ratio of twenty-five men to one woman.[35] Thus the few Japanese prostitutes also found themselves in demand as potential wives. During the same period, there were at least twenty Chinese men for every Chinese woman in California. However, unlike Japanese immigrants who later could exploit loopholes in the Gentlemen's Agreement of 1908 to bring their wives to the United States, Chinese male sojourners faced stringent and discriminatory immigration laws. These restrictions barred the entry of married women of most classes, with the exception of wives (and daughters) of the elite, such as officials, teachers, students, and merchants.[36] In contrast to the Chinese but more similar to the Japanese, Korean male emigrants had little trouble bringing in more than a thousand Korean picture brides between 1910 and 1924; consequently, relatively few Korean women entered as prostitutes.[37]

Chinese men who wished to set down permanent roots in the United States ruled out interracial marriages with Euro-American women. The sociologist Stanford M. Lyman has proposed that "the mutual peculiarities of dress, language, habits, customs, and diet, not to mention the physical distinctiveness of racial identities," kept the number of intermarriages low. Most Chinese men considered it beneath them to maintain any social ties with white women. One xenophobic Chinese male emigrant deplored Euro-American relationships generally — "men and women [living] together like animals, without any marriage or faithfulness, and even . . . shameless enough to walk the streets arm in arm in daylight."[38]

Those Chinese male emigrants who had no compunctions about pairing up with white women discovered that the legal system did not recognize such unions. Antimiscegenation laws in California passed as early as 1850 made interracial marriage illegal. An 1880 statute amendment stated that California officials vested with the power to solemnize marriages "shall not issue a license authorizing the marriage of a white person with a negro, mulatto, or Mongolian."[39] It was not until 1948 that the Supreme Court ruled such laws unconstitutional.

Although they carried no penal sanctions, antimiscegenation laws discouraged Chinese–Euro-American unions. Rev. A. W. Loomis claimed in 1876 that San Francisco had, at the most, five cases of Chinese men living with white women.[40] An 1885 San Francisco board of supervisors' investigation into the living conditions of the Chinese revealed ten cases of "white women living and cohabiting with Chinamen in the relation of wives or mistresses."[41] Contemporary newspapers reported the existence of only a handful of Chinese-white marriages. In 1883, the *Morning Call* mentioned three such cases, and in 1903, the *San Francisco Chronicle* identified twenty white women in Chinatown in marital relationships with Chinese emigrants.[42]

Further, the cultural differences, the segregation of the two races, and extreme anti-Chinese sentiments combined to discourage Chinese men

from marrying white women. Not unlike their countrymen, Chinese prostitutes received and accepted
few American offers of marriage. One prostitute,
Kit Ti Wong, did cross racial lines, marrying a white
sailor and moving out of Chinatown into a white
neighborhood. The sole newspaper account of her
marriage, curiously enough, contained no critical
remarks despite strong anti-Chinese sentiments
among white San Franciscans of that time.[43] Perhaps her marginal position led whites to ignore her
actions. However, research into conjugal ties between Mexican women and whites has shown that
the former suffered hostility and isolation from
their white neighbors.[44]

On the West Coast, miscegenation was strongly
condemned. Short stories depicting miscegenation
in a bad light abounded in popular literature. "The
Haunted Valley" (1871) by Ambrose Bierce features
Ah Wee, a cook in the employment of a supposedly
temperamental man, Jo Dunbar. Quickly, the reader
learns of rumors that Dunbar, displeased with Ah
Wee's work, had killed his servant in a fit of rage.
Thus far perhaps a commentary on anti-Chinese
prejudice, the story surprisingly reveals more. Ah
Wee turns out to be married to Dunbar and only
masquerading as a servant. Her death, in actual fact,
resulted from a brawl involving her husband and
some enemies. Caught in between, she was cut
down during the scuffle. The lesson here is simple:
any woman who dares to cross over the threshold of
prejudice must forsake openness and truthfulness;
otherwise, the flames of racial hatred will consume
her.[45]

For Chinese prostitutes, the American West
presented opportunities to control one's circum-

stances. The exigencies of an isolated existence on the frontier did not Americanize these women but, nevertheless, gave them a chance to discard cultural habits of the past. The absence of parents and in-laws, a result of the fragmentation of families as some members went to Gold Mountain, allowed them to ignore the hierarchical kinship system and its concomitant structure of authority. Companion-ate marriage replaced arranged wedlock. Prostitutes weighed their options; the job market was essen-tially closed to Chinese single women, and interra-cial union had to be ruled out. Thus marriage with Chinese men emerged as the logical choice, and the demand for wives made it even more compelling.

During the nineteenth century, some of the Chinese women succeeded in leaving prostitution behind, but others failed. A former prostitute named Hy Tee, recently married to Ah Long, was kid-napped from her home during her husband's ab-sence.[46] Miss Donaldina Cameron, the well-known matron of the San Francisco Presbyterian Mission Home, alleged that "highbinders have even stolen married girls from their husbands after they have gone to small country places."[47] Another prosti-tute, Sing Fung, though prevented from uniting with her lover by her owner, who moved her from one town to another, lost little of her buoyant spir-its, confident that her suitor would come through. Disappointment awaited her, however. Her desper-ate lover, Ah Pung, instituted litigation to reclaim her but eventually met defeat.[48]

Newspapers of that time frequently tantalized their readers with stories of Chinese women run-ning off with their lovers and chased by enraged highbinders bent on recovering their lost "property."

One tragic tale involved Kum Ho and her admirer, Low Sing, a member of the Suey Sin Tong. Enamored with her, he scraped together enough cash to buy out the owner. Unfortunately, a member of another tong, Ming Long, was also smitten with Kum Ho. Ming Long ambushed the couple and had Low Sing killed. The death of their comrade agitated members of the Suey Sin Tong. Bent on revenge, they challenged their enemies to a head-on confrontation, which took place late one night in 1875, leaving ten dead. With few clues available, Kum Ho's fate remained unknown.[49]

In contrast, one determined woman joined her husband to-be, Ah Kim, by sending herself in a box on board a train to a prearranged rural area.[50] One Cantonese folk rhyme told the tale of a one hundred men's wife who loved a man with so much passion that her "emotions burned the lacquer and glue." Unfortunately for her, "the pimp hears about this, and scolds her and beats her up," but luckily, "she runs off and makes back to China with her lover."[51]

Behind these romantic tales lay deep-seated problems that challenged prostitutes and their lovers. Men visited brothel residents and then became attached to them. Some of these suitors, however, lacked the financial standing to redeem their fiancées. Prostitutes had even less financial means to pay off their owners. Thus running away, even at the risk of retribution from owners and their associates, became one option.

Prostitutes and suitors on occasion would use the judiciary system to challenge the right of owners. Lin Chong's beau, Ah Tong, failed to raise the $600 fee set to redeem her. He then sued to release her from the agreement she had signed with the owner. The judge presiding over the case granted their petition and declared the contract for prostitution null and void. Then he solemnized their union.

Women sought to make their marriages more secure by taking their vows before a judge or clergyman.[52] But Lin Chong's case was unique. More often, prostitutes and their lovers found the system ineffectual. Sometimes the court would unwittingly return the female runaways to their owners. Brothel proprietors could also manipulate the law to their advantage. They lodged reports with the police and made trumped-up charges, frequently theft, against prostitutes and their companions. After they had been arrested, owners would drop the charges against the prostitutes. With their suitors still locked up, owners could then reclaim the women.[53]

Notwithstanding the emotional and physical hazards of trying to leave the trade and the stormy circumstances surrounding attempts to find security and stability through permanent relationships, prostitutes' desire for companionship and domestic stability led them to pair off with men through traditional marriages or common-law arrangements. Unfortunately, the prostitutes sometimes chose disreputable men who had few qualms about making them vend their one commodity. Unwilling to forgo any chance of escaping prostitution, they rushed into shaky relationships. When the true intentions of these men came to light, the final chance to extricate themselves from the entanglement of fraudulent wedlock had long passed, and they were forced to return to prostitution.[54]

This seems to support the contention that, instead of severing her relation to prostitution, marriage sometimes further tied a woman to it.[55] There is undoubtedly enough statistical evidence on non-

Chinese prostitutes to legitimize that argument. Two separate studies in the 1880s — one funded by the state of California and the other commissioned by the federal government — concluded that close to a quarter of the white prostitutes surveyed were married, divorced, or widowed.[56] Statutes against adultery, which would provide another means (in addition to anti-prostitution statutes) of prosecuting married women who worked as prostitutes, entered into California law only in the early years of the twentieth century. Thus nineteenth-century married women could remain in the profession without living in fear of legal prosecution via adultery laws. In the East, married prostitutes were not uncommon; most could be found in slums or ethnic neighborhoods.[57]

Chinese prostitutes, however, differed from their white counterparts in that fewer married Chinese women remained in the profession. In 1880, census takers identified 12 Chinese women as wives of Chinese men from an aggregate total of 305 prostitutes. This 4 percent fits well with the statistical profile of prostitutes outside San Francisco. Sucheng Chan, who studied 1880 census schedules for selected northern California counties outside San Francisco, has tabulated the number of married Chinese prostitutes. Based on her statistics, 2 to 4 percent of the women fell into this category, possibly slightly more.[58] The difference between Chinese and non-Chinese prostitutes is accounted for by the simple fact that only affluent people could redeem indentured Chinese prostitutes. Secured in a comfortable marriage, most Chinese women who left the trade rarely had to face the bleak prospect of returning to prostitution.

While some showed little compunction at putting themselves at risk in order to leave prostitution, others sought the help of sympathetic individuals or organizations. During the last third of the century, benevolent agencies flourished in San Francisco. The social ills of the city cried out for collective action, and an absence of unemployment offices or welfare programs opened the door for humanitarian institutions to step in and respond. Prostitutes looked to these social agencies for protection; typically, the women had run away from brothels when their plans to marry collapsed following their suitors' failure to buy out their contracts or purchase them out of slavery.

One organization that extended aid to underage prostitutes was the Society for the Prevention of Cruelty to Children. Members of this voluntary organization committed themselves to rescuing young girls forced into prostitution regardless of their ethnicity, though they left the task of rehabilitation to others.[59] In 1874, their work received a boost from the California legislature, which passed a law that made it a felony to force girls below the age of eighteen into prostitution, although the law proved unenforceable if brothel owners could prove their victims had willingly acquiesced. Later the legislature removed the loophole but also lowered the age of a minor to sixteen. The municipal administration itself in 1876 passed an ordinance to suppress prostitution for children below the age of fourteen. These laws and the organization entrusted with the task of helping to enforce them, unfortunately, touched the lives of few Chinese prostitutes. As the age of minority dropped, Chinese prostitutes, most of whom were not minors, stood outside the law's protection and, simultaneously, the assistance offered by the society.[60]

One agency that did offer aid to prostitutes of all ethnic origins was the Magdalen Asylum established in 1868 by the Catholic Sisters of Charity. Unlike organizations that advocated moral redemption as the panacea for prostitutes' problems (the Salvation Army, the Society for the Restoration of Fallen Women, the San Francisco Ladies Protection and Relief Society), the Sisters of Charity designed a rehabilitation program that offered removal from prostitution through a new environment. Asylum residents learned, in addition to religious lessons, domestic skills such as sewing and gardening for eventual entry into the job market. An obvious demand existed for such a program; in 1871, a newspaper noted that the asylum had started to turn away women because of a lack of space.[61] But again, few Chinese prostitutes found refuge here aside from a negligible number sent by the police for a temporary stay while awaiting transportation back to China.[62] Since the asylum sat on a property south of Market Street in a predominantly white neighborhood, many prostitutes did not know of its existence. Those who did probably balked at venturing into such an area.[63]

Closer to home were church missions located in the vicinity of Chinatown and geared to serve the Chinese population. Missionaries prayed and labored for the conversion of as many sojourners as possible so that on their return to China these new believers could help spread the gospel.[64]

In the mid-1850s, concerned Southern Baptists struggled to build a kingdom of God among the Chinese. They met indifference from the church leaders who, on the whole, sought to bring more whites rather than Chinese into the flock. After a few unsuccessful attempts, plans to revive the Chinese mission finally reached fruition in 1878. Shortly after, the female benevolent organization of the church, the Woman's Baptist Home Mission Society, followed their male brethen to California and in 1884 began a home visitation program for Chinese mothers and children to "lift them out of their idolatry and sin" and help them "strive to attain to higher and nobler things."[65]

For late-nineteenth-century female missionaries working in the cities, home visitation formed the core element in their varied agenda. Directed toward significant new immigrant groups, the visitation program was designed to transmit good moral values that would lead immigrants away from poverty and degradation.[66] Women of the Congregational church also embarked on home visitations, but they arrived on the scene much later, in 1894. Although both the Baptists and the Congregationalists came to the succor of the Chinese poor, they ignored the specific plight of Chinese prostitutes. One Congregational report admitted that both the Baptists and Congregationalists chose not to "care for all those who could in any way be rescued from their lives of shame."[67] They believed Chinese women could be "saved" but wanted to avoid competing with the other major denominations in San Francisco, the Methodists and the Presbyterians.

Chinese members of the demimonde found their haven mainly in Methodist and Presbyterian rescue homes run by female missionaries. These rescue homes were offshoots of general missionary work in San Francisco. Though the Presbyterians were the first to establish a Chinese Mission—in 1853—in the city, they lagged behind the Methodists in the development of a rescue home to provide care to homeless, wayward, and criminal girls and women. In 1870, the Methodists opened their Mission House, which occupied the whole length of the third floor of their Chinese Mission building on Washington Street. In contrast, the Presbyterians' rescue home, called the Mission Home, began operating in 1874 from cramped rented quarters. Shortly after, the Presbyterians moved to a twenty-five-room tenement on Sacramento Street.[68]

Chinese brothel residents fled to either the Mission House or Mission Home when owners mistreated them or when they lacked protection to marry safely. Some found their way to the missions with the help of their lovers. In the summer of 1873, three Chinese women escaped a brothel and headed for the Methodist mission with the help of an admirer by the name of Yat Seng, who later married one of them and secured proposals for the other two. In another case, Loi Kum, with her own fiancé, fled to the Presbyterian home.[69]

Those ignorant of the existence of such establishments arrived following the direct intervention of mission officials. Jin Ho had slipped out of her crib, run several blocks, and then thrown herself into the cold waters of the bay. Rescued in the nick of time, she was brought to the police station. She made it clear that she would readily go anywhere, except back to the "vile den." Later, Reverend Gibson dropped by the station and offered her refuge in the Methodist rescue home. Placing her trust in Gibson and having nowhere else to turn, she agreed to go with him.[70]

The mission officials who cared for women like Jin Ho viewed their charges' sinful behavior as endemic to the general moral decay of the American West.[71] They believed that women of the underclasses, needed to learn Protestant middle-class values that defined the moral sphere of Victorian America. Home officials shared nationalistic and Christian emotions and worked to provide surroundings that replaced mayhem with order, bedlam with routine, and abuse with comity.[72]

Convinced of their special feminine ability to empathize with the weak and the dependent and goaded by the desire to put in motion "the process of deliverance," these female missionaries planned a rehabilitation program that betrayed didactic elements of Victorian culture.[73] These proselytizers of Victorian family life—women possessed of "true mother spirit"—built their program on the basic assumption that the Chinese were inferior and primitive.[74] Certainly, the aim of establishing the rescue homes was not simply altruism; one Methodist annual report made it clear that work among these "idolatrous heathen women" guaranteed "safety for our children and succeeding generations."[75] By making immigrant women imitate the family and gender roles of white, middle-class culture, evangelical women could guarantee the salvation of their own families, communities, and nation.

To achieve both idealistic and self-serving goals, missionaries structured their programs along the precepts of "true womanhood," that is, purity, piety, and domesticity.[76] Mission officials desired their charges to achieve "passionlessness"—the absence of female sexuality and, conversely, an overflow of intuitive morality—to tame male lust, the source of

Western moral degeneration.[77] Officials had hoped that a large dose of Victorian values would stimulate the dormant nurturing qualities of their residents. These ethnic women could then serve as moral authorities for their future families. Missionary women considered the emancipation of prostitutes a step toward modern marriages in which husbands' traditional powers could be curtailed through their wives' moral influence.[78]

Their attitude toward those under their care reflected the general ambivalence of Gilded Age reformers. On the one hand, they showed an incipient understanding of the roots of prostitution by opening refuges to prostitutes, teaching them new trades, and finding employment. On the other hand, they failed to move away from the profoundly moralistic perspective of their age.[79]

Missionaries placed Christianization ahead of Americanization. The cultivation of white bourgeois manners, which served as an instrument of inclusion and socialization in American society, lagged slightly behind in their agenda.[80] Officials accepted those who desired to maintain their diet, dress, and other traditional accoutrements. Missionaries hesitated to introduce radical changes in their daily habits for fear of antagonizing them and jeopardizing their foremost goal — salvation. The "first and chief aim," as one missionary emphasized, "was to teach them something of the religion of Christ."[81] Following their rehabilitation, former residents were to return to China and help to spread the good news.[82]

Immigrant women, unskilled in the arts of domesticity, required more attention. Residents had to learn Euro-American ways of bringing up children and running a household before the transformation of the heathen home into a Christian one could begin. Evangelical women placed in those rescue homes taught their wards "not only to read and write, but [also] to keep house neatly, to cook, and to be good wives and Christian mothers," according to one religious organization publication.[83] In truth, both elements, acculturation and Christianization, confronted the women during the period of residence. Christianization, however, received more attention than acculturation.

Residents in the homes followed a prescribed hectic daily routine of early rising for prayers, school lessons in the morning and afternoon, domestic duties, and more prayers at night—all designed to stimulate dormant natural instincts for tenderness and motherliness. In school, the curriculum went beyond Western subjects and included Chinese language, training in calligraphy, and, occasionally, Chinese history.[84] Few pupils took their classroom work in stride. After all, few had received any form of education prior to stepping through the doors of the mission. However, at least one student at the Methodist Mission House, Doris Dong, attained some measure of success. Asked to participate in a statewide children's essay contest on the theme, "My Favorite Revolutionary Character," Dong chose Nathan Hale and went on to capture the gold medal.[85] School lessons offered by missionary teachers constituted the only formal education available to Chinese women living in San Francisco until the mid-1880s and survived as their most important contribution.[86]

School life for Chinese women included some extracurricular activities. Musical programs featured prominently during holidays. All students had an opportunity to take center stage during the annual Christmas celebrations at the mission and then again at Easter. They sang hymns and recited verses from the Bible and, in return, received gifts of nuts, fruits, and candy. Sometimes they even put on small plays that imparted an obvious message: they should be grateful for the benevolence showered on them. One such piece, "A New Life for Ling Wang," depicted how the love and sympathy of missionaries "healed [the] wounds" of the girl. The narrator told the audience that "she awakened mentally . . . and became ambitious to learn."[87]

Mission home officials made arrangements with business interests for residents to take in sewing work, as much to nurture feminine qualities as to pay for their living expenses in these poor, struggling establishments. Perhaps this represented one challenge that Protestant women made against the Victorian ideal of female economic dependence. To further reduce the financial pressure on the treasury, missionaries placed selected longtime residents in white households to work as domestic helpers. Officials expected the pious environment in these Christian homes to transform Chinese women into Victorian mothers possessing moral authority.[88]

The work program fell short of success because employers objected to the presence of "heathen women" in their homes. Yet thousands of "heathen" Chinese men worked in them. No concrete evidence has been uncovered to explain this contradiction. Possibly, employers could not set aside their prejudices against former prostitutes, who were seen as defiled persons.[89] The Chinese women, according to one white female employer, used "nails or teeth upon each other to enforce their rights." News of the home work program appeared in two or three annual reports and then disappeared until the early years of the twentieth century.[90] Even when it was reestablished, one church employee, a former Chinese resident, admitted that "after the girls were with us for over a year, we could scarcely find any employment for them."[91] Furthermore, some of the women, found it impossible to adjust to life in white households and vented their frustrations on their employers, thus rupturing their relationship with these families.

Rules and regulations, framed to prevent the supposed threat of predatory men bent on kidnapping as many women as possible for prostitution, kept them in a cloistered environment and restricted their movements. To prevent backsliding, missionaries invited interested female parishioners to be "American mammies" to all the "girls" and to provide material support and spiritual guidance.[92] In the words of one Methodist missionary, the rescue home "ministers in modern ways to modern girls who must have the intensive home training."[93] Such a program corresponded with the didactic paternalism of Victorian culture. At the end of their stay in the homes, Protestant women planned to pair residents with Chinese Christian men for companionate marriages.

Missionaries had good intentions. Yet in their enthusiasm to protect residents, they also exhibited a disrespectful attitude toward them and a failure to cast aside the Victorian framework of a moral hierarchy of cultures. These proselytizers had to contend with an ideology that defined their race and country, an ideology that scoffed at the idea of

equality of cultures. As a result, few transcended
the moral imperatives that defined their generation.

The Chinese who lived in these homes were
never consulted on serious matters affecting their
well-being because missionaries saw them as inferi-
or, hapless women and stereotyped them as passive,
subservient, and self-effacing. Missionaries were a
contradiction of sorts. They preached the efficacious-
ness of Christianity and acculturation but also doubt-
ed their charges could fully subscribe to the heights of
Western civilization.[94] In the end, these Protestant
women denied them the autonomy necessary to
work for their own liberation. Instead, exhibiting
extreme paternalism toward their charges, they tried
to be faithful to their promise to draw Chinese
women "from filth and vice to cleanliness and godli-
ness, from idleness to industry, from Satan to God.[95]

Women who came to the homes without suitors
found themselves cajoled into accepting Chinese
Christian men — missionaries ruled out white men —
as husbands. Mission officials justified this on the
grounds that too many Chinese men had passed
themselves off as sincere husbands-to-be only to
make off with the women to the interior and sell
them to new owners. Not surprisingly, officials tried
to convince women to end their ties to the men who
accompanied them to the homes and when they
failed, subjected the suitors to endless rounds of oral
interviews designed to ferret out the disreputable.[96]
This is perhaps understandable, if claims of the
constant threat of violence were accurate. Writers of
missionary literature told terrifying tales of dyna-
mite sticks on doorsills, on window ledges, and on
the floor. Readers also learned of enraged highbinders
who broke the windows of the mission, crashed

through the door, and heckled "respectable" white women.[97]

However, internal missionary society records indicate that violent attacks against missionaries and their wards were infrequent. More substantive would be the fears missionaries harbored about the well-being of their charges after they left the home. To their credit, officials attempted to eliminate those prospective husbands with little economic standing. To discourage the indigent, officials collected a modest sum from each suitor, which also helped to offset the cost of running the institution.[98]

Chinese women saw themselves as willing residents at the home but were treated more like prisoners. Missionaries instructed them to wear only cotton clothes and provided them with simple food. Male visitors were carefully screened. To separate the women from their old life-style, mission officials introduced routine and regimentation. A typical morning schedule included a prescribed set of chores. Then the "children [formed] double lines in the hall . . . marching into the dining hall, singing hymns." After more chores, "each girl was inspected as she pass[ed] out the front door" of the living quarters.[99] The isolation and rigid circumscription of the daily routine differed only in kind from the life led by prostitutes. Although order replaced disorder and civility supplanted abuse, the women remained outcasts. The ordinary experiences of human existence and social interaction were denied them. Thus they relied on home officials for material and emotional support.[100]

Annual missionary reports usually included a few anecdotal accounts of Chinese women who

accepted Christianity. One such account told the
dramatic story of sixteen-year-old Ah Tsun, who
ran away from her owner just before he sold her into
prostitution. Presbyterian missionaries kept their
patrons informed of her progress from "slave girl" to
"native helper" (a mission assistant who helped
with the teaching and proselytizing). Proud of her
achievements, home officials also pointed out the
domestic bliss she shared with her Chinese Christian husband.[101] Another prostitute, Ah Gum, sought
refuge in the Methodist mission home and later
married a doctor. In the opinion of officials, the
eventual baptism of her family served as an example
of "reaping the seeds" missionaries had sown earlier.[102] Chy Hay, after a year in the home, married a
"heathen" man, moved to Sacramento, and lost contact with Methodist officials. Four years later, according to the annual report, a native helper found
her. Missionaries claimed that Chy Hay had not
forgotten the lessons her teachers taught in the
mission school, and within a few months, she was
baptized and received the "glory of God."[103] These
stories sometimes tended toward the melodramatic; one eighteen-year-old woman afflicted by tuberculosis somehow dragged herself to the Methodist
Mission and struggled to stay alive for the next few
weeks. She accepted Christ on her deathbed moments before she passed away.[104]

Writings aimed at the uninformed public often
extolled Chinese women who had embraced Christianity and reported that a number of the "girls" had
been "saved, soul and body."[105] In reality, many
prostitutes rejected the Protestant women's proselytizing. Missionaries who labored among these
women complained that "their work sometimes

seems difficult."[106] Mrs. Stephen Baldwin, a Presbyterian missionary, revealed the tension felt by some of her co-workers: "One who had not had the experience can hardly realize the consecrated patience required, . . . the patience which the loving mother gives to her child."[107] Mrs. E. V. Robbins, a colleague, echoed her words: "a most difficult work — to tame barbarians."[108] They lamented that older Chinese persons did not speak English nearly as well as the younger women. They reported that more of the latter were baptized than the former.[109] Home officials bemoaned the difficulty of rehabilitating "rebellious" mature women. Later they mandated that the acceptance of a woman into the home rested on agreement to stay for at least a year.[110]

Perhaps a few young women developed affection for their guardians. Annual reports of the rescue missions presented a number of anecdotes of dying, grateful women. Commenting on the work of Mrs. Jane Walker, the principal of the Methodist school, Mrs. Otis Gibson wrote, "More than once or twice or thrice, I have seen the dying one turn to Mrs. Walker, and while struggling for breath, thank her teacher for all care, love, and instruction."[111] Yet, their penchant for portraying themselves in a favorable light seems to betray a hint of insecurity about their relationship with the residents. At the least, some women, particularly the older ones, resented the pressures exerted on them and rebelled against their matrons. Many of these women had sought help from home officials when treated badly by their owners or when marriage prospects seemed dim.[112] In the words of one historian, Chinese prostitutes "used the mission home to limit their vulnerability."[113] For these women, involvement in the vice trade was not a lifelong moral shame but more of an unpleasant and—it was hoped—temporary necessity until they had gained some leverage against their owners.

The number of baptized converts never represented a large percentage of the women who sought refuge in mission homes. In their annual report for 1882, Methodist officials reported that 34 Chinese women had been baptized over the last ten years. During the same period, more than 140 women had stayed in the mission. The Presbyterian rescue home had even fewer converts. From 1873 to 1881, about a hundred women found protection in this home, but only 10 percent accepted Christianity.[114] The low number of new believers mirrored the numerically insignificant Christian population among the Chinese in the United States during the nineteenth century. Potential converts had to overcome traditional and nationalistic barriers to conversion. Christianity represented a foreign, heterodox faith that attempted to subvert traditional Chinese society, while the hostility of friends and family also discouraged women from accepting the overtures of proselytizers. Many of them severed their ties with the missions after entering matrimony and continued to resist evangelists.[115]

Missionaries themselves offered an explanation for the indifference. In their estimate, Chinese women, embittered by the xenophobia of white society, predictably rejected its religion.[116] The agitation surrounding their daily lives gave credence to rumors that Americans trying to aid them had ulterior motives and were as untrustworthy as their owners. In short, the rejection of the Christian faith, in the eyes of the evangelical women, grew out of fear for their personal security.[117]

❧

In summary, most Chinese prostitutes never received aid from social organizations. Some simply were ignorant of the existence of rescue homes, and officials of the rescue homes themselves had few viable means of publicizing their institutions.[118] For those who were aware of the rescue homes, misconceptions about missionaries became an obstacle. Women who believed the word of their keepers that "white men want girls . . . to pickle their eyes and eat their brains," who accepted the allegations of ill-treatment in these mission homes, seldom turned to these institutions.[119]

The few who, despite trepidation, turned to churches and benevolent organizations faced frustration as these institutions lacked empowering, respectful programs for social care. Female missionary societies offered protection, but their programs exposed prostitutes to the moral restrictiveness of Victorian culture. These programs, although to some degree efficacious in helping prostitutes adjust to life outside the vice world, did little to help them join Euro-American society. The end result was perpetuation of racial segregation. Residents nevertheless used these supportive institutions to their own benefit — to facilitate their exit from the trade through marriage.

Quite a few of those Chinese prostitutes who struggled on without outside intervention eventually also left the trade through marriage. Some escaped with their suitors into the interior of the American West. Others followed a more conventional path: redeemed by their clients who took them as marriage partners, they moved into the wider society. The success of these women challenges the argument that all of them were passive victims. Despite the physical and emotional hazards of the trade, a number of Chinese prostitutes found a way to leave the exploitative sphere into which they had been thrown.

Conclusion

The second half of the nineteenth century saw the arrival of new immigrant groups into the American West: Chinese, Japanese, Eastern European, and Hispanic. Eventually, the multifarious strands of these cultures conflicted with the dominant Euro-American culture, setting off a struggle for control of the limited resources in the region. Strife and contention for power within each ethnic group augmented the disorder.

Chinese men often exploited their own people, which dispels the idealistic notion of solidarity among the oppressed. In *The Legacy of Conquest: The Unbroken Past of the American West* (1987), Patricia Nelson Limerick has argued that class, in

addition to race, "complicated matters within the
Chinese population."[1] Rivalries between various
groups in power, particularly the Chinese Consolidated Benevolent Association (or Chinese Six Companies) versus the fighting tongs, involved people at
all levels of the hierarchy. Caught between this
struggle for preeminence were Chinese prostitutes.

Almost all Chinese prostitutes came from the
poorest groups of the peasantry class in Kwangtung
in southern China. Most had few skills and little
education. Though they had limited means to alter
lives marked by poverty and exploitation, many
worked to help their families survive the difficult
conditions of the region. When all else failed, some
parents sold their daughters, many quite young, into
indentured servitude. Others cajoled them to accept
offers of marriage. In a few cases, women had been
simply abducted by procuring agents.

On the voyage to America, most of the women
no doubt wrestled with a range of deep-felt emotions: anxiety, loneliness, fear, anger, and despair.
Women probably coped with their situation by rely-
ing on the friendship of fellow passengers. Almost
all of them withdrew into themselves and reflected
on the past; they anguished over leaving their family and friends behind. For some women, however,
the complete truth still eluded them; duped by the
promise of marriage or employment, these women
shared with their male emigrants the Gum Saan
dream, the dream of a better life in the promised
land. This dream was shattered when they finally
arrived in America and felt the bitter pain of hostility from within their community and without.

By the time most of these women entered the
United States, the era of independent Chinese pros-

titutes had passed, and they felt the full weight of the social ills afflicting San Francisco. They were cast into a vice enterprise controlled by male owners under the protection of tongs. While poverty was not alien to their life experiences, the social ostracism and their marginal status very likely proved more difficult to accept.

Treated with derision by Euro-American society, these public women had to endure physical and psychological torment. Sporadic raids and arrests led to their segregation in a clearly defined neighborhood. Avoidance of mainstream society became a pattern of behavior for these minority women. Many of those who failed to come to terms with their predicament followed the road of drug abuse or suicide. These attempts to escape from prostitution were, of course, self-defeating.

From the evidence available, it seems that quite a few discovered more constructive ways of coping with their lives. In spite of the prospect of a bleak future, many prostitutes did not cave in under societal pressures. These women resisted their exploiters, and some found a means to escape their circumstances.

Prostitutes maintained some control over their lives. Owners sometimes physically abused them, but with some restraint, as serious harm might limit the women's earning potential. Most ill-treatment fell on young charges who lacked the means to retaliate. Clients, for fear of undue publicity, preferred to slip in and out of brothels without leaving a trail of lawlessness. Thus prostitutes were able to avoid the widespread serious violence popularly associated with powerless groups. Their physical and cultural separation from society, voluntary or otherwise, ironically afforded protection against further harm.

Some women took it on themselves to alter their lives. They accepted the proposals of wealthy suitors and vanished into the interior of the West or simply remained in San Francisco; others took their chances and escaped with indigent husbands-to-be. Some succeeded; others experienced total failure and returned to the sexual trade.

Less fortunate prostitutes had to depend on the limited services of social agencies in the city. A number gravitated to the mission rescue homes Protestant women established to offer protection to so-called deviants. Prostitutes sought these agencies to help tip the balance between vulnerability and opportunity, but the prostitutes' goals diverged considerably from those of the missionaries. While the cultural conflict generally resulted in failure for the missionaries, prostitutes benefited from their stay in those homes. Mission officials facilitated their marriages and invoked the protection of the police and judiciary system. Of course, a significant number of the Chinese women went through their daily routines without ever meeting any of these benevolent reformers.

Segregation, which placed a comfortable distance between Chinese prostitutes and the wider society, doomed any effort to remove the badge of inferiority from them. In the years following the passage of the Chinese Exclusion Act of 1882, the negative perception of these women intensified. It was expressed in all writings, nonfiction or otherwise.

In response to the arrest of sixty Chinese prostitutes, an editorial in the *San Francisco Chronicle* in 1897 condemned the "systematic infraction [slavery] of the Federal Constitution."[2] Even publications based in the East lashed out at the "Oriental brothel slavery." One writer, George Kibbe Turner, whose articles appeared regularly at the turn of the century in the respectable *McClure's Magazine*, blamed the flourishing red-light districts of America on alien women, the Chinese included.[3] Indeed, as late as the 1950s, popular writers were still churning out sensationalized works on the Chinese. Many wrote of the "subterranean passageways" that supposedly housed activities such as "the smoking of opium, the keeping of concubines, [and] large scale gambling."[4]

The nativist assault on prostitution and prostitutes extended into fiction and then into film. Short stories such as "A Partly Celestial Tale" (1895), "The Conversion of Ah Lew Sing" (1897), "The Revenge of Ching Chow" (1924), and "Dead Yellow Women" (1925) depicted Chinese brothel residents as nothing more than slave girls who lived in secret passageways and who would betray others at the slightest chance.[5]

Of the many writings about Chinese women that appeared in the early years of the twentieth century, none had as strong an impact on popular characterization of the Chinese woman as *Daughter of Fu Manchu* (1931). The protagonist, Fah Lo Suee, continues her father's work, told in the earlier Fu Manchu series, as the champion of Asian hegemony over the white race. Her character, to borrow the words of William F. Wu, an American studies scholar, exhibited "exotic sensuality, sexual availability to a white man, and a treacherous nature."[6]

The portrayal of Asian women in American films has perpetuated that stereotype. The image of Asian women as sensuous, promiscuous, and unreliable creatures was evident in the 1950s films *Tea-*

house of the August Moon and *The World of Suzi Wong*. These films developed dichotomous stereotypes of the Asian woman: either she is the Dragon Lady or the China Doll. The former is dangerous and untrustworthy, the latter submissive and powerless.[7] Either way, Asian women have been reduced to one-dimensional caricatures.

For most of the first half of this century, Euro-Americans often shrouded Chinese women in an aura of forbidden and illicit eroticism and delighted in imagining the decadent torturing of women in the hidden tunnels or dens of Chinatown. Early twentieth-century tourists to the Chinese neighborhood of San Francisco insisted on visiting these places of disrepute in the hope of confirming the stories. But as one Chinese male long-time resident who trotted behind the Chinese guides accompanying visitors to Chinatown recalled, "I never saw an underground tunnel, just *mah-jongg* rooms in the basements."[8]

The misconceptions about Chinese women stemmed from a lack of understanding of their role as active, thinking, indentured workers in the urban American West. In truth, these unsubmissive women rose to the challenge of adapting to a circumscribed life, and many eventually overcame their oppressors. Though rejected by American society at large, these women built a place for themselves in the mainstream, and in the process, demonstrated an enduring spirit of resistance and unflinching courage. Their history testifies to the power of marginal groups.

Bills of Sale
of Chinese
Prostitutes

An Agreement Paper by the Person Mee Yung

At this time there is a prostitute woman, Yut Kum, who has borrowed from Mee Yung $470. It is distinctly understood that there shall be no interest charged on the money and no wages paid for services. Yut Kum consents to prostitute her body to receive company to aid Mee Yung for the full time of four years. When the time is fully served, neither service nor money shall be longer required.

If Yut Kum should be sick fifteen days she shall make up one month. If she conceives, she shall serve one year more. If during the time any man wishes to redeem her body, she shall make satisfactory arrangements with the mistress, Mee Yung. If Yut Kum should herself escape and be recovered, then her time shall never expire. Should the mistress become very wealthy and return to China with glory, then Yut Kum shall fulfill her time, serving another person.

This is a distinct agreement made face to face, both parties willingly consenting. But lest the words of the mouth should be without proof, the agreement-paper is executed and placed in her hands for proof. There are four great sicknesses against which Mee Yung is secured for one hundred days, namely, leprosy, epilepsy, conception, and "stone-woman," i.e., inability to have carnal intercourse with men. For any of these four diseases she may be returned within one hundred days.

Truly with her own hands Mee Yung hands over $470.

Tung Chee 12th year, 8th month, 14th day. The agreement is executed by Mee Yung.

SOURCE: *Congressional Record*, 43d Cong., 2d sess., March 1875, 3, pt. 3: 41.

Contract Between Ah Ho and Yee-Kwan

An agreement to assist the woman Ah Ho, because coming from China to San Francisco she became indebted to her mistress for passage. Ah Ho herself asks Mr. Yee-Kwan to advance for her $630, for which Ah Ho distinctly agrees to give her body to Mr. Yee for services as a prostitute for a term of four years.

There shall be no interest on the money. Ah Ho shall receive no wages. At the expiration of four years Ah Ho shall be her own master. Mr. Yee-Kwan shall not hinder or trouble her. If Ah Ho runs away before her time is out her mistress shall find her and return her, whatever expense is incurred in finding and returning her Ah Ho shall pay.

On this day of the agreement Ah Ho with her own hands has received from Mr. Yee-Kwan $630.

If Ah Ho shall be sick at any time for more than ten days she shall make up by an extra month of service for any ten days' sickness.

Now this agreement has proof. This paper received by Ah Ho is witness.

TUNG CHEE.

Twelfth year, ninth month, fourteen day.

SOURCE: "Chinese Immigration," *Senate Report 689*, 44th Cong., 2d sess. (serial 1734): 145.

An Agreement to Assist a Young Girl Named Loi Yau

Because she became indebted to her mistress for passage, food, &c., and has nothing to pay, she makes her body over to the woman Sep Sam, to serve as a prostitute to make out the sum of $503. The money shall draw no interest, and Loi Yau shall receive no wages. Loi Yau shall serve four and a half years. On this day of agreement Loi Yau receives the sum of $503 in her own hands. When the time is out Loi Yau may be her own master, and no man shall trouble her. If she runs away before the time is out and any expense is incurred in catching, then Loi Yau must pay that expense. If she is sick fifteen days or more, she shall make up one month for every fifteen days. If Sep Sam should go back to China, then Loi Yau shall serve another party till her time is out. If in such service she should be sick one hundred days or more, and cannot be cured, she may return to Sep Sam's place. For a proof of this agreement this paper.

LOI YAU.

Dated second day sixth month of the present year.

SOURCE: "Chinese Immigration," *Senate Report 689*, 44th Cong., 2d sess. (serial 1734): 146.

Notes

Introduction

1. Ho Ping-ti, *Studies on the Population of China, 1368–1953* (Cambridge: Harvard University Press, 1959): 167.

2. "The Celestials at Home and Abroad," *Littell's Living Age*, August 14, 1852, 290.

3. Marlon K. Hom, "Chinatown High Life: A Literary Pride," in *Chinese America: History and Perspectives 1988* (San Francisco: Chinese Historical Society of America, 1988): 125; Confucius, *The Analects of Confucius*, trans. Arthur Waley (London: George Allen & Unwin, 1964): 105–6.

4. Stanford M. Lyman, "Red Guard on Grant Avenue: The Rise of Youthful Rebellion in Chinatown," in

Asian Americans: Psychological Perspectives, eds. Stanley Sue and Nathaniel N. Wagner (Ben Lomond, Calif.: Science & Behavior Books, 1973): 21; Stanford M. Lyman, "Marriage and the Family Among Chinese Immigrants to America, 1850–1960," *Phylon* 29 (Winter 1968): 324.

    5. George Anthony Peffer, "From Under the Sojourner's Shadow: A Historiographical Study of Chinese Female Immigration to America, 1852–1882," *Journal of American Ethnic History* 11 (Spring 1992): 59.

    6. "Letter of the Chinamen to His Excellency, Gov. Bigler," San Francisco, 28 April 1852, reprinted in *Littell's Living Age*, 3 July 1852, 33.

    7. George M. Blackburn and Sherman L. Ricards, "The Chinese of Virginia City, Nevada: 1870," *Amerasia Journal* 7, no. 1 (1980): 53.

    8. Evelyn Nakano Glenn, "Split Household, Small Producer, and Dual Wage Earner: An Analysis of Chinese-American Family Strategies," *Journal of Marriage and Family* 45 (February 1983): 38.

    9. Victor G. Nee and Brett de Bary Nee, *Longtime Californ': A Documentary Study of an American Chinatown* (New York: Pantheon Books, 1972): 24.

    10. Linda Gordon, *U.S. Women's History*, New American History Series, ed. Eric Foner (Washington, D.C.: American Historical Association, 1990): 3.

**One: Chinese Prostitutes
in the West, 1849–1882**

    1. "The Chinese in San Francisco," *Daily Evening Picayune,* June 4, 1851, reprinted in *San Francisco as It Is: Gleanings from the Picayune*, ed. Kenneth M. Johnson (Georgetown, Calif.: Talisman Press, 1984): 146.

    2. "Celestials at Home and Abroad," 291.

    3. California Legislature, *Population Schedules of California, 1852: City and County of San Francisco* (Family History Department of the Church of Jesus Christ of Latter-Day Saints, microfilm copy) [hereafter cited as

Population Schedules].

4. Stanford M. Lyman, "The Chinese Diaspora in America, 1850–1943," in *The Life, Influence, and the Role of the Chinese in the United States, 1776–1960* (San Francisco: Chinese Historical Society of America, 1976): 133.

5. E. S. Capron, *History of California from Its Discovery to the Present Time* (Boston: John P. Jewett, 1854): 146–47.

6. D. B. Bates, *Incidents on Land and Water* (Boston: James French, 1857): 317.

7. Marlon K. Hom, ed. and trans., *Songs of Gold Mountain: Cantonese Rhymes from San Francisco Chinatown* (Berkeley: University of California Press, 1987): 309, 322.

8. Philip D. Jordan, *Frontier Law and Order: Ten Essays* (Lincoln: University of Nebraska Press, 1970): 116. "Celestial" was a pejorative term for Asians.

9. Jacqueline Baker Barnhart, *The Fair but Frail: Prostitution in San Francisco, 1849–1900* (Reno: University of Nevada Press, 1986): 16–17.

10. Christiane Fischer, "Women in California in the Early 1850s," *Southern California Quarterly* 60 (Fall 1978): 242.

11. Elisha Oscar Crosby, "Statement of Events in California as Related by Judge Elisha Oscar Crosby for Bancroft Library, 1878," AMs, 121, 123, Bancroft Manuscript Collection, Bancroft Library, University of California, Berkeley [CU-B].

12. Fischer, "Women in California," 243.

13. Henry Perrin Coon, "Annals of San Francisco," AMs, Bancroft Manuscript Collection, CU-B; Gunther Barth, *Instant Cities: Urbanization and the Rise of San Francisco and Denver* (New York: Oxford University Press, 1975): 133.

14. J. F. Elliott, "The Great Western: Sarah Bowman, Mother and Mistress to the U.S. Army," *Journal of Arizona History* 30 (Spring 1989): 1, 18.

15. Janet LeCompte, "La Tules and the Americans," *Arizona and the West* 20 (Autumn 1978): 215–30;

Deena J. Gonzales, "The Spanish-Mexican Women of Santa Fe: Patterns of Their Resistance and Accommodation, 1820–1880" (Ph.D. diss., University of California, Berkeley, 1985): 75–77.

16. Curt Gentry, *The Madams of San Francisco* (Garden City, N.Y.: Doubleday, 1954): 51, 57; *Alta California*, December 14, 15, 16, 24, 1851.

17. Barbara Welter, "The Cult of True Womanhood, 1820–1860," *American Quarterly* 18 (Summer 1966): 151–74; Mary Murphy, "The Private Lives of Public Women: Prostitution in Butte, Montana, 1878–1917," in *The Women's West*, eds. Susan Armitage and Elizabeth Jameson (Norman: University of Oklahoma Press, 1987): 196.

18. *Alta California*, July 1, 1851, November 8, 9, 15, 1851, December 14, 15, 16, 24, 1851.

19. Albert Benard de Russailh, *Last Adventure*, trans. Clarkson Crane (San Francisco: Westgate, 1931): 89; *Alta California*, July 1, 1851.

20. Gentry, *Madams of San Francisco*, 52; J. M. Parker, *The San Francisco Directory for the Year 1852–1853: Embracing a General Directory of Citizens, a Street Directory* (San Francisco: J. M. Parker, 1852): 45.

21. *Population Schedules*, 398; Gentry, *Madams of San Francisco*, 52.

22. Roger W. Lotchin, *San Francisco, 1846–1856: From Hamlet to City* (New York: Oxford University Press, 1974): 22, 256; *Population Schedules*, 398.

23. Gentry, *Madams of San Francisco*, 57; Ronald D. Miller, "Hell's Belles," *Brandbook: Los Angeles Corral of Westerners* 12 (1965): 161; Frank Soulé, John H. Gibon, and James Nisbet, *The Annals of San Francisco* (New York: D. Appleton, 1854): 384.

24. *Alta California*, December 14, 1853; Herbert Asbury, *The Barbary Coast* (New York: Garden City Publishing, 1933): 172.

25. Fischer, "Women in California," 232.

26. A. W. Loomis, "Chinese in California," AMs,

Augustus Ward Loomis Papers, CU-B; Crosby, "Statement of Events in California," 124.

27. Ronald Takaki, *Strangers from a Different Shore* (Boston: Little, Brown, 1989; New York: Penguin Books, 1990): 119; Laurence Dicker Mau, *The Chinese in San Francisco: A Pictorial History* (New York: Dover Publications, 1979): 8; John J. Manion, "Tongs," paper presented at the Peace Officers' Association of the State of California, Proceedings, 17th Annual Convention, Sacramento, California, Nov. 14–16, 1927, TMs, John J. Manion Papers, CU-B; Eve L. Armentrout-Ma, *Revolutionaries, Monarchists and Chinatowns: Chinese Politics in the Americas and the 1911 Revolution* (Honolulu: University of Hawaii Press, 1990): 19, 27–28.

28. Douglas W. Lee, "Sacred Cows and Paper Tigers: Politics in Chinese America, 1880–1900," in *Annals of the Chinese Historical Society of the Pacific Northwest*, ed. Douglas W. Lee (Seattle: Chinese Historical Society of the Pacific Northwest, 1983): 89; Him Mark Lai, "Historical Development of the Chinese Consolidated Benevolent Association/*Huiguan* System," in *Chinese America: History and Perspectives, 1987* (San Francisco: Chinese Historical Society of America, 1987): 14.

29. Hubert Howe Bancroft, *The Works of Hubert Howe Bancroft*, vol. 36, *Popular Tribunals* (San Francisco: History Publishers, 1887): 378–79.

30. Mary Roberts Coolidge, *Chinese Immigration* (New York: Henry Holt, 1909): 502; *Alta California*, April 20, 1854.

31. *Alta California*, December 14, 15, 16, 24, 1851, February 20, 1852; "The Chinese in San Francisco," *Daily Evening Picayune*, June 4, 1851, 146.

32. *Alta California*, March 6, 8, May 1, 16, 1851, February 20, July 2, August 13, 15, 29, 1852.

33. Gentry, *Madams of San Francisco*, 37–38; *California Police Gazette*, March 20, 1859; C. Y. Martin, *Whiskey and Wild Women* (New York: Hart Publishing, 1974): 71.

34. Randall E. Rohe, "After the Gold Rush: Chinese Mining in the Far West, 1850–1890," *Montana: The Magazine of Western History* 32 (Autumn 1980): 9, 19; P. Scott Corbett and Nancy Parker Corbett, "The Chinese in Oregon, c. 1870–1880," *Oregon Historical Society Quarterly* 78, no. 1 (1977): 73, 84.

35. Edward Gould Buffum, *Six Months in the Gold Mines* (Philadelphia: C. Sherman, 1850; repr., Ann Arbor: UMI Microfilms, 1966): 182; J. D. Borthwick, *Three Years in California, 1851–1854* (Edinburgh: Blackwood & Sons, 1857): 44.

36. Lyman, "Marriage and the Family Among Chinese Immigrants," 327.

37. Elliot West, "Scarlet West: The Oldest Profession in the Trans-Mississippi West," *Montana: The Magazine of Western History* 31 (Spring 1981): 18.

38. Douglas McDonald, *The Legend of Julia Bulette and the Red Light Ladies of Nevada* (Las Vegas: Stanley Paher, 1983): 17.

39. David Dufault, "The Chinese in the Mining Camps of California, 1848–1870," *Historical Society of Southern California Quarterly* 41 (June 1959): 157; Louis J. Rasmussen, comp., *San Francisco Ship Passenger Lists*, 5 vols. (Colma, Calif.: San Francisco Historic Records, 1965): 2:ix; see also Moon L. Lee, *Cathay in Eldorado: The Chinese in California* (Weaverville: California Book Club, 1972).

40. Judy Yung, *Chinese Women of America: A Pictorial History* (Seattle: University of Washington Press, 1986): 19; Glenn, "Split Household," 37–39.

41. Lawrence B. de Graaf, "Race, Sex, and Region: Black Women in the American West, 1850–1920," *Pacific Historical Review* 49 (May 1980): 304; Glenda Riley, "American Daughters: Black Women in the West," *Montana: The Magazine of Western History* 38 (Spring 1988): 23–24.

42. Dufault, "Chinese in the Mining Camps," 165–66; Lucie Cheng Hirata, "Chinese Immigrant Women in

Nineteenth-Century California," in *Women in America*, eds. Carol Ruth Berkins and Mary Beth Norton (Boston: Houghton Mifflin, 1979): 227; Thomas W. Chinn, Him Mark Lai, and Phillip P. Choy, eds., *A History of the Chinese in California: A Syllabus* (San Francisco: Chinese Historical Society of America, 1969): table 6, 21.

43. David Beesley, "From Chinese to Chinese American: Chinese Women & Families in a Sierra Nevada County," *California History* 67 (September 1988): 171; Dufault, "Chinese in the Mining Camps," 166; Mary Lou Locke, "'Like a Machine or an Animal': Working Women of the Late Nineteenth-Century Urban Far West, in San Francisco, Portland, and Los Angeles" (Ph.D. diss., University of California, San Diego, 1982): 243.

44. Ella Cain, *The Story of Bodie* (San Francisco: Fearon Publishers, 1956): 96.

45. Corbett and Corbett, "Chinese in Oregon," 73, 84; Rohe, "After the Gold Rush," 15–16.

46. Gregg Lee Carter, "Social Demography of the Chinese in Nevada, 1870–1880," *Nevada Historical Society Quarterly* 18 (Summer 1975): 73, table 3, 79, table 4, 80–81; table 5, "Territory of Nevada, Nativities of Population: 1860," U.S. Bureau of the Census, *Eighth Census of the United States: 1860*, 3 vols., compendium (Washington, D.C.: Government Printing Office, 1864): 1:564–65.

47. Walter Van Tilburg Clark, ed., *The Journals of Alfred Doten, 1849–1903*, 3 vols. (Reno: University of Nevada Press, 1973): 2:867.

48. Ibid., 2:817, 839, 866–67.

49. Carter, "Social Demography of the Chinese," 80–81.

50. Marion Goldman, "Prostitution and Virtue in Nevada," *Society* 10 (November 1972): 32, 37; Marion Goldman, *Gold Diggers and Silver Miners: Prostitution and Social Life on the Comstock Lode* (Ann Arbor: University of Michigan Press, 1981): 95.

51. George M. Blackburn and Sherman L. Ricards, "The Prostitutes and Gamblers of Virginia City, Nevada:

1870," *Pacific Historical Review* 38 (May 1979): 250; Goldman, *Gold Diggers and Silver Miners*, 95.

52. Russell M. Magnaghi, "Virginia City's Chinese Community, 1860–1880," *Nevada Historical Society Quarterly* 24 (Summer 1981): 146, 139; Loren B. Chan, "The Chinese in Nevada: An Historical Survey, 1856–1970," *Nevada Historical Society Quarterly* 25 (Winter 1982): 269, 279, 288, 298.

53. Anne M. Butler, *Daughters of Joy, Sisters of Misery: Prostitutes in the American West, 1865–1890* (Urbana: University of Illinois Press, 1985): 15; Carter, "Social Demography of the Chinese," 73.

54. Blackburn and Ricards, "Prostitutes and Gamblers of Virginia City," 240, 246–47.

55. Butler, *Daughters of Joy*, 6; table 5, "Territory of Colorado, Nativities of the Population: 1860," *Eighth Census*, 1:549; table 21, "The Table of Sex: 1870," U.S. Bureau of the Census, *Ninth Census of the United States: 1870*, 3 vols., compendium (Washington, D.C.: Government Printing Office, 1872): 2:538–39; table 53, "Sex of the Chinese Population with General Nativity," *Ninth Census*, compendium, 551.

56. Butler, *Daughters of Joy*, 6.

57. Rohe, "After the Gold Rush," 13–14; Rodman Wilson Paul, *Mining Frontiers of the Far West, 1848–1880* (New York: Holt, Rinehart & Winston, 1963): 127; Barth, *Bitter Strength*, 135, 150; table 19, "Sex of the Colored, Chinese, and Japanese, and Civilized Indian Population, with General Nativity, 1880," U.S. Bureau of the Census, *Tenth Census of the United States: 1880*, 22 vols., compendium (Washington, D.C.: Government Printing Office, 1883): 1:544–45.

58. Robert R. Swartout, Jr., "Kwangtung to Big Sky: The Chinese in Montana, 1864–1900," *Montana: The Magazine of Western History* 38 (Winter 1988): 48–49.

59. Rose Hum Lee, "Social Institutions of a Rocky Mountain Chinatown," *Social Forces* 27 (October 1948):

6; table 8, "Population by Counties at each Census, Territory of Montana: 1870," *Ninth Census*, compendium, 108; Rose Hum Lee, *The Growth and Decline of Chinese Communities in the Rocky Mountain Region* (New York: Arno Press, 1978): 152.

60. Blackburn and Ricards, "Chinese of Virginia City," 67.

61. Paul, *Mining Frontiers*, 144; F. Ross Peterson, *Idaho: A Bicentennial History* (New York: W. W. Norton, 1976): 60.

62. For a biographical novel on her life, see Ruthanne Lum McCunn, *Thousand Pieces of Gold* (San Francisco: Design Enterprises, 1981). See also Sister M. Alfreda Elsensohn, *Idaho Chinese Lore* (Cottonwood: Idaho Corporation of Benedictine Sisters, 1971): 81–88.

63. Elsensohn, *Idaho Chinese Lore*, 81–82.

64. Ibid., 83–87.

65. Gary P. Tipton, "Men Out of China: Origins of the Chinese Colony in Phoenix," *Journal of Arizona History* 18 (Autumn 1977): 342; table 21, "The Table of Sex: 1870," *Ninth Census*, 2:538–39; table 19, "Sex of the Colored, Chinese, Japanese and Civilized Indian Population," *Tenth Census*, 1:544–45.

66. Lawrence Michael Fong, "Sojourners and Settlers: The Chinese Experience in Arizona," *Journal of Arizona History* 21 (Autumn 1980): 250.

67. "Sanborn Fire Insurance Maps of Phoenix, 1889" (New York: Sanborn Map Publishing, 1890; repr., Palo Alto, Calif.: Vladshurkin, 1982); "Sanborn Fire Insurance Maps of Tombstone, 1883" (New York: Sanborn Map Publishing, 1890; repr., Palo Alto, Calif.: Vladshurkin, 1982); Florence C. Lister and Robert H. Lister, *The Chinese of Early Tucson: Historic Archaeology from the Tucson Urban Renewal Project* (Tucson: University of Arizona Press, 1989): 5; "Federal Census — Territory of New Mexico and Territory of Arizona," *Senate Executive Document* [hereafter *SED*] 13, 89th Cong., 1st sess. (Serial 12668–1).

68. Fong, "Sojourners and Settlers," 250–51.

69. Ibid., 248; Lister and Lister, *Chinese of Early Tucson*, 69.

70. Yung, *Chinese Women of America*, 19; John Shertzer Hittell, A *History of the City of San Francisco and Incidentally of the State of California* (San Francisco: A. L. Bancroft, 1878): 101.

71. Pauline Minke, *Chinese in the Mother Lode* (San Francisco: R & E Research Associates, 1974): 37.

72. Clarence W. Kellogg, Major, U.S. Army, Retired, "Early Day Family Life in California Mining Camps," TMs, CU-B; Sylvia Sun Minnick, *Sam Fow: The San Joaquin Chinese Legacy* (Fresno, Calif.: Panorama Publishing, 1988): 59.

73. Kellogg, "Early Day Family Life," 66.

74. Robert E. Riegel, "Changing American Attitudes Toward Prostitution (1800–1920)," *Journal of the History of Ideas* 29 (July/September 1968): 439–40; John S. Haller and Robbin M. Haller, "Sex in Victorian America," in *The Social Fabric: American Life from the Civil War to the Present*, eds. John H. Cary, Julius Weinberg, and Thomas L. Hartshorne (Glenview, Ill.: Scott, Foresman, 1987): 98–99; Howard I. Kushner, "Nineteenth-Century Sexuality and the 'Sexual Revolution' of the Progressive Era," *Canadian Review of American Studies* 9 (Spring 1978): 35–36.

75. Chinn, Lai, and Choy, *Syllabus*, 31–32.

76. Elizabeth Jameson, "Women as Workers, Women as Civilizers: True Womanhood in the American West," in *The Women's West*, eds. Susan Armitage and Elizabeth Jameson (Norman: University of Oklahoma Press, 1987): 147.

77. Chen Chang-fang, "Barbarian Paradise: Chinese Views of the United States, 1784–1911" (Ph.D. diss., Indiana University, 1985): 19, 49.

78. James W. Buel, *Metropolitan Life Unveiled* (San Francisco: A. L. Bancroft, 1882): 277; Dufault, "Chinese in Mining Camps," 162.

79. William Acton, *Prostitution: Considered in Its Moral, Social and Sanitary Aspects in London and Other Garrison Towns* (London: John Churchill & Sons, 1870): 166; Soulé, Gibon, and Nisbet, *Annals of San Francisco*, 384.

80. Peter L. Tylor, "'Denied the Power to Choose the Good': Sexuality and Mental Defect in American Medical Practice, 1850–1920," *Journal of Social History* 10 (June 1977): 472; John Berdan Gardner, "The Image of the Chinese in the United States" (Ph.D. diss., University of Pennsylvania, 1961): 26; Judy M. Tachibana, "Outwitting the Whites: One Image of the Chinese in California Fiction and Poetry, 1849–1924," *Southern California Quarterly* 61 (Winter 1979): 387.

81. Jameson, "Women as Workers, Women as Civilizers," 147.

82. Roy Lubove, "The Progressives and the Prostitute," *Historian* 24 (May 1962): 311.

83. Judy Yung, "The Social Awakening of Chinese American Women as Reported in *Chung Sai Yat Po*, 1900–1911," in *Chinese America: History and Perspectives 1988* (San Francisco: Chinese Historical Society of America, 1988): 83; Hom, *Songs of Gold Mountain*, 285–86.

84. Marlon K. Hom, ed. and trans., "A *Muk-yu* from Gold Mountain," in *Chinese America: History and Perspectives 1989* (San Francisco: Chinese Historical Society of America, 1989): 24, 39.

85. Jeff Gillenkirk and James Motlow, *Bitter Melon: Stories from the Last Rural Chinese Town in America* (Seattle: University of Washington Press, 1987): 113.

86. Paul C. P. Siu, "The Chinese Laundryman: A Study of Social Isolation" (Ph.D. diss., University of Chicago, 1953): 323.

87. Barnhart, *Fair but Frail*, 59.

88. Table 26, "Persons in Each Class of Occupations, with Sex," *Ninth Census*, 1:671; table 29, "The

Number of Persons in the United States Engaged in Each Class of Occupation with Distinctions of Sex, by States and Territories: 1880," *Tenth Census*, 1:712–13; Locke, "'Like a Machine or an Animal,'" xiii.

89.   Table 22, "The Table of Sex: 1870," *Ninth Census*, 1:608–9; table 26, "Occupations by Classes, with Age and Sex, and Nativity: 1870," *Ninth Census*, 1:700.

90.   Hirata, "Chinese Immigrant Women," 228, 236. Figures given in the text were extrapolated from the data Hirata provides. By eliminating 1,445 persons identified as "keeping house" or housewives from 3,171 (the total number of Chinese females for the state), an estimated 1,726 of the women could be termed wage earners. Of that figure, 759, or 44 percent, of the women were prostitutes.

91.   Peter Dexter, *Deadwood* (New York: Random House, 1986).

92.   Telegrams reprinted in Albert Dressler, ed., *California Chinese Chatter* (San Francisco: Albert Dressler, 1927): 14–27.

93.   Ralph Mann, "Frontier Opportunity and the New Social History," *Pacific Historical Review* 53 (November 1984): 463–91.

**Two: Unwilling Travelers
to Gum Saan**

1.   Immanuel C. Y. Hsu, *The Rise of Modern China* (New York: Oxford University Press, 1983): 27; Jonathan D. Spence, *The Search for Modern China* (New York: W. W. Norton, 1990): 165.

2.   Him Mark Lai, "The Guangdong Historical Background, with Emphasis on the Development of the Pearl River Delta Region," in *Chinese America: History and Perspectives, 1991* (San Francisco: Chinese Historical Society of America, 1991): 88; Robert G. Lee, "The Origins of Chinese Immigration to the United States,

1848–1882," in *The Life, Influence, and the Role of the Chinese in the United States, 1776–1960* (San Francisco: Chinese Historical Society of America, 1976): 185; Ho, *Studies on the Population of China*, table 1, 281–82, table 2, 283.

3. Lee, "Origins of Chinese Immigration," 185; Hsu, *Rise of Modern China*, 27; Wen Djang-chu, "The Background of the Chinese Immigration into the United States" (M.A. thesis, University of Washington, 1949): 48; Zo Kil Young, "Chinese Immigration into the United States, 1850–1880," (Ph.D. diss., Columbia University, 1971): 62.

4. Peng Yu Ling, "Peng Kang-chih-kung tsou-kao" (The Memorial of Peng Yu-ling), in Wen, "Background of the Chinese," 56.

5. U.S. Department of State, *Dispatches from Consuls in Tientsin, 1868–1906* [hereafter *Tientsin Dispatches*] (National Archives microfilm copy, reel 1), dispatch 8, December 4, 1871; June Mei, "Socioeconomic Origins of Emigration: Guangdong to California, 1850–1882," in *Labor Immigration Under Capitalism*, eds. Lucie Cheng and Edna Bonacich (Berkeley: University of California Press, 1984): 230.

6. Wong Ah So, "Story of Wong Ah So — Experiences as a Prostitute," in Social Science Institute, *Orientals and Their Cultural Adjustment* (Nashville: Fisk University, 1946): 31; table 10, "Wages of the Pacific Coast Compared with Those in Kwangtung," in Wen, "Background of the Chinese," 69.

7. Elizabeth Wong, "Leaves from the Life History of a Chinese Immigrant," *Social Process in Hawaii* 2 (1936): 39–42.

8. "Cities of Sin," TMs, in Miner Chapman Papers, Hoover Institution Archives, Stanford University, Stanford, California.

9. Table 8, "Floods, Droughts, Famines, Local Rebellions, and Other Troubles in the Districts from which the Chinese Immigrants Came, 1832–1881," in Wen,

"Background of the Chinese," 58; Chinn, Lai, and Choy, *Syllabus*, 20.

10. Quotation of an unknown memorial to the Emperor, in "Celestials at Home and Abroad," 294.

11. Rose [pseud.], "Experiences of 'Rose'—A Slave Girl," Social Science Institute, *Orientals and Their Cultural Adjustment* (Nashville: Fisk University, 1946): 36–38.

12. William Hung, Interview by Kathleen Chinn and Theodore Chang, Combined Asian American Resource Project, San Francisco, California, 1977, Regional Oral History Office, CU-B; *En-p'ing hsien-chih* (The Gazette of En-p'ing District), quotation reprinted in Zo, "Chinese Immigration," 70.

13. *Tientsin Dispatches* (reel 2), dispatch 24, November 20, 1878; unnamed Nien chant from Pohsien, Anhwei, reprinted in Wei Min She Labor Committee, *Chinese Working People in America: A Pictorial History* (San Francisco: United Front Press, 1974): 7; Ning Lao T'ai-t'ai, *A Daughter of Han: The Autobiography of a Chinese Working Woman*, ed. Ida Pruitt (Stanford: Stanford University Press, 1945): 55.

14. Mother Teng [pseud.], "Life History," in *The Sandalwood Mountains: Readings and Stories of the Early Chinese in Hawaii*, ed. Tin-Yuke Char (Honolulu: University of Hawaii Press, 1975): 248; Lin Yu-shih, deposition, in "The Consulate at Hong Kong," *House Report Executive Document* [hereafter *HRD*] 20, 46th Cong., 2d sess. (Serial 1913): 76; Huie Kin, *Reminiscences* (Peiping: San Yu Press, 1909): 7.

15. Deborah Davis-Friedmann, "Village Wives," in *Lives: Chinese Working Women*, eds. Mary E. Sheridan and Janet W. Salaff (Bloomington: Indiana University Press, 1984): 72.

16. *Sunning hsien-chih* (Gazette of the Sunning District), 10 August 1864, quotation reprinted in Him Mark Lai, Joe Huang, and Don Wong, *The Chinese of America, 1785–1980* (San Francisco: Chinese Culture Center, 1980): 15.

17.   Arthur P. Wolf and Huang Chieh-shan, *Marriage and Adoption in China, 1845–1945* (Stanford: Stanford University Press, 1980): 230; Yan Phou Lee, *When I Was a Boy in China* (Boston: D. Lothrop, 1887): 43.

18.   Elizabeth Cooper, *My Lady of the Chinese Courtyard* (New York: Frederick A. Stokes, 1914): 13–14.

19.   Nee and Nee, *Longtime Californ'*, 83; Rose, "Experiences of 'Rose,'" 36.

20.   Francis L. K. Hsu, *The Challenge of the American Dream: The Chinese in the United States* (Belmont, Calif.: Wadsworth Publishing, 1971): 20, 22; Ginger Chih, "Immigration of Chinese Women to the United States, 1900–1940" (M.A. thesis, Sarah Lawrence College, 1977): 11.

21.   Amy Ling, *Between Worlds: Women Writers of Chinese Ancestry* (New York: Pergamon Press, 1990): 2.

22.   Maurice Freedman, "The Family in China, Past and Present," *Pacific Affairs* 34 (Winter 1961/62): 328–29; *Tientsin Dispatches* (reel 2), dispatch 101, September 30, 1875.

23.   Judith Stacey, *Patriarchy and Socialist Revolution in China* (Berkeley: University of California Press, 1983): 23; H. K. Wong, *Gum Sahn Yun: Gold Mountain Men* (n.p.: for the author, 1987): 32.

24.   Julia Kristeva, *About Chinese Women*, trans. Anita Barrows (London: Marion Boyars, 1974): 71; Lucie Cheng Hirata, "Free, Indentured, Enslaved: Chinese Prostitutes in Nineteenth-Century America," *Signs* 5 (Autumn 1979): 5.

25.   Wolf and Huang, *Marriage and Adoption in China*, 260.

26.   Ibid., 257–58; Yuji Ichioka, "*Ameyuki-san*: Japanese Prostitutes in Nineteenth-Century America," *Amerasia Journal* 4, no. 1 (1977): 3.

27.   McCunn, *Thousand Pieces of Gold*, 25; Wong Ah So, "Letter from Wong Ah So to Her Mother," in Social Science Institute, *Orientals and Their Cultural Adjustment* (Nashville: Fisk University, 1946): 34; Elis-

abeth Croll, *Wise Daughters from Foreign Lands: European Women Writers in China* (London: Pandora Press, 1989): 37–38.

28. "Expatriation and Slavery in China," *HRD 60*, 46th Cong., 2d sess. (Serial 1925): 23, 27–29.

29. U.S. Department of State, *Dispatches from Consuls in Hong Kong, 1873–1881 [Hong Kong Dispatches]* (National Archives microfilm copy, reel 10), dispatch 307, enclosure 6, August 28, 1875; Sue Gronewold, *Beautiful Merchandise: Prostitution in China, 1860–1936* (New York: Haworth Press, 1982): 26–36; Maria Jaschok, *Concubines and Bondservants: The Social History of a Chinese Custom* (London: Zed Books, 1989): 8.

30. Charles R. Shepherd, "Chinese Girl Slavery in America," *Missionary Review* 46 (1923): 894.

31. "Consulate in Hong Kong," *HRD 20*, 76–77; Wong Ah So, "Story of Wong Ah So," 31; Chun Ho, interview in *Makers of America—Natives and Aliens, 1894–1903*, ed. Wayne Moquin (New York: William Benton, 1971): 118.

32. Shepherd, "Chinese Girl Slavery," 896–97; Charles Caldwell Dobie, *San Francisco: A Pageant* (New York: D. Appleton, 1933): 69; Ira M. Condit, *The Chinaman as We See Him and Fifty Years of Work for Him* (Chicago: Fleming H. Revell, 1900): 147.

33. Sieh Fu-ching, "Chinese Emigrants Abroad," *China Review* 21 (1894–95): 140.

34. Mei, "Socioeconomic Origins," 234.

35. Zo, "Chinese Immigration," 23, 30; *Ta-Ch'ing hui-tien shih-li* (Precedents and Edicts Pertaining to the Collected Statutes) (Peking, 1886): 775:1a, quoted in Henry Shih-shan Tsai, *China and the Overseas Chinese in the United States, 1868–1911* (Fayetteville: University of Arkansas Press, 1983), 9; William Alexander Parsons Martin, *Cycle of Cathay; or China, South and North, with Personal Reminiscences* (New York: Fleming H. Revell, 1896): 160.

36. *Chia-ch'ting ta'ch'ing hui-tien shih-li* (Prece-

dents and Edicts Pertaining to the Collected Statutes of the Ch'ing Government) (Peking: Government Printing Office, 1818): 775:1–2, in Wen, "Background of the Chinese," 110; Chen Liang-shih, deposition, "Consulate at Hong Kong," *HRD 20*, 76; George F. Seward, "Memo on the Chinese Question from Minister G. F. Seward to Mr. Evarts," ALS, March 26, 1879, Rutherford B. Hayes Collections, Rutherford B. Hayes Presidential Center, Fremont, Ohio.

37. Sucheng Chan, *This Bittersweet Soil: The Chinese in California Agriculture, 1860–1910* (Berkeley: University of California Press, 1986): 24.

38. "Expatriation and Slavery in China," *HRD 60*, 21–22, 28–29.

39. "Consulate at Hong Kong," *HRD 20*, 3–4, 11; "Memorial of the Chinese Companies," 1876, reprinted in Otis Gibson, *The Chinese in America* (Cincinnati: Hitchcock & Walden, 1877): 318; *Alta California*, September 14, 1867, January 21, 1869; "Importation of Chinese Coolies," *SED 116*, 41st Cong., 2d sess. (Serial 1407): 3.

40. "Importation of Chinese Coolies," *SED 116*, 3; "Consulate at Hong Kong," *HRD 20*, 4, 9.

41. Roger Daniels, *Asian America: Chinese and Japanese in the United States Since 1850* (Seattle: University of Washington Press, 1988): 44.

42. An Act Supplementary to the Act in relation to Immigration [Page Law]," U.S. *Statutes at Large* 477 (1875): 477–78.

43. "Chinese Immigration," *Senate Report* [hereafter *SR*] 689, 44th Cong., 2d sess. (Serial 1734): 395.

44. "Consulate at Hong Kong," *HRD 20*, 28; Coolidge, *Chinese Immigration*, 502; William Adam Piper, *Immigration of Chinese into the United States: Speech in the House of Representatives, May 18, 1876* (Washington, D.C.: Government Printing Office, 1876): 12.

45. *Daily Evening Bulletin*, December 9, 1875; *Morning Call*, October 29, 1877.

46. "Consulate at Hong Kong," *HRD 20*, 28; *Hong Kong Dispatches* (reel 10), dispatch 307, August 28, 1875.

47. *Hong Kong Dispatches* (reel 12), dispatch 485, enclosures 2–3, July 26, 1878; Seward, "Memo on the Chinese Question."

48. *Hong Kong Dispatches* (reel 14), dispatch 200, May 23, 1882; James B. Angell, "James B. Angell Diary, 1880–1881," TMs, 20, James B. Angell Papers, box 13, Michigan Historical Collections, Bentley Library, University of Michigan, Ann Arbor; Coolidge, *Chinese Immigration*, 502.

49. U.S. Department of State, *Diplomatic Instructions of the Department of State, 1801–1906: China* (National Archives microfilm copy, reel 40), dispatch 1, June 7, 1880; *Hong Kong Dispatches* (reel 10), dispatch 307, enclosure 5, August 28, 1875.

50. George Anthony Peffer, "Forbidden Families: Emigration Experiences of Chinese Women Under the Page Law, 1875–1882," *Journal of American Ethnic History* 6 (Fall 1986): 32.

51. Charles Frederick Holder, "Chinese Slavery in America," *North American Review* 165 (1897): 290–91; Nee and Nee, *Longtime Californ'*, 84.

52. "Chinese Exclusion," *SR 776*, 52th Cong., 1st sess. (Serial 4265): 228.

53. *San Francisco Chronicle*, August 27, 1873.

54. Rasmussen, *San Francisco Ship Passenger Lists*, gives time taken by each ship to travel from Hong Kong or Canton or Shanghai to San Francisco (see vols. 5 and 6); *Alta California*, August 6, 1874; Pacific Mail Steamship Company advertisement, Bancroft Scraps: Pacific Mail Steamship Company and Ship Building, v. 105, CU-B; Robert A. Weinstein, "North from Panama, West to the Orient: The Pacific Mail Steamship Company," *California History* 57 (Spring 1978): 51; Robert J. Schwendinger, *Ocean of Bitter Dreams: Maritime Relations Between China and the United States, 1850–1915* (Tucson: Westernlore Press, 1988): 66–76.

55. *San Francisco Chronicle*, January 21, 1869, August 27, 1873; *Evening Post*, December 22, 1876.

56. "Memorial of the Anti-Coolie and Anti-Monopoly Association of San Francisco, California," *Senate Report Miscellaneous Document* [hereafter *SRD*] *34*, 41st Cong., 2d sess. (Serial 1408): 29; "Foreign Relations: China," *HRD 1*, 42d Cong., 2d sess. (Serial 1502): 207–9.

57. Robert J. Schwendinger, "Chinese Sailors: America's Invisible Merchant Marine, 1876–1906," *California History* 57 (Spring 1978): 62.

58. Henry Hiram Ellis, *From the Kennebec to California: Reminiscences of a California Pioneer*, ed. Laurence R. Cook (Los Angeles: Warren F. Louis, 1959): 60.

59. *Alta California*, 26 February 1869.

60. *The Oriental/Tung Ngai San-Luk*, January 4, 1855; *San Francisco Examiner*, August 28, 1888.

61. Robert J. Schwendinger, "Investigating Chinese Immigrant Ships and Sailors," in *The Chinese American Experience*, ed. Genny Lim (San Francisco: Chinese Historical Society of America and Chinese Culture Center, 1984): 16–25; John H. Kemble, ed., "Andrew Wilson's Jottings on Civil War in California," *California Historical Society Quarterly* 32, no. 2 (September 1953): 213; *Alta California*, July 12, 1869; *Morning Call*, October 20, 1878.

62. Chen Liang-shih, deposition, "Consulate at Hong Kong," *HRD 20*, 76; Lin Yu-shih, deposition, "Consulate at Hong Kong," *HRD 20*, 77.

63. Wong Ah So, "Story of Wong Ah So," 32; "Consulate at Hong Kong," *HRD 20*, 74.

Three: Arrival in America

1. Gibson, *Chinese in America*, 135; Takaki, *Strangers from a Different Shore*, 236; *Morning Call*, October 20, 1878.

2. Imperial Maritime Customs, Treaties, Conven-

tions, etc., *Between China and Foreign States*, 3 vols. (Shanghai: Statistical Department of the Inspectorate General of Customs, 1905): 1:627; Augustus Layres, *Facts upon the Other Side of the Chinese Question with a Memorial to the President of the United States from Representative Chinamen in America* (San Francisco: n.p., 1876): 18.

3. Shepherd, "Chinese Girl Slavery in America," 896–97.

4. M. G. C. Edholm, "A Stain on the Flag," *Californian* (February 1892): 163; "Consulate at Hong Kong," *HRD 20*, 74.

5. Huie Kin, *Reminiscences*, 24.

6. Wong Ah So, "Story of Wong Ah So," 31.

7. "Consulate at Hong Kong," *HRD 20*, 74.

8. "The Old Oriental Warehouse in San Francisco," *Bulletin of the Chinese Historical Society of America* 25 (November 1990): 1.

9. "Consulate at Hong Kong," *HRD 20*, 75–77; Lui Nee U and Chan Nee Leung, testimonies, in "Consulate at Hong Kong," *HRD 20*, 71.

10. Ibid.

11. Lee, "Sacred Cows and Paper Tigers," 96–97.

12. "Old Oriental Warehouse," 2; "Sanborn Fire Insurance Maps of San Francisco: 1887" (New York: Sanborn Map Publishing, 1890), no. 192, Library of Congress, Washington D.C.; U.S. Department of the Treasury, *Letters Received by the Secretary of the Treasury from Collectors of Customs, 1833–1869* (National Archives microfilm copy, reel 219), dispatch 119, May 2, 1868.

13. Vincente Tang, "Chinese Women Immigrants and the Two-Edged Sword of Habeas Corpus," in *The Chinese American Experience*, ed. Genny Lim (San Francisco: Chinese Historical Society of America and Chinese Culture Center, 1984): 49; *Alta California*, August 24, 1876.

14. *Alta California*, August 24, 26, 27, 1874; California *Statutes* 23 (1870): 300–31; William J. Courtney,

San Francisco's Anti-Chinese Ordinances, 1850–1900 (San Francisco: R & E Research Associates, 1974): 22.

15. Christian G. Fritz, "Due Process, Treaty Rights, and Chinese Exclusion, 1882–1891," in *Entry Denied: Exclusion and the Chinese Community in America, 1882–1943*, ed. Sucheng Chan (Philadelphia: Temple University Press, 1991): 26; Christian G. Fritz, "Bitter Strength (*k'u-li*) and the Constitution: The Chinese Before the Federal Courts in California," *Historical Reporter* 1 (Autumn 1980): 9–10; *Alta California*, September 11, 14, 24, 1874.

16. Shirley Hune, "Politics of Chinese Exclusion: Legislative-Executive Conflict, 1876–1882," *Amerasia Journal* 9, no. 1 (1982): 9.

17. *Alta California*, August 28, 1974.

18. Ibid., January 18, 1874.

19. Ibid., September 26, 1874.

20. "Sanborn Fire Insurance Maps of San Francisco, 1887"; "The Bitter Society: *Kushehui*, a translation, Chapters 37–46," trans. June Mei and Jean Pang Yip with Russell Leong, *Amerasia Journal* 8, no. 1 (1981): 45.

21. Condit, *Chinaman as We See Him*, 86–87.

22. "Chinese Immigration," *HRD 62*, 45th Cong., 3d sess. (Serial 1866): 390; California Chinese Exclusion Convention, *Proceedings and Lists of Delegates, California Chinese Exclusion Convention Held at Metropolitan Temple, San Francisco, November 21 and 22, 1901* (San Francisco: Star Press, 1901): 3.

23. Chun Ho, interview in *Makers of America*, 118.

24. *Alta California*, August 24, 1874.

25. *San Francisco Chronicle*, September 21, 1878; "Consulate at Hong Kong," *HRD 20*, 73.

26. John J. Manion, "Slave Women," TMs, John J. Manion Papers, CU-B.

27. F. A. Bee to John S. Mosby, letter in "Chinese Consulate at Hong Kong," *HRD 20*, 74.

28. Eve L. Armentrout-Ma, "Big and Medium Businesses of Chinese Emigrants to the United States, 1850–

1890: An Outline," *Bulletin of the Chinese Historical Society of America* 13 (September 1978): 1; *San Francisco Chronicle*, February 19, 1870; *Daily Morning Chronicle*, January 23, 1869; *San Francisco Chronicle*, November 9, 1869.

29. Sum Yee Kaw to his father, letter printed in *Alta California*, July 17, 1869; *Alta California*, December 11, 1871.

30. *California Police Gazette*, July 24, 1869.

31. *Collectors of Custom* (reel 206), dispatch 603, April 27, 1865, dispatch 600i, April 27, 1865, (reel 214), dispatch 105a, March 18, 1867, dispatch 116, June 7, 1867; "Immigration," TMs, Miner Chapman Papers, box 2, Hoover Institution Archives, Stanford University, California.

32. Charles R. Shepherd, *The Ways of Ah Sin: A Composite Narrative of Things as They Are* (Chicago: Fleming H. Revell, 1923): 204.

33. *Alta California*, February 23, 1869.

34. Ivan Light, "From Vice District to Tourist Attraction: The Moral Career of American Chinatowns, 1880–1940," *Pacific Historical Review* 43 (August 1974): 379.

35. *The Oriental/Tung Ngai San Luk*, February 1, 1855.

36. Lai Chun Chuen, *Remarks of the Chinese Merchants of San Francisco upon Governor Bigley's Messages, and Some Common Objections with Some Explanations of the Character of the Chinese Companies and the Laboring Class in California* (San Francisco: Whitton, Towne, 1855): 4.

37. Michael L. Stahler, "William Speer: Champion of California's Chinese, 1852–1857," *Journal of Presbyterian History* 48 (Summer 1970): 126; *Alta California*, September 14, 1867; Thomas J. Vivian, "John Chinaman in San Francisco," *Scribner's Monthly* 12 (October 1876): 862; Gibson, *Chinese in America*, 145.

38. Richard H. Dillon, *The Hatchet Men* (Sau-

salito, Calif.: Comstock, 1962): 85; Social Science Institute, *Orientals and Their Cultural Adjustment* (Nashville: Fisk University, 1946): 22–23.

39. Richard White, *It's Your Misfortune and None of My Own: A History of the American West* (Norman: University of Oklahoma Press, 1991): 316; Yung, "Social Awakening of Chinese American Women," 87–88.

40. *San Francisco Evening Bulletin*, May 12, 1864, March 28, 1867; *Alta California*, January 21, 1869, January 5, 1870, September 21, 1878; *San Francisco Chronicle* August 5, 1873; Frederick A. Bee, *Opening Argument of F. A. Bee Before the Joint Committee of the Houses of Congress on Chinese Immigration* (San Francisco: n.p., 1876): 24.

41. Jacqueline Baker Barnhart, "Working Women: Prostitution in San Francisco from the Gold Rush to 1900" (Ph.D. diss., University of California, Santa Cruz, 1976): 123.

42. *Alta California*, December 11, 1871.

43. Lee Chew, "Life Story of a Chinaman," in *The Life Stories of Undistinguished Americans as Told by Themselves*, ed. Hamilton Holt (New York: James Pott, 1906): 285; *San Francisco Chronicle*, February 27, 1879; Paul Jacobs, Saul Landau, and Eve Pell, *To Serve the Devil: Colonials and Sojourners* (New York: Vintage Books, 1971): 134.

44. Albert S. Evans, *A la California: Sketches of Life in the Golden State* (San Francisco: A. L. Bancroft, 1874): 319.

45. Wong Ah So, "Story of Wong Ah So," 31; Rose, "Experiences of 'Rose,'" 36.

46. *Alta California*, December 11, 1871; G. B. Densmore, *The Chinese in California: Description of Chinese Life in San Francisco, Their Habits, Morals and Manners* (San Francisco: Petitt & Russ, 1890): 78.

47. Densmore, *Chinese in California*, 78; Holder, "Chinese Slavery in America," 292; *San Francisco Daily Morning Chronicle*, August 15, 1869; *Alta California*,

December 11, 1871.

48. *San Francisco Chronicle*, March 6, 1878.

49. Glenn, "Split Household," 39.

50. Loomis, "Chinese in California."

51. Anthony Chan, *Gold Mountain: The Chinese in the New World* (Vancouver: New Star Books, 1983): 80.

52. *Daily Morning Chronicle*, March 15, 1868.

53. Ibid., December 9, 1869, February 13, 1879.

54. *Alta California*, March 15, 1873.

55. See Appendix.

56. See Appendix.

57. See Appendix.

58. Gibson, *Chinese in America*, 145–46.

59. *Alta California*, August 13, 1873.

60. Occidental Branch (Woman's Foreign Missionary Society), *Annual Report*, 1878, 9 [hereafter OB-WFMS, *AR*].

61. *San Francisco Chronicle*, August 13, 1873.

62. Condit, *Chinaman as We See Him*, 150.

63. A. W. Loomis, "Chinese Women in California," *Overland Monthly* 2 (April 1869): 347.

64. Christopher Lee Yip, "San Francisco's Chinatown: An Architectural and Urban History" (Ph.D. diss., University of California, Berkeley, 1985): 114.

65. Benjamine E. Lloyd, *Lights and Shades in San Francisco* (San Francisco: A. L. Bancroft, 1876): 257.

66. Ibid.

67. Buel, *Metropolitan Life Unveiled*, 277; Nee and Nee, *Longtime Californ'*, 85.

68. Densmore, *Chinese in California*, 83; Takaki, *Strangers from a Different Shore*, 87.

69. Wong Ah So, "Story of Wong Ah So," 31–32; Rose, "Experiences of 'Rose,'" 36; Chun Ho, interview in *Makers of America*, 118.

70. Tsoi Yee, interview in "Chinese Exclusion," *SRD* 776, 228.

71. Data compiled from *San Francisco Chronicle*,

1869–73; San Francisco (Calif.) Board of Supervisors, *Municipal Reports,* 1869–70, 95.

72. Wong Ah So, "Wong Ah So to Her Mother," 34.

Four: Adjusting to Life in Chinatown

1. Unless otherwise noted, all numbers and demographic characteristics in this chapter concerning women of all ethnic origins in San Francisco during the nineteenth century are computed from U.S. Bureau of the Census, Eighth Census (1860), *Population Schedules, San Francisco,* M-683, reel 67–68; Ninth Census (1870), *Population Schedules, San Francisco,* M-593, reel 79–85; and Tenth Census (1880), *Population Schedules, San Francisco,* T-9, reel 72–79.

2. Coolidge, *Chinese Immigration,* 502; Chan, *Bittersweet Soil,* 389–90.

3. Paul M. Ong, "Chinese Labor in Early San Francisco: Racial Segmentation and Industrial Expansion," *Amerasia Journal* 8, no. 1 (1981): 73–74.

4. Coolidge, *Chinese Immigration,* 502; Margo Anderson Conk, "Occupational Classification in the United States Census, 1870–1940," *Journal of Interdisciplinary History* 9 (Summer 1978): 111; George Anthony Peffer, "Forbidden Families" (M.A. thesis, San Francisco State University, 1981): 11; table 24, "Selected Statistics of Age and Sex by Counties," *Ninth Census,* 1:624; Margo Anderson, *The American Census: A Social History* (New Haven: Yale University Press, 1988): 78.

5. Henry Shih-shan Tsai, *The Chinese Experience in America* (Bloomington: Indiana University Press, 1986): 41.

6. Helen Virginia Carter, *The History of San Francisco's Chinatown* (San Francisco: R & E Research Associates, 1974): 33.

7. Coolidge, *Chinese Immigration,* 502.

8. *Morning Call,* October 21, 1879; Him Mark Lai

and Phillip P. Choy, *History of the Chinese in America* (San Francisco: H. M. Lai & P. P. Choy, 1971): 97.

9. California Bureau of Labor Statistics, *Third Biennial Report of the Bureau of Labor Statistics of the State of California for the Years 1887–1888* (Sacramento: State Printing Office, 1889): 107–9.

10. A. W. Loomis, "How Our Chinamen Are Employed," *Overland Monthly* 2 (March 1869): 235.

11. John W. Stephens, "A Quantitative History of Chinatown, San Francisco, 1870 and 1880," in *The Life, Influence, and the Role of the Chinese in the United States, 1776–1960* (San Francisco: Chinese Historical Society of America, 1976): 78–79; William Issel and Robert I. Cherny, *San Francisco, 1865–1932: Politics, Power, and Urban Development* (Berkeley: University of California Press, 1986): 76–77; Paul Ong, "An Ethnic Trade: The Chinese Laundries in Early California," *Journal of Ethnic Studies* 8, no. 4 (1981): 100; Chinn, Lai, and Choy, *Syllabus*, 50–55.

12. Loomis, "Chinese Women in California," 349–50.

13. Table 26, "Persons in Each Class of Occupations, with Sex: 1870," *Ninth Census*, 670–71; table 24, "The Number of Persons in the United States Engaged in Each Class of Occupations with Distinctions of Sex by States and Territories: 1880," *Tenth Census*, 712.

14. Blackburn, "Prostitutes and Gamblers of Virginia City," 247.

15. Stephens, "Quantitative History," 76. Stephens's assumption can be rebutted. Given the Chinese preference for having several generations living under one roof, it can be argued that the more well-to-do the household, the larger would be the number of people in it.

16. Fernando Henriques, *Prostitution and Society: A Survey* (New York: Citadel Press, 1963): 257.

17. Hirata, "Chinese Immigrant Women," 234.

18. Rose, "Experiences of 'Rose,'" 37.

19. Takaki, *Strangers from a Different Shore*, 122;

Daily Evening Bulletin, July 4, 1876.

20.   Lorna E. Logan, *Ventures in Mission: The Cameron House Story* (Castro Valley, Calif.: Lorna E. Logan, 1976): 9.

21.   Asbury, *Barbary Coast*, 174. A "crib" prostitute operated from a small room that often opened onto the street by door and window, allowing solicitation of potential customers. A courtesan, by contrast, a prostitute of the highest class, lived in elegant surroundings.

22.   California Department of Public Health, *First Biennial Report of the State Board of Health of California for the Years 1870 and 1871* (San Francisco: D. W. Gelwicks, 1871): 46; *The Chinese Hospital of San Francisco* (Oakland: Carruth & Carruth, 1899): 1; *San Francisco Chronicle*, July 1, 1871.

23.   Joan B. Trauner, "The Chinese as Medical Scapegoats in San Francisco, 1870–1905," *California History* 57 (Spring 1978): 82–83; Ninth Census (1870), *Population Schedules, San Francisco*; Tenth Census (1880), *Population Schedules, San Francisco*.

24.   Chinese Hospital, San Francisco, *Chinese Hospital Medical Staff Archives, 1978–1981* (San Francisco: Chinese Hospital, 1981): 1–4.

25.   Kemble, "Andrew Wilson's Jottings," 306; Lloyd, *Lights and Shades in San Francisco*, 260; Myriam F. Leslie, *California: A Pleasure Trip from Gotham to the Golden Gate* (New York: C. W. Carleton, 1877), selection reprinted in *Let Them Speak for Themselves: Women in the American West, 1849–1900*, ed. Christiane Fischer (Hamden, Conn.: Archon Books, 1977): 319.

26.   A. W. Loomis, "Medical Art in the Chinese Quarter," *Overland Monthly* 2 (June 1869): 496; A. W. Loomis, "Chinese in California: Their Signboard Literature," *Overland Monthly* 1 (August 1868): 154; William M. Tisdale, "Chinese Physicians in California," *Lippincott's Magazine* 63 (March 1899): 412.

27.   Trauner, "Chinese as Medical Scapegoats," 81.

28.   Evans, *A la California*, 302.

29. *Morning Call*, December 3, 1869; *Daily Morning Chronicle*, March 4, 1869; *San Francisco Chronicle*, October 12, 1870; Logan, *Ventures in Mission*, 25; *California Police Gazette*, May 16, 1868; *Evening Post*, March 25, 1879; *San Francisco Chronicle*, July 16, 1873; Chapman, "Chinese Immigration"; Densmore, *Chinese in California*, 78; *Alta California*, April 26, 1873.

30. Soulé, Gibon, and Nisbet, *Annals of San Francisco*, 384; *California Police Gazette*, February 27, May 14, 1859; William J. Hoy, "Chinatown Devises Its Own Street Names," *California Folklore Quarterly* 2 (April 1943): 72.

31. *Alta California*, April 20, 1854; "Map of San Francisco, 1852," in Parker, *San Francisco Directory*; *California Police Gazette*, June 25, 1859; *Alta California*, July 26, 1859; *San Francisco Chronicle*, July 26, 1878.

32. Lotchin, *San Francisco*, 256–58; California State Automobile Association, *A Map of San Francisco* (San Francisco: California State Automobile Association, 1979).

33. Timothy J. Gilfoyle, "The Urban Geography of Commercial Sex: Prostitution in New York City, 1790–1860," *Journal of Urban History* 13 (August 1987): 384–87; Ivan Light, "The Ethnic Vice Industry, 1880–1944," *American Sociological Review* 38 (May 1979): 470–71.

34. William P. Humphery, *San Francisco Map* (San Francisco: Britton & Ray, 1870); William Ingram Kip, "The Chinese in California," *Spirit of Missions* 20 (March 1855): 85–90.

35. Stahler, "William Speer," 126.

36. Neil Larry Shumsky and Larry M. Springer, "San Francisco's Zone of Prostitution, 1880–1934," *Journal of Historical Geography* 7, no. 1 (1981): 74.

37. Kip, "Chinese in California," 87–88.

38. San Francisco (Calif.) Board of Supervisors, *Municipal Reports*, 1869–70, 139.

39. Kushner, "Nineteenth-Century Sexuality," 39.

40. Soulé, Gibon, and Nisbet, *Annals of San Francisco*, 550; *California Police Gazette*, August 20, 1859;

James F. Richardson, "The Police in the City: A History," in *The Urban Experience: Themes in American History*, eds. Raymond A. Mohl and James F. Richardson (Belmont, Calif.: Wadsworth, 1973): 173; James F. Richardson, *Urban Police in the United States* (Port Washington, N.Y.: Kennikat Press, 1974): 155; John Young, *San Francisco: A History of the Pacific Coast Metropolis*, 2 vols. (San Francisco: S. J. Clarke Publishing, 1912): 1:228–29.

41. Sucheng Chan, *Asian Americans: An Interpretive History* (Boston: Twayne Publishers, 1991): 56.

42. Alvin Auerbach, "San Francisco's South of Market District, 1850–1950: The Emergence of a Skid Row," *California Historical Quarterly* 52 (Fall 1973): 206.

43. *California Police Gazette*, June 1, 1866.

44. Neil Larry Shumsky, "Tacit Acceptance: Respectable Americans and Segregated Prostitution, 1870–1910," *Journal of Social History* 19 (Summer 1986): 665.

45. Barth, *Bitter Strength*, 155; John F. Kasson, *Rudeness and Civility: Manners in Nineteenth-Century Urban America* (New York: Hill & Wang, 1990): 128; Eric H. Monkkonen, *Police in Urban America, 1860–1920* (Cambridge: Cambridge University Press, 1981): 55; *Municipal Reports*, 1866, 124–25; *Municipal Reports*, 1874–75, 498–99; California Senate, Special Committee on Chinese Immigration, *Chinese Immigration: Its Social, Moral, and Political Effect* (Sacramento: State Printing Office, 1878): 47; Workingmen's Party of California, *Chinatown Declared a Nuisance!* (San Francisco: Workingmen's Party of California, 1880): 15.

46. Tenth Census (1880), *Population Schedules, San Francisco*; *Evening Post*, April 30, 1878; *Alta California*, April 10, 1874; Gibson, *Chinese in America*, 259; *California Police Gazette*, January 20, 1866.

47. Densmore, *Chinese in California*, 82.

48. "Sanborn Fire Insurance Maps of San Francisco, 1887"; San Francisco (Calif.) Board of Supervisors, "The Official Chinatown Map: 1885," CU-B.

49. Blackburn and Ricards, "Prostitutes and Gam-

blers of Virginia City," 250, 257; Goldman, *Gold Diggers and Silver Miners,* 69; de Graaf, "Race, Sex, and Region," 304; Asbury, *Barbary Coast,* 257.

50. Pacific Union Express Company, *Address of Principal Chinese Merchants of San Francisco, in Chinese and English, for the Guidance of Our Agents in Addressing Letters, for 1868 and 1869,* reprinted in Gladys C. Hansen, *The Chinese in California: A Brief Bibliographic History* (Portland, Oreg.: R. Abel, 1970), frontispiece; Wells Fargo & Company's Express, *Directory of Chinese Business Houses* (San Francisco: Britton & Ray, 1878); Wells Fargo & Company's Express, *Directory of Chinese Merchants in San Francisco and Sacramento* (San Francisco: Britton & Ray, 1873); "Chinese Classified Business Directory," in *D. M. Bishop Annual Directory of the City and County of San Francisco for 1877* (San Francisco: B. C. Vandall, 1877): 1426–31.

51. Sucheng Chan, "The Exclusion of Chinese Women, 1870–1943," in *Entry Denied: Exclusion and the Chinese Community in America, 1882–1943,* ed. Sucheng Chan (Philadelphia: Temple University Press, 1991): 97–98.

52. *Municipal Reports,* 1869–70, 94–95; 1874–75, 504; 1878–79, 36.

53. Ibid., 1874–75, 498–99.

54. Connie Young Yu, "A History of San Francisco Chinatown Housing," *Amerasia Journal* 8, no. 1 (1981): 99; Benjamin S. Brooks, *Appendix to the Opening Statement and Brief of B. S. Brooks on the Chinese Question* (San Francisco: Women's Cooperative Printing Union, 1877): 78; *Morning Call,* March 14, 1878; "The Foul Contagious Disease" (editorial) *Medico-Literary Journal* 1 (November 1878): 4; *California Police Gazette,* January 20, June 9, 1866.

55. *Municipal Reports,* 1866–68, 124–25; *Municipal Reports,* 1869–70, 139; *California Police Gazette,* March 21, 1868; *San Francisco Chronicle* May 5, 1869; *Morning Call,* August 13, 1878.

56.   Ruth Rosen, *The Lost Sisterhood: Prostitution in America, 1900–1918* (Baltimore: Johns Hopkins University Press, 1982): 4; Helen Reynolds, *The Economics of Prostitution* (Springfield, Ill.: Charles C Thomas, 1986): 35; Lloyd, *Lights and Shades in San Francisco*, 142–43; Kushner, "Nineteenth-Century Sexuality," 39.

57.   Joel Best, "Keeping the Peace in St. Paul: Crime, Vice, and Police Work, 1869–1874," *Minnesota History* 47 (Summer 1981): 248; West, "Scarlet West," 19; Paula Petrik, "Capitalists with Rooms: Prostitution in Helena, Montana, 1865–1900," *Montana: The Magazine of Western History* 31 (Spring 1981): 32.

58.   Barnhart, *Fair but Frail*, 49; Harvey J. Graff, "'Pauperism, Misery, and Vice': Illiteracy and Criminality in the Nineteenth Century," *Journal of Social History* 11 (Winter 1977): 264; Brooks, *Appendix to the Opening Statement*, 78; *Alta California*, March 4, 1870; Carolina H. Dalls, *My First Holiday; or, Letters Home* (Boston: Roberts Bros., 1981): 126; Esther Jerman Baldwin, *Must the Chinese Go? An Examination of the Chinese Question* (Boston: Rand, Avery, 1886): 38.

59.   Chan, "Exclusion of Chinese Women," 97; Chan, *Asian Americans*, 56.

60.   *Municipal Reports*, 1866–67, 483; *California Statutes* 505 (1866): 641–42; San Francisco Police Department, "Chinese Criminal Photography Key: 1875–78," San Francisco History Room, San Francisco Public Library, San Francisco, California.

61.   Lawrence H. Larsen, The *Urban West at the End of the Frontier* (Lawrence: Regents Press of Kansas, 1978): 88.

62.   Chan, "Exclusion of Chinese Women," 106–7.

63.   Theodore N. Frederick, "Politics, the Police, and Arresting Policies in Salem, Massachusetts, and the Civil War," *Social Problems* 19 (Spring 1972): 577; Frank Prassel, *The Western Peace Officer: A Legacy of Law and Order* (Norman: University of Oklahoma Press, 1972): 80; Eve L. Armentrout-Ma, "Urban Chinese at the Sinet-

ic Frontier: Social Organizations in United States' Chinatowns, 1849–1898," *Modern Asian Studies* 17, no. 1 (1983): 117.

64. Stanford M. Lyman, "Conflict and the Web of Group Affiliation in San Francisco's Chinatown, 1850–1910," *Pacific Historical Review* 43 (November 1974): 489.

65. Data compiled from *San Francisco Chronicle* for 1872 and 1873.

66. Courtney, *San Francisco's Anti-Chinese Ordinances*, 23; Gilfoyle, "Urban Geography of Commercial Sex," 387; Roger Lane, *Policing the City: Boston, 1822–1885* (New York: Atheneum Books, 1977): 115; *Municipal Reports*, 1859–60, 42.

67. Butler, *Daughters of Joy*, 76; *San Francisco Chronicle*, March 27, 1872.

68. Loomis, "Chinese in California"; Wu Chengtsu, ed., *Chink! A Documentary History of Anti-Chinese Prejudice in America* (New York: World Publishing, 1972): 36; California Senate, Special Committee on Chinese Immigration, *Chinese Immigration*, 93; Mark Twain, *Mark Twain's San Francisco*, ed. Bernard Taper (New York: McGraw-Hill, 1963): 172–73. For more information on *People v. Hall* and the relationship between race and permissible evidence, see my discussion on page XXX.

69. *California Police Gazette*, August 20, 1859.

70. *Municipal Reports*, 1866–67, 463; *Daily Morning Chronicle*, June 26, 1869; *San Francisco Chronicle*, March 30, April 29, 1873.

71. Monkkonen, *Police in Urban America*, 67; Jordan, *Frontier Law and Order*, 139; *Daily Evening Bulletin*, February 14, 1878; *San Francisco Chronicle*, October 17, 1871; *Morning Call*, March 9, 1879; *San Francisco Chronicle*, October 10, 1869, June 17, 1873; *California Police Gazette*, August 26, 1875; *San Francisco Chronicle*, August 13, 1871, September 29, 1871; Dillon, *Hatchet Men*, 11.

72. John C. Schneider, "Public Order and the Geography of the City: Crime, Violence, and the Police in

Detroit, 1845–1875," *Journal of Urban History* 4 (February 1978): 184, 199–200; *Morning Call*, March 14, 1878.

73. Emily M. Ahern, "The Power and Pollution of Chinese Women," in *Women in Chinese Society*, eds. Margery Wolf and Roxane Witke (Stanford: Stanford University Press, 1975): 195, 205, 209.

74. A peipa girl was a prostitute trained to play the stringed musical instument, *peipa*, to entertain patrons. Hom, *Songs of Gold Mountain*, 318, 320.

75. Lois Rodecape, "Celestial Drama in the Golden Hills: The Chinese Theatre in California, 1849–1869," *California Historical Quarterly* 23 (June 1944): 112; Ronald Riddle, *Flying Dragons, Flowing Streams: Music in the Life of San Francisco's Chinese* (Westport, Conn.: Greenwood Press, 1983): 32.

76. Gillenkirk, *Bitter Melon*, 112–13.

77. Loomis, "Chinese Women in California," 347; Dillon, *Hatchet Men*, 155.

78. Loomis, "Chinese in California."

79. Dalls, *My First Holiday*, 382.

80. "Chinese Exclusion," *SR 776*, 229.

Five: Violence and Public Women

1. Luther W. Spoehr, "Sambo and the Heathen Chinee: Californians' Racial Stereotypes in the Late 1870s," *Pacific Historical Review* 42 (May 1973): 186.

2. Larsen, *Urban West*, 88; Prassel, *Western Peace Officer*, 22; Harry N. Anderson, "Deadwood, South Dakota: An Effort at Stability," *Montana: The Magazine of Western History* 20 (January 1970): 40–47; Robert R. Dykstra, *The Cattle Towns* (New York: Knopf, 1968): 142–48; W. Eugene Hollon, *Frontier Violence: Another Look* (New York: Oxford University Press, 1974): x, 125; Richard Maxwell Brown, "Western Violence: Structure, Values, Myth," *Western Historical Quarterly* 24 (Febru-

ary 1993): 6; Roger D. McGarth, *Gunfighters, Highwaymen, and Vigilantes: Violence on the Frontier* (Berkeley: University of California Press, 1984): 149–62. For other works on the involvement of women in western violence, see Melody Graulich, "Violence Against Women: Power Dynamics in Literature of the Western Family," in *The Women's West*, eds. Susan Armitage and Elizabeth Jameson (Norman: University of Oklahoma Press, 1987): 111–25; Anne M. Butler, "Still in Chains: Black Women in Western Prisons, 1865–1910," *Western Historical Quarterly* 20 (February 1989): 18–35; David Peterson, "Wife Beating: An American Tradition," *Journal of Interdisciplinary History* 23 (Summer 1992): 97–118.

3. McGarth, *Gunfighters, Highwaymen, and Vigilantes*, 149. See Melody Graulich, "Violence Against Women," for a discussion on violence against women in the home and how few cases of familial violence surfaced in the male-dominated society of the American West. McGarth's analysis fails to adequately admit this phenomenon.

4. Butler, *Daughters of Joy*, 154; David Hammack, "Problems of Power in the Historical Study of Cities, 1800–1960," *American Historical Review* 83 (April 1978): 333–36.

5. Dan Caldwell, "The Negroization of the Chinese Stereotype in California," *Southern California Quarterly* 53 (June 1971): 125–26, 128.

6. Gardner, "Image of the Chinese," 28–29.

7. Elmer C. Sandmeyer, *The Anti-Chinese Movement in California* (Berkeley: University of California Press, 1939): 35; Baldwin, *Must the Chinese Go?*, 21; Mark Thomas Connelly, *The Response to Prostitution in the Progressive Era* (Chapel Hill: University of North Carolina Press, 1980): 6; Henry Harris, *California's Medical Story* (Springfield, Ill.: Grabhorn Press, 1932): 156; Tylor, "'Denied the Power to Choose the Good,'" 473.

8. Elizabeth Lomax, "Infantile Syphilis as an Example of Nineteenth-Century Belief in the Inheritance

of Acquired Characteristics," *Journal of the History of Medicine and Allied Sciences* 34 (January 1979): 24; "Foul Contagious Disease," 3–4.

9. *Communication from the Mechanics State Council of California in Relation to Chinese Immigration to the Honorable Legislature of the State of California* (San Francisco: D. W. Gelwicks, n.d.): 4.

10. Kay A. Holmes, "Reflections by Gaslight: Prostitution in Another Age," *Issues in Criminology* 7 (Winter 1972): 83.

11. *San Francisco Chronicle,* May 17, 1873; *California Police Gazette,* January 30, 1869; *Municipal Reports,* 1872–73, 340.

12. U.S. Bureau of the Census, *The Social Statistics of Cities,* 2 vols. (Washington, D.C.: Government Printing Office, 1886; repr., New York: Arno Press, 1970): 2:811; Trauner, "Chinese as Medical Scapegoats," 73, 75.

13. Frederick A. Bee, *The Other Side of the Chinese Question* (San Francisco, 1886; repr., San Francisco: R & E Research Associates, 1971): 50; California Department of Public Health, *First Biennial Report,* 46–47; Jay Marion Read and Mary E. Mathes, *The History of the San Francisco Medical Society, 1850–1900,* 2 vols. (San Francisco: San Francisco Medical Society, 1958): 1:136.

14. Yu, "History of San Francisco Chinatown Housing," 98.

15. Angell, "Diary," 17; Leslie, *California,* 318.

16. *Evening Post,* February 24, 1879; Peggy Pascoe, *Relations of Rescue: The Search for Female Moral Authority in the American West, 1874–1939* (New York: Oxford University Press, 1990): 54; Eric Goldman, *Rendezvous with Destiny* (New York: Knopf, 1972): 71, 78; Robert Seager II, "Some Denominational Reactions to Chinese Immigration to California, 1856–1892," *Pacific Historical Review* 28 (1959): 55, 61.

17. Otis Gibson, testimony, "Chinese Immigration," *HRD 62,* 457.

18. Wong Sam and Assistants, *An English-Chinese Phrase Book* (San Francisco: Cubery, 1875): 151, 274.

19. President U. S. Grant, "Sixth Message to the Senate and House of Representatives, December 7, 1874," in James D. Richardson, comp., *Messages and Papers of the Presidents, 1789–1897*, 11 vols. (Washington, D.C.: Government Printing Office, 1907): 7:288; Harry T. Williams, ed., *Hayes: The Diary of a President, 1875–1881* (New York: D. McKay, 1964): 192.

20. *Congressional Record*, 44th Cong., 1st sess., May 1876, 16, pt. 3:3101.

21. See Lynwood Carranco, "Chinese Expulsion from Humboldt County," *Pacific Historical Review* 30 (November 1961): 329–40.

22. *Daily Evening Bulletin*, October 25, 1871.

23. Nee and Nee, *Longtime Californ'*, 48.

24. Hom, *Songs of Gold Mountain*, 109–10.

25. *California Police Gazette*, February 27, 1859.

26. *California Police Gazette*, May 14, 1859; Charles J. McClain, Jr., "The Chinese Struggle for Civil Rights in Nineteenth Century America: The First Phase, 1850–1870," *California Law Review* 72 (July 1974): 549–51.

27. Charles J. McClain and Laurene Wu McClain, "The Chinese Contribution to the Development of American Law," in *Entry Denied: Exclusion and the Chinese Community in America, 1882–1943*, ed. Sucheng Chan (Philadelphia: Temple University Press, 1991): 8–9.

28. *Alta California*, March 30, 1879.

29. Tang, "Chinese Women Immigrants," 48.

30. Layres, *Chinese Question*, 30.

31. Richard C. Wade, "Violence in the Cities: A Historical View," in *Cities in American History*, eds. Kenneth Jackson and Stanley K. Schultz (New York: Knopf, 1972): 479; Lawrence Friedman and Robert V. Percival, *The Roots of Justice: Riots and Punishments in Alameda County, California, 1870–1910* (Chapel Hill: University of North Carolina Press, 1981): 105.

32. *San Francisco Chronicle*, November 21, 1872.

33. Ibid., December 30, 1872, May 28, 1873; Chinn, Lai, and Choy, *Syllabus*, 24.

34. U.S. Treasury Department, Bureau of Narcotics, "Specialized Illegal Activities in Chinese Communities in the United States," Memorandum, TLS, August 16, 1945, 24, CU-AAS.

35. The Tilly-Gamson thesis argues that violence is a regular and integral part of the fight for power in any society and that more often than not, the use of violence will succeed. See Charles Tilly, "Collective Violence in European Perspective," in *Violence in America*, eds. Hugh Davis Graham and Ted Robert Gurr (Beverley Hills, Calif.: Sage, 1979): 4–45; William A. Gamson, *The Strategy of Social Protest* (Homewood, Ill.: Dorsey, 1975).

36. W. N. Davis, "Research Uses of County Court Records, 1850–1879: and Incidental Intimate Glimpses of California Life and Society, Part I," *California Historical Quarterly* 52 (Fall 1973): 245; Murphy, "The Private Lives of Public Women," 202; Goldman, *Gold Diggers and Silver Miners*, 114–15.

37. *San Francisco Chronicle*, September 25, 1872.

38. Ibid., March 30, 1872, April 2, 1872.

39. McClain, "Chinese Struggle for Civil Rights," 567.

40. *San Francisco Chronicle*, May 15, 1872.

41. Ibid., December 23, 1872.

42. Edholm, "A Stain on the Flag," 165.

43. Loomis, "Chinese Women in California," 347; Rev. Arthur J. Brown, "'Lo Mo' of San Francisco: Donaldina Cameron and Her Work for the Rescue of Chinese Girls," *Missionary Review* 55 (May 1932): 263.

44. Yung, *Chinese Women of America*, 19; Jules Becker, *The Course of Exclusion, 1882–1924: San Francisco Newspaper Coverage of the Chinese and Japanese in the United States* (San Francisco: Mellen Research University Press, 1991): 21, 52, 88.

45. Takaki, *Strangers from a Different Shore*, 122–23; Gibson, *Chinese in America*, 220–21.

46. *San Francisco Chronicle*, March 13, 1873.

47. Rosen, *Lost Sisterhood*, 131, 133–34, 98.

48. West, "Scarlet West," 25; Butler, *Daughters of Joy*, 154.

49. White, *It's Your Misfortune*, 332; Graulich, "Violence Against Women," 122.

50. *San Francisco Chronicle*, July 30, 1873.

51. Chun Ho, interview in Moquin, *Makers of America*, 119; D. Kelly Weisberg, *Children of the Night: A Study of Adolescent Prostitution* (Lexington, Mass.: D.C. Heath, 1985): 109.

52. Major works on prostitution in the American West offer scant analysis of the rate of male abuse. See Butler, *Daughters of Joy*, 107, 110–11, 113; Goldman, *Gold Diggers and Silver Miners*, 113–15.

53. Davis, "Research Uses of County Court Records," 245.

54. Minnick, *Sam Fow*, 220; *San Francisco Chronicle*, September 13, 1869.

55. *Daily Morning Chronicle*, February 17, May 4, 1869; *San Francisco Chronicle*, August 21, 1872.

56. *San Francisco Chronicle*, July 26, 1872.

57. Ibid., January 3, 30, 1872; April 29, 1873.

58. *Daily Morning Chronicle*, September 24, 1868; *San Francisco Chronicle*, February 3, 1871, September 11, 1879.

59. San Francisco Police Department, Chinese Criminal Photograph Key.

60. Table 126, "The Defective, Dependent, and Delinquent Classes: The Foreign-born Prisoners of the United States: 1880," in Frederick Howes Wines, *Report on the Dependent, and Delinquent Classes of the Population of the United States as Returned at the Tenth Census, June 1, 1880* (Washington, D.C.: Government Printing Office, 1880): 516–17.

61. Friedman, *Roots of Justice*, 106; Light, "Ethnic Vice Industry," 471; Julia Kirk Blackwelder, "Crime, Policing, and the Dangerous Classes," *Journal of Urban*

History 10 (May 1984): 335.

62. Prassel, *Western Peace Officer*, 21.

63. McGarth, *Gunfighters, Highwaymen, and Vigilantes*, 162; *San Francisco Chronicle*, July 26, 1872.

64. *San Francisco Chronicle*, July 24, November 2, December 18, 31, 1872.

65. Table 14, "The Chinese Population by Counties: 1890, 1880, and 1870," U.S. Bureau of the Census, *Compendium of the Eleventh Census of the United States: 1890*, 3 vols. (Washington, D.C.: Government Printing Office, 1892): 1:516; Ninth Census (1870): *Population Schedules, San Francisco*.

66. Rosen, *Lost Sisterhood*, 131–32.

67. *Daily Morning Chronicle*, October 9, 1868.

68. Tachibana, "Outwitting the Whites," 385.

69. Frank Norris, "The Third Circle," in *The Third Circle, A Deal in Wheat, and Other Stories of the New and Old West* (Garden City, N.Y.: Doubleday, Doran, 1928): 1–10.

70. Jacob Riis, *How the Other Half Lives* (New York, 1890; repr., New York: Hill & Wang, 1957): 70–71.

71. Ida M. Van Etten, "The House of Dragons," *Cosmopolitan* (March 1893): 615–25.

72. Frederick K. Grittner, *White Slavery: Myth, Ideology, and American Law* (New York: Garland Publishing, 1990): 108.

73. Chapman, "Chinese Immigration"; *California Police Gazette*, May 21, 1859.

74. *San Francisco Chronicle*, March 26, 1872.

75. Ibid., May 17, 1872.

76. Minnick, *Sam Fow*, 96.

77. *San Francisco Chronicle*, January 17, March 31, July 9, September 27, 1872, January 22, 1873, October 30, 1870; *Daily Morning Chronicle*, October 9, 1868.

78. *San Francisco Chronicle*, March 30, 1872; October 23, 1871.

79. Manion, "Tongs"; American Federation of Labor, *Some Reasons for Chinese Exclusion: Meat vs. Rice;*

American Manhood Against Asiatic Coolieism: Which Shall Survive? (Washington, D.C.: American Federation of Labor, 1901): 26; *San Francisco Chronicle*, February 10, 1872; *Daily Evening Bulletin*, January 1, 1878.

80. *San Francisco Chronicle*, February 10, 1872.

81. Ibid., June 17, 1873; *Alta California*, May 27, 1876; *Daily Evening Bulletin*, June 6, 1878.

82. Margery Wolf, "Women and Suicide in China," in *Women in Chinese Society*, eds. Margery Wolf and Roxane Witke (Stanford: Stanford University Press, 1975): 112.

83. *San Francisco Chronicle*, July 16, 1873.

84. *Evening Post*, March 25, 1879.

85. Read and Mathes, *History of the San Francisco Medical Society*, 1:89.

86. West, "Scarlet West," 26–27; Petrik, "Capitalists with Rooms," 36; Murphy, "Private Lives of Public Women," 200; Butler, *Daughters of Joy*, 68.

87. *San Francisco Chronicle*, November 27, 1870.

88. Ibid., December 25, 1873.

89. Tsai, *Chinese Experience in America*, 56; Harris, *California's Medical Story*, 271.

90. Ben Hong, interview by Jeffrey Paul Chan, Combined Asian American Resource Project, 1975, Regional Oral History Office, CU-B; Hart H. North, "Chinese Highbinder Societies in California," *California Historical Society Quarterly* 27 (March 1948): 25; Riddle, *Flying Dragons, Flowing Streams*, 66; *San Francisco Chronicle*, December 5, 1869; Buel, *Metropolitan Life Unveiled*, 277; Lloyd, *Lights and Shades in San Francisco*, 258.

91. Herman Scheffaner, "The Old Chinese Quarter," *Living Age*, 10 August 1907.

92. Leslie, *California*, 129.

93. Mary Hardy, *Through Cities and Prairie Lands* (New York: R. Worthington, 1881; repr., New York: Arno Press, 1974): 194.

94. Schneider, "Public Order," 199.

95. *San Francisco Chronicle*, September 29, 1871,

March 29, 1872; Ellis, *From the Kennebec to California*, 61; Prassel, *Western Peace Officer*, 79.

96. Loomis, "Chinese in California"; "Chinese Immigration," *HRD 240*, 45th Cong., 2d sess. (Serial 1822): 3.

97. "Argument of Joseph C. G. Kennedy Adverse to Legislation by Congress," *Senate Miscellaneous Document* [hereafter *SMD*] *36*, 45th Cong., 2d sess. (Serial 1786): 22; Edwin R. Meade, "Speech of Hon. E. R. Meade of New York," *Congressional Record*, 44th Cong., 2d sess., February 1877, 28, pt. 3:117.

98. *California Police Gazette*, August 20, 1859.

99. Workingmen's Party, *Chinatown Declared a Nuisance!* 5.

Six: Leaving the Trade

1. Unless otherwise noted, all numbers and demographic characteristics in this chapter regarding prostitutes in San Francisco during the nineteenth century are computed from U.S. Bureau of the Census, Eighth Census (1860), *Population Schedules, San Francisco*, M-683, reel 67–68; Ninth Census (1870), *Population Schedules, San Francisco*, M-593, reel 79–85; and Tenth Census (1880), *Population Schedules, San Francisco*, T-9, reel 72–79.

2. Coolidge, *Chinese Immigration*, 502.

3. Michael A. Smith, testimony, "Chinese Immigration," *HRD 62*, 192.

4. *Municipal Reports*, 1875–76, 232–39; *Municipal Reports*, 1876–77, 354–59.

5. *San Francisco Chronicle*, December 16, 1878.

6. Butler, *Daughters of Joy*, 15.

7. Gerda Lerner, ed., *The Female Experience: An American Documentary* (Indianapolis: Bobbs-Merrill, 1977), 273.

8. William Laird MacGregor, *San Francisco, California in 1876* (Edinburgh: T. Laurie, 1876): 68.

9. Carter, *History of San Francisco's Chinatown*,

36; Takaki, *Strangers from a Different Shore*, 87; Stephens, "Quantitative History," 80, 85.

10. *Morning Call*, March 27, 1870.

11. Loomis, "How Our Chinamen Are Employed," 235.

12. Yung, *Chinese Women of America*, 30; Loomis, "Chinese Women in California," 350.

13. Barnhart, *Fair but Frail*, 58; Florence Ayscough, *Chinese Women: Yesterday and Today* (Shanghai: Modern Books, 1930): 93; Reay Tannahill, *Sex in History* (New York: Stein & Day, 1980): 194; James Hundley Wiley, "A Study of Chinese Prostitution" (M.A. thesis, University of Chicago, 1928): 75.

14. Hirata, "Free, Indentured, Enslaved," 19.

15. Hom, *Songs of Gold Mountain*, 318; Hom, "Chinatown High Life," 127.

16. Otis Gibson, testimony, "Investigation of Causes of General Depression in Labor and Business; and Chinese Immigration," *HMD 5*, 46th Cong., 2d sess. (Serial 1928): 343.

17. Gibson, testimony, in Canada, Royal Commission on Chinese Immigration, *Report and Evidence* (Ottawa: Printed by Order of the Commission, 1885): 38; Yan, *When I Was a Boy in China*, 49.

18. Peggy Pascoe, "Gender Systems in Conflict: The Marriages of Mission-Educated Chinese American Women, 1874–1939," *Journal of Social History* 22 (Summer 1989): 633.

19. Kay Ann Johnson, *Women, the Family, and Peasant Revolution in China* (Chicago: University of Chicago Press, 1983): 13; Wolf, *Marriage and Adoption in China*, 77, 79.

20. Mrs. F. I. Chin, interview by Kathleen Chinn, Combined Asian American Resource Project, 1977, CU-B.

21. Lorraine Dong and Marlon K. Hom, "Defiance or Perpetuation: An Analysis of Characters in *Mrs. Spring Fragrance*," in *Chinese America: History and Perspectives 1987* (San Francisco: Chinese Historical Society of

America, 1987): 148; Amaury de Reincourt, *Sex and Power in History* (New York: D. McKay, 1974): 183; Johnson, *Women, the Family, and Peasant Revolution*, 8; Yung, *Chinese Women of America*, 30; Wu Ting-fang, *America Through the Spectacles of an Oriental Diplomat* (New York: Frederick A. Stokes, 1914): 129–30; Diane Mei Lin Mark and Ginger Chih, *A Place Called America* (San Francisco: Organization of Chinese Americans, 1982): 61.

22. Johnson, *Women, the Family, and Peasant Revolution*, 10.

23. Kristeva, *About Chinese Women*, 71; Mary E. Sheridan and Janet W. Salaff, "Introduction," in *Lives: Chinese Working Women*, eds. Mary Sheridan and Janet W. Salaff (Bloomington: Indiana University Press, 1984):6.

24. Hsu, *Challenge of the American Dream*, 21–22; Stacey, *Patriarchy and Socialist Revolution in China*, 39, 54; Wolf, *Marriage and Adoption in China*, 86.

25. Freedman, "Family in China, Past and Present," 328–29.

26. Stacey, *Patriarchy and Socialist Revolution in China*, 58; Albert Richard O'Hara, *The Position of Woman in Early China* (Washington, D.C.: Catholic University of America Press, 1945; repr., Westport, Conn.: Hyperion Press, 1981): 261; Chao Buwei, *Autobiography of a Chinese Woman* (Westport, Conn.: Greenwood Press, 1974): 9–11.

27. Zo, "Chinese Emigration," 81.

28. Marjorie Topley, "Marriage Resistance in Rural Kwangtung," in *Women in Chinese Society*, eds. Margery Wolf and Roxane Witke (Stanford: Stanford University Press, 1975): 78.

29. Freedman, "Family in China, Past and Present," 328–29; Croll, *Wise Daughters from Foreign Lands*, 14, 39.

30. Chen, "Barbarian Paradise," 136.

31. Ning, *Daughter of Han*, 55, 72–73.

32. Wong Ah So, "Letter from Wong Ah So to Her

Mother," 34; Pascoe, "Gender Systems in Conflict," 632–33.

33. Yung, "Social Awakening of Chinese American Women," 80; Ono Kazuko, *Chinese Women in a Century of Revolution, 1850–1950*, trans. Joshua A. Fogel and others (Stanford: Stanford University Press, 1978): 26, 42, 91; Marilyn B. Young, ed., *Women in China: Studies in Social Change and Feminism* (Ann Arbor: Center for Chinese Studies, University of Michigan, 1973): 33; Soong Ching-ling, "Women's Liberation," in *Women in China*, 201.

34. Stacey, *Patriarchy and Socialist Revolution in China*, 50–52.

35. Ichioka, "*Ameyuki-san*," 2, 17; Joan Hori, "Japanese Prostitution in Hawaii During the Immigration Period," *Hawaiian Journal of History* 15 (1980): 122.

36. Table 3, "Number of Chinese Males Per 100 Females: 1860–1900," in Tsai, *Chinese Experience in America*, 40; Vincente Tang, "Chinese Women Immigrants," 48–49. See also Edwin C. Brandenburg, ed., *Official Opinions of the Attorneys-General of the United States* (Washington, D.C.: Government Printing Office, 1900): 260–64.

37. Eun Sik Yang, "Korean Women of America: From Subordination to Partnership, 1903–1930," *Amerasia Journal* 11, no. 2 (1984): 3.

38. Lyman, "Marriage and the Family Among Chinese Immigrants," 325–26; Linda Perrin, *Coming to America: Immigrants from the Far East* (New York: Delacorte Press, 1980): 8.

39. Irving G. Tragen, "Statutory Prohibitions Against Interracial Marriage," *California Law Review* 32 (1944): 272, 276; Megumi Dick Osumi, "Asians and California's Anti-Miscegenation Laws," in *Asian and Pacific American Experiences: Women's Perspectives*, ed. Nobuya Tsuchida (Minneapolis: University of Minnesota Press, 1932): 2, 6.

40. Loomis, "Chinese in California."

41. Willard B. Farwell, *The Chinese at Home and Abroad* (San Francisco: A. L. Bancroft, 1885): 15–16.

42. Coolidge, *Chinese Immigration*, 441.

43. *Evening Post*, April 4, 1877.

44. Susan L. Johnston, "Sharing Bed and Board: Cohabitation and Cultural Difference in Central Arizona Mining Towns, 1863–1873," in *The Women's West*, eds. Susan Armitage and Elizabeth Jameson (Norman: University of Oklahoma Press, 1987): 88.

45. William F. Wu, *The Yellow Peril: Chinese Americans in American Fiction, 1850–1940* (Hamden, Conn.: Archon Books, 1984): 57.

46. *California Police Gazette*, August 27, 1859.

47. Shepherd, *Ways of Ah Sin*, 205.

48. *Daily Evening Bulletin*, June 11, 1878.

49. Stephen Longstreet, *The Wilder Shore* (Garden City, N.Y.: Doubleday, 1968): 168.

50. *Morning Call*, September 13, 1879.

51. Hom, *Songs of Gold Mountain*, 317.

52. Royal Commission on Chinese Immigration, *Report and Evidence*, 38; Magnaghi, "Virginia City's Chinese Community," 146.

53. *Alta California*, April 10, 1874; "Chinese Immigration," *HRD 62*, 11, 14, 148; Gibson, testimony, "Investigation of Causes," *HMD 5*, 343; Gibson, *Chinese in America*, 140–43; *Alta California*, December 10, 1875.

54. *Evening Post*, April 4, 1877; *San Francisco Chronicle*, April 1, 1877; *Evening Post*, March 23, 1877; "Chinese Immigration," *HRD 62*, 14.

55. Butler, *Daughters of Joy*, 28.

56. California Bureau of Labor Statistics, *Third Biennial Report, 1887–1888*, 105; Caroll Wright, *Fourth Annual Report of the Commissioner of Labor, 1888: Working Women in Cities* (Washington, D.C.: Government Printing Office, 1889): 75.

57. Ronald A. St. Laurence, "The Myth and the Reality: Prostitution in San Francisco, 1880–1913" (M.A.

NOTES TO PAGES 175–79

thesis, California State University, Hayward, 1974): 117–18; Rosen, *Lost Sisterhood*, 143.

58. Gronewold, *Beautiful Merchandise*, 28; Chan, *Bittersweet Soil*, 392–93.

59. *Daily Evening Bulletin*, August 13, 1880.

60. California *Statutes* 266 (1866): 76–77; California *Statutes* 111 (1880): 202–3; Order No. 1291, "Relating to and Affecting Children," *San Francisco Ordinances, etc., the General Orders of the Board of Supervisors, Providing Regulations for the Government of the City and County of San Francisco and the Ordinances of the Park Commission* (San Francisco: W. M. Hinton, 1878): 114–15.

61. *San Francisco Chronicle*, December 10, 1871.

62. Asbury, *Barbary Coast*, 168–69, 183; *San Francisco Chronicle*, March 29, 1870.

63. Langley, *Directory*, 1869, 130.

64. Seager, "Some Denominational Reactions to Chinese Immigration," 50; Wesley S. Woo, "Protestant Work Among the Chinese in San Francisco Bay Area, 1850–1920" (Ph.D. diss., Graduate Theological Union, University of California, Berkeley, 1983): 31.

65. Lawrence B. Davis, *Immigrants, Baptists, and the Protestant Mind in America* (Urbana: University of Illinois Press, 1973): 16; Southern Baptist Convention, *Annual Report*, 1855, 16, 32; Woman's Baptist Home Mission Society, *Annual Report*, 1879, 25 [hereafter WBHMS, *AR*]; WBHMS, *AR*, 1884, 28; WBHMS, *AR*, 1887, 37. Quotations are from WBHMS, *AR*, 1887. See also WBHMS, *AR*, 1897, 50.

66. Paul Boyer, *Urban Masses and Moral Order in America, 1820–1920* (Cambridge.: Harvard University Press, 1978): 100, 122.

67. California Chinese Mission (American Missionary Association), *Annual Report*, 1894, 45; Woo, "Protestant Work," 162.

68. *San Francisco Chronicle*, December 27, 1870; Edward A. Wicher, *The Presbyterian Church in Califor-*

nia, 1849–1927 (New York: Frederick H. Hitchcock, 1927): 289–90.

69. Gibson, *Chinese in America*, 141–42; Pascoe, "Gender Systems in Conflict," 638.

70. Gibson, *Chinese in America*, 204–5.

71. *San Francisco Chronicle*, July 30, 1872; Charles V. Anthony, *Fifty Years of Methodism: A History of the Methodist Episcopal Church, Within the Bounds of the California Annual Conference from 1847–1897* (San Francisco: Methodist Book Concern, 1901): 297.

72. Pascoe, "Gender Systems," 634–35.

73. Jill Conway, "Women Reformers and American Culture, 1870–1930," *Journal of Social History* 5 (Winter 1971/72): 166; Anthony, *Fifty Years of Methodism*, 297.

74. C. P. Colegrove, *Among the Chinese* (Cincinnati: Woman's Home Missionary Society, n.d.): 10.

75. OB-WFMS, *AR*, 1880, 76; Methodist Episcopal Church, Missionary Society, *Annual Report*, 1874, 152 [hereafter MEMS, *AR*].

76. Gibson, *Chinese in America*, 202–3, 206–7; Stella Wyatt Brummitt, *Looking Backward, Thinking Foward: The Jubilee History of the Woman's Home Missionary Society of the Methodist Episcopal Church* (Cincinnati: Woman's Home Missionary Society, 1930): 93–95; Anthony, *Fifty Years of Methodism*, 298–99.

77. Nancy Cott, "Passionlessness: An Interpretation of Victorian Sexual Ideology, 1790–1850," *Signs* 4 (Winter 1978): 233–34, 236; Caroll-Smith Rosenberg and Charles Rosenberg, "The Female Animal: Medical and Biological Views of Woman and Her Role in Nineteenth-Century America," *Journal of American History* 60 (September 1973): 334.

78. *San Francisco Chronicle*, December 27, 1870; Pascoe, "Gender Systems in Conflict," 634–35; *Occident*, April 13, 1881.

79. Conway, "Women Reformers and American Culture," 166–67; Sheila A. Rothman, *Woman's Proper Place*

(New York: Basic Books, 1978): 63; Rosen, *Lost Sisterhood*, 8.

80. Patricia Hill, "'Heathen Women's Friends': The Role of the Methodist Episcopal Women in the Women's Foreign Mission Movement, 1869–1915," *Methodist History* 19, no. 3 (1981): 151; Kasson, *Rudeness and Civility*, 43–44.

81. Mrs. Otis Gibson, "Woman's Missionary Society of the Pacific Coast (Methodist Episcopal)," in *Historical Sketches of Woman's Missionary Societies in America and England* (Boston: Mrs. L. H. Daggett, 1879): 139.

82. James Eells, "The Chinese in America," *Presbyterian Review* 1 (April 1880): 254; William C. Pond, *Gospel Pioneering: Reminiscences of Early Congregationalism in California, 1833–1920* (Oberlin, Ohio: William C. Pond, 1921): 143.

83. Patricia R. Hill, *The World Their Household: The American Woman's Foreign Mission Movement and Cultural Transformation, 1870–1920* (Ann Arbor: University of Michigan Press, 1985): 3; Hill, "'Heathen Women's Friends,'" 152; Colegrove, *Among the Chinese*, 262.

84. California Branch, Woman's Foreign Missionary Society, *Annual Report*, 1876, 20–21 [hereafter CB-WFMS, *AR*]; Woman's Occidental Board of Foreign Missions, *Annual Report*, 1895, 58–59 [hereafter WOBFM, *AR*]; OB-WFMS, *AR*, 1878, 7; WOBFM, *AR*, 1896, 66; Mrs. E. V. Robbins, "Chinese Slave Girls: A Bit of History," *Overland Monthly* 51 (1908): 100; Gibson, *Chinese in America*, 206; *Alta California*, March 30, 1876; Mrs. Gibson, "Woman's Missionary Society of the Pacific Coast," 139; MEMS, *AR*, 1875, 150; OB-WFMS, *AR*, 1880, 7; MEMS, *AR*, 1880–81, 11, 22; Woman's Foreign Missionary Society of the Presbyterian Church, *Historical Sketches of the Mission Under the Care of the Board of Foreign Missions of the Presbyterian Church* (Philadelphia: Woman's Foreign Missionary Society of the Presbyterian Church, 1886): 261–62; OB-WFMS, *AR*, 1878, 7.

85. Colegrove, *Among the Chinese*, 10.

86. Victor Low, *The Unimpressible Race: A Century of Educational Struggle by the Chinese in San Francisco* (San Francisco: East/West, 1982): 33, 50; Hill, "'Heathen Women's Friends,'" 152; Janet Harbison Penfield, "Women in the Presbyterian Church—An Historical Overview," *Journal of Presbyterian History* 55, no. 2 (1977): 122.

87. *Alta California*, January 8, 1876; Bertha M. Stephenson, *A New Life for Ling Wang* (Cincinnati: Woman's Home Missionary Society, n.d.): 5–6.

88. *Alta California*, January 8, 1876; MEMS, *AR*, 1873, 168; OB-WFMS, *AR*, 1880, 7; OB-WFMS, *AR*, 1881, 11, 22.

89. "Chinese Characteristics," William Johnston to Rutherford B. Hayes, March 3, 1879, Rutherford B. Hayes Papers, RBH Collections, Rutherford B. Hayes Presidential Center, Fremont, Ohio.

90. OB-WFMS, *AR*, 1878, 8; MEMS, *AR*, 1873, 168; MEMS, *AR*, 1889, 13.

91. Nee and Nee, *Longtime Californ'*, 88.

92. Gibson, "Woman's Missionary of the Pacific Coast," 139; *Alta California*, May 27, 1870; OB-WFMS, *AR*, 1881, 26–28, 34–41.

93. Brummitt, *Looking Backward*, 96.

94. Daniel W. Howe, "American Victorianism as a Culture," *American Quarterly* 27 (December 1975): 526–28; MEMS, *AR*, 1883, 177; William Stewart Young, *William Stewart Young, 1859–1937: Builder of California Institutions: An Intimate Biography*, ed. Nellie Mary Young (Glendale, Calif.: Arthur H. Clark, 1967): 51.

95. OB-WFMS, *AR*, 1880, 28, 35.

96. CB-WFMS, *AR*, 1875, 19; Occidental Board (Woman's Foreign Missionary Society), *Annual Report*, 1883, 41 [hereafter OCB-WFMS, *AR*].

97. Robbins, "Chinese Slave Girls," 100; Brown, "'Lo Mo' of San Francisco," 265.

98. *Alta California*, May 27, 1870.

99. Colegrove, *Among the Chinese*, 9.

100. Mildred Crowl Martin, *Chinatown's Angry Angel: The Story of Donaldina Cameron* (Palo Alto, Calif.: Pacific Books, 1977): 44; Nee and Nee, *Longtime Californ'*, 88.

101. OB-WFMS, *AR*, 1878, 8; Logan, *Ventures in Mission*, 11–12.

102. MEMS, *AR*, 1880, 206.

103. Ibid. 1881, 256.

104. Ibid., 1882, 178.

105. J. G. Kerr, "Missions to Chinese in California," *Chinese Recorder* 10 (1879): 440.

106. MEMS, *AR*, 1880, 205.

107. Esther E. Baldwin, "Christian Work for Chinese in America," *Missionary Review* 34 (February 1911): 121.

108. Woo, "Protestant Work," 274.

109. MEMS, *AR*, 1881, 255–56.

110. *Occident*, September 6, 1876, 285; MEMS, *AR*, 1880, 177.

111. Anthony, *Fifty Years of Methodism*, 299.

112. Carol Green Wilson, *Chinatown Quest: The Life Adventures of Donaldina Cameron* (Stanford: Stanford University Press, 1950): 44; Nee, *Longtime Californ'*, 87–88.

113. Pascoe, *Relations of Rescue*, 161.

114. Data compiled from WFMS annual reports from 1873 to 1881 and MEMS annual reports from 1873 to 1882.

115. MEMS, *AR*, 1882, 177; Woo, "Protestant Work," 277, 264; OB-WFMS, *AR*, 1880, 7.

116. Presbyterian Church in the U.S.A., *Report of the Presbyterian Mission to the Chinese of California* (San Francisco: George Spaulding, 1881): 95; OB-WFMS, *AR*, 1878, 1–5; OB-WFMS, *AR*, 1880, 37; Loomis, "Chinese in California."

117. Manion, "Slave Women"; Robbins, "Chinese Slave Girls," 100; Arnold Genthe, *Old Chinatown: A*

Book of Pictures, with text by Will Irwin (New York: Mitchell Kennerley, 1913): 166.

118. *Alta California*, April 3, 1876; *San Francisco Chronicle*, March 3, 1871; Gibson, "Woman's Missionary Society of the Pacific Coast," 137.

119. Genthe, *Old Chinatown*, 166; Gibson, *Chinese in America*, 208.

Conclusion

1. Patricia Nelson Limerick, *The Legacy of Conquest: The Unbroken Past of the American West* (New York: W. W. Norton, 1987): 268.

2. Becker, *Course of Exclusion*, 71.

3. Egal Feldman, "Prostitution, the Alien Woman and the Progressive Imagination, 1910–1915," *American Quarterly* 19 (Summer 1967): 195.

4. G. B. Densmore, *Curious Lore of Chinatown* (San Francisco: Henry Evans, 1955): 6.

5. Wu, *Yellow Peril*, 48, 52, 53, 116, 186–90.

6. Ibid., 190–92.

7. Ling, *Between Worlds*, 11–12.

8. Caroll Cook to Chinese Consolidated Benevolent Association of San Francisco, July 21, 1911, Caroll Cook Collection, CU-AAS; Stan Steiner, *Fushang: The Chinese Who Built America* (New York: Harper & Row, 1979): 206, 208.

Bibliography

Primary Sources

ARCHIVAL COLLECTIONS

Angell, James B. Papers. Michigan Historical Collections, Bentley Library, University of Michigan, Ann Arbor.

Bancroft, Hubert Howe. Papers. Bancroft Collections, Bancroft Library, University of California, Berkeley [hereafter CU-B].

Bancroft Scraps: Pacific Mail Steamship Company and Ship Building, vol. 105. CU-B.

Chapman, Miner. Papers. Hoover Institution Archives, Stanford University, Stanford, California.

Combined Asian American Resource Project, San Francisco,California, 1977. Transcripts of interviews. Regional Oral History Office, CU-B.

Cook, Caroll. Papers. Asian American Library, University of California, Berkeley [hereafter CU-AAS].

Coon, Henry Perrin. "Annals of San Francisco." Autograph manuscript [hereafter AMs]. Bancroft Manuscript Collection, CU-B.

Crosby, Elisha Oscar. "Statement of Events in California as Related by Judge Elisha Oscar Crosby for Bancroft Library, 1878." AMs. Bancroft Manuscript Collection, CU-B.

Hayes, Rutherford B. Papers. Rutherford B. Hayes Collections, Rutherford B. Hayes Presidential Center, Fremont, Ohio.

Kellogg, Clarence W, Major, U.S. Army, Retired. "Early Day Family Life in California Mining Camps." Typewritten manuscript [hereafter TMs]. Bancroft Manuscript Collection, CU-B.

Loomis, Augustus Ward. Papers. CU-B.

Manion, John J. Papers. CU-B.

San Francisco (Calif.) Board of Supervisors. "The Official Chinatown Map: 1885." CU-B.

San Francisco Police Department. Chinese Criminal Photography Key: 1875–1878. San Francisco History Room, San Francisco Public Library, San Francisco, California.

"Sanborn Fire Insurance Maps of San Francisco: 1887." New York: Sanborn Map Publishing, 1890, no. 192. Library of Congress, Washington, D.C.

U.S. Treasury Department, Bureau of Narcotics. "Specialized Illegal Activities in Chinese Communities in the United States," Memorandum, TLS, August 16, 1945. CU-AAS.

FEDERAL, STATE, AND LOCAL GOVERNMENT PUBLICATIONS

Brandenburg, Edwin C., ed. *Official Opinions of the Attorneys-General of the United States.* Washington, D.C.: Government Printing Office, 1900.

California Bureau of Labor Statistics. *Third Biennial Report of the Bureau of Labor Statistics of the State* of California for the Years 1887–1888. Sacramento: State Printing Office, 1889.

California Department of Public Health. *First Biennial Report of the State Board of Health of California for the Years 1870 and 1871.* San Francisco: D. W. Gelwicks, 1871.

California Legislature. *Population Schedules of California, 1852: City and County of San Francisco.* Family History Department of the Church of Jesus Christ of Latter-Day Saints. Microfilm copy.

California Senate, Special Committee on Chinese Immigration. *Chinese Immigration: Its Social, Moral, and Political Effect.* Sacramento: State Printing Office, 1878.

California *Statutes,* 1866, 1870, 1880.

Canada, Royal Commission on Chinese Immigration. *Report and Evidence.* Ottawa: Printed by Order of the Commission, 1885.

Piper, William Adam. *Immigration of Chinese into the United States: Speech in the House of Representatives, May 18, 1876.* Washington, D.C.: Government Printing Office, 1876.

Richardson, James D., comp. *Messages and Papers of the Presidents, 1789–1897.* 11 vols. Washington, D.C.: Government Printing Office, 1907.

San Francisco (Calif.) Board of Supervisors. *Municipal Reports,* 1859–90. 31 vols.

San Francisco. *San Francisco Ordinances, etc., the General Orders of the Board of Supervisors, Providing Regulations for the Government of the City and County of San Francisco and the Ordinances of the Park Commission.* San Francisco: W. M. Hinton, 1878.

United States. *Statutes at Large,* 1875.

U.S. Bureau of the Census. *Eighth Census of the United States: 1860.* 3 vols., compendium. Washington, D.C.: Government Printing Office, 1864.

_____. Eighth Census of the United States, 1860. *Population Schedules, San Francisco.* Washington, D.C.:

National Archives and Records Services. M-683, reel 67–68.

————. *Ninth Census of the United States: 1870.* 3 vols., compendium. Washington, D.C.: Government Printing Office, 1872.

————. Ninth Census of the United States, 1870. *Population Schedules, San Francisco.* Washington, D.C.: National Archives and Records Services. M-593, reel 79–85.

————. *Tenth Census of the United States: 1880.* 22 vols., compendium. Washington, D.C.: Government Printing Office, 1883.

————. Tenth Census of the United States, 1880. *Population Schedules, San Francisco.* Washington, D.C.: National Archives and Records Services. T-9, reel 72–79.

————. *Compendium of the Eleventh Census of the United States: 1890.* 3 vols. Washington, D.C.: Government Printing Office, 1892.

————. *The Social Statistics of Cities.* 2 vols. Washington, D.C.: Government Printing Office, 1886; repr., New York: Arno Press, 1970.

U.S. Congress. *Congressional Record,* 1876–78.

————. House. "Chinese Immigration." *House Report Document 62.* 45th Cong., 3d sess. (Serial 1866).

————. "Chinese Immigration." *House Report Document 240.* 45th Cong., 2d sess. (Serial 1822).

————. "The Consulate at Hong Kong." *House Report Executive Document 20.* 46th Cong., 2d sess. (Serial 1913).

————. "Expatriation and Slavery in China." *House Report Document 60.* 46th Cong., 2d sess. (Serial 1925).

————. "Foreign Relations: China." *House Report Executive Document 1,* 42d Cong., 2d sess. (Serial 1502).

————. "Investigation of Causes of General Depression in Labor and Business; and Chinese Immigration." *House Miscellaneous Document 5.* 46th Cong., 2d sess. (Serial 1928).

_____. Senate. "Argument of Joseph C. G. Kennedy Adverse to Legislation by Congress." *Senate Miscellaneous Document 36.* 45th Cong., 2d sess. (Serial 1786).

_____. "Chinese Exclusion." *Senate Report 776.* 52d Cong., 1st sess. (Serial 4265).

_____. "Chinese Immigration." *Senate Report 689.* 44th Cong., 1st sess. (Serial 1734).

_____. "Federal Census — Territory of New Mexico and Territory of Arizona." *Senate Executive Document 13.* 89th Cong., 1st sess. (Serial 12668–1).

_____. "Importation of Chinese Coolies." *Senate Executive Document 116.* 41st Cong., 2d sess. (Serial 1407).

_____. "Memorial of the Anti-Coolie and Anti-Monopoly Association of San Francisco, California." *Senate Report Miscellaneous Document 34.* 41st Cong., 2d sess. (Serial 1408).

U.S. Department of State. *Diplomatic Instructions of the Department of State, 1801–1906: China.* Washington, D.C.: National Archives and Records Services. M-77, reel 38–40.

_____. *Dispatches from Consuls in Hong Kong, 1873–1881.* Washington, D.C.: National Archives and Records Services. M-92, reel 10–14.

_____. *Dispatches from Consuls in Tientsin, 1868–1906.* Washington, D.C.: National Archives and Records Services, M-92, reel 1–2.

U.S. Department of the Treasury. *Letters Received by the Secretary of the Treasury from Collectors of Customs, 1833–1869.* Washington, D.C.: National Archives and Records Services. M-174, reels 206, 214, 219.

Wines, Frederick Howes. *Report on the Dependent, and Delinquent Classes of the Population of the United States as Returned at the Tenth Census, June 1, 1880.* Washington, D.C.: Government Printing Office, 1880.

Wright, Caroll. *Fourth Annual Report of the Commis-*

sioner of Labor, 1888: Working Women in Cities. Washington, D.C.: Government Printing Office, 1889.

ANNUAL REPORTS OF MISSIONARY ORGANIZATIONS
American Baptist Home Mission Society. *Annual Report,* 1833–1920. Roberts Library, Southwestern Baptist Theological Seminary, Fort Worth, Texas [hereafter SBTS-RL].
California Chinese Mission (American Missionary Association). *Annual Report,* 1875–1906. CU-B.
Methodist Episcopal Church. Missionary Society. *Annual Report,* 1871–1907. Bridwell Library, Southern Methodist University, Dallas, Texas [hereafter SMU-BL].
————. Woman's Missionary Society of the Pacific Coast. *Annual Report,* 1883–84. SMU-BL.
Presbyterian Church in the U.S.A. California Branch (Woman's Foreign Missionary Society). *Annual Report,* 1874–76. CU-B.
————. Occidental Board (Woman's Foreign Missionary Society). *Annual Report,* 1882–88. CU-B.
————. Occidental Branch (Woman's Foreign Missionary Society). *Annual Report,* 1877–81. CU-B.
————. *Report of the Presbyterian Mission to the Chinese of California.* San Francisco: George Spaulding, 1881.
————. Woman's Occidental Board of Foreign Missions. *Annual Report,* 1889–1900. CU-B.
Southern Baptist Convention. *Proceedings,* 1854–84. SBTS-RL.
Woman's Baptist Home Mission Society. *Annual Report,* 1879–1900. SBTS-RL.
Woman's Union Mission to Chinese Women and Children. *Annual Report,* 1880, 1883, 1888. CU-B.

ARTICLES
Baldwin, Esther E. "Christian Work for Chinese in America." *Missionary Review* 34 (February 1911): 121–23.

BIBLIOGRAPHY

"The Celestials at Home and Abroad." *Littell's Living Age*, 14 August 1852, 289–98.

"The Chinese in San Francisco," *Daily Evening Picayune*, June 4, 1851, reprinted in *San Francisco as It Is: Gleanings from the Picayune*, ed. Kenneth M. Johnson (Georgetown, Calif.: Talisman Press, 1984): 145–46.

Edholm, M. G. C. "A Stain on the Flag." *Californian* (February 1892): 159–70.

Eells, James. "The Chinese in America." *Presbyterian Review* 1 (April 1880): 247–67.

"The Foul Contagious Disease" (editorial). *Medico-Literary Journal* 1 (November 1878): 1–6.

Gibson, Mrs. Otis. "Woman's Missionary Society of the Pacific Coast (Methodist Episcopal)." In *Historical Sketches of Woman's Missionary Societies in America and England*, 136–41. Boston: Mrs. L. H. Daggett, 1879.

Holder, Charles Frederick. "Chinese Slavery in America." *North American Review* 165 (1897): 288–94.

Kerr, J. G. "Missions to Chinese in California." *Chinese Recorder* 10 (1879): 433–44.

Kip, William Ingram. "The Chinese in California." *Spirit of Missions* 20 (March 1855): 85–90.

Lee Chew. "Life Story of a Chinaman." In *The Life Stories of Undistinguished Americans as Told by Themselves*, ed. Hamilton Holt, 284–99. New York: James Pott, 1906.

"Letter of the Chinamen to His Excellency, Gov. Bigler," San Francisco, 28 April 1852. Reprinted in *Littell's Living Age*, 3 July 1852, 32–34.

Loomis, A. W. "Chinese in California: Their Signboard Literature." *Overland Monthly* 1 (August 1868): 152–56.

———. "Chinese Women in California." *Overland Monthly* 2 (April 1869): 344–51.

———. "How Our Chinamen Are Employed." *Overland Monthly* 2 (March 1869): 232–40.

BIBLIOGRAPHY

_____. "Medical Art in the Chinese Quarter." *Overland Monthly* 2 (June 1869): 496–506.

_____. "The Six Chinese Companies." *Overland Monthly* 1 (October 1868): 360–67.

Robbins, Mrs. E. V. "Chinese Slave Girls: A Bit of History." *Overland Monthly* 51 (1908): 100–102.

Scheffaner, Herman. "The Old Chinese Quarter." *Living Age*, 10 August 1907, 359–66.

Shepherd, Charles R. "Chinese Girl Slavery in America." *Missionary Review* 46 (1923): 893–98.

Sieh Fu-ching. "Chinese Emigrants Abroad." *China Review* 21 (1894–95): 138–41.

Tisdale, William M. "Chinese Physicians in California." *Lippincott's Magazine* 63 (March 1899): 411–16.

Vivian, Thomas J. "John Chinaman in San Francisco." *Scribner's Monthly* 12 (October 1876): 862–72.

BOOKS AND PAMPHLETS

Acton, William. *Prostitution: Considered in Its Moral, Social and Sanitary Aspects in London and Other Garrison Towns.* London: John Churchill & Sons, 1870.

American Federation of Labor. *Some Reasons for Chinese Exclusion: Meat vs. Rice; American Manhood Against Asiatic Coolieism: Which Shall Survive?* Washington, D.C.: American Federation of Labor, 1901.

Anthony, Charles V. *Fifty Years of Methodism: A History of the Methodist Episcopal Church, Within the Bounds of the California Annual Conference from 1847–1897.* San Francisco: Methodist Book Concern, 1901.

Baldwin, Esther Jerman. *Must the Chinese Go? An Examination of the Chinese Question.* Boston: Rand, Avery, 1886.

Bancroft, Hubert Howe. The *Works of Hubert Howe Bancroft.* Vol. 36, *Popular Tribunals.* San Francisco: History Publishers, 1887.

Bee, Frederick A. *Opening Argument of F. A. Bee Before*

the Joint Committee of the Houses of Congress on Chinese Immigration. San Francisco: n.p., 1876.

_____. *The Other Side of the Chinese Question.* San Francisco, 1886; repr., San Francisco: R & E Research Associates, 1971.

Brooks, Benjamin S. *Appendix to the Opening Statement and Brief of B. S. Brooks on the Chinese Question.* San Francisco: Women's Cooperative Printing Union, 1877.

Brummitt, Stella Wyatt. *Looking Backward, Thinking Forward: The Jubilee History of the Woman's Home Missionary Society of the Methodist Episcopal Church.* Cincinnati: Woman's Home Missionary Society, 1930.

Buel, James W. *Metropolitan Life Unveiled.* San Francisco: A. L. Bancroft, 1882.

California Chinese Exclusion Convention. *Proceedings and Lists of Delegates, California Chinese Exclusion Convention Held at Metropolitan Temple, San Francisco, November 21 and 22, 1901.* San Francisco: Star Press, 1901.

Capron, E. S. *History of California from Its Discovery to the Present Time.* Boston: John P. Jewett, 1854.

The Chinese Hospital of San Francisco. Oakland: Carruth & Carruth, 1899.

Colegrove, C. P. *Among the Chinese.* Cincinnati: Woman's Home Missionary Society, n.d.

Communication from the Mechanics State Council of California in Relation to Chinese Immigration to the Honorable Legislature of the State of California. San Francisco: D. W. Gelwicks, n.d.

Condit, Ira M. *The Chinaman as We See Him and Fifty Years of Work for Him.* Chicago: Fleming H. Revell, 1900.

Confucius. *The Analects of Confucius,* trans. Arthur Waley. London: George Allen & Unwin, 1964.

Cooper, Elizabeth. *My Lady of the Chinese Courtyard.* New York: Frederick A. Stokes, 1914.

Densmore, G. B. *The Chinese in California: Description*

of *Chinese Life in San Francisco, Their Habits, Morals and Manners*. San Francisco: Petitt & Russ, 1890.

————. *Curious Lore of Chinatown*. San Francisco: Henry Evans, 1955.

Evans, Albert S. *A la California: Sketches of Life in the Golden State*. San Francisco: A. L. Bancroft, 1874.

Farwell, Willard B. *The Chinese at Home and Abroad*. San Francisco: A. L. Bancroft, 1885.

Genthe, Arnold. *Old Chinatown: A Book of Pictures*. With text by Will Irwin. New York: Mitchell Kennerley, 1913.

Gibson, Otis. *The Chinese in America*. Cincinnati: Hitchcock & Walden, 1877.

Hardy, Mary. *Through Cities and Prairie Lands*. New York: R. Worthington, 1881; repr., New York: Arno Press, 1974.

Hittell, John Shertzer. *A History of the City of San Francisco and Incidentally of the State of California*. San Francisco: A. L. Bancroft, 1878.

Lai Chun Chuen. *Remarks of the Chinese Merchants of San Francisco upon Governor Bigley's Messages, and Some Common Objections with Some Explanations of the Character of the Chinese Companies and the Laboring Class in California*. San Francisco: Whitton, Towne, 1855.

Layres, Augustus. *Facts upon the Other Side of the Chinese Question with a Memorial to the President of the United States from Representative Chinamen in America*. San Francisco: n.p., 1876.

Lloyd, Benjamine E. *Lights and Shades in San Francisco*. San Francisco: A. L. Bancroft, 1876.

Pond, William C. *Gospel Pioneering: Reminiscences of Early Congregationalism in California, 1833–1920*. Orbelin, Ohio: William C. Pond, 1921.

Riis, Jacob. *How the Other Half Lives*. New York, 1890; repr., New York: Hill & Wang, 1957.

Shepherd, Charles R. *The Ways of Ah Sin: A Composite*

Narrative of Things as They Are. New York: Fleming H. Revell, 1923.

Social Science Institute. *Orientals and Their Cultural Adjustment.* Nashville: Fisk University, 1946.

Soulé, Frank, John H. Gibon, and James Nisbet. *The Annals of San Francisco.* New York: D. Appleton, 1854.

Wicher, Edward A. *The Presbyterian Church in California, 1849–1927.* New York: Frederick H. Hitchcock, 1927.

Woman's Foreign Missionary Society of the Presbyterian Church. *Historical Sketches of the Mission Under the Care of the Board of Foreign Missions of the Presbyterian Church.* Philadelphia: Woman's Foreign Missionary Society of the Presbyterian Church, 1886.

Workingmen's Party of California. *Chinatown Declared a Nuisance!* San Francisco: Workingmen's Party of California, 1880.

Young, John. *San Francisco: A History of the Pacific Coast Metropolis.* 2 vols. San Francisco: S. J. Clarke Publishing, 1912.

JOURNALS AND MEMOIRS

Bates, D. B. *Incidents on Land and Water.* Boston: James French, 1857.

Benard de Russailh, Albert. *Last Adventure.* Translated by Clarkson Crane. San Francisco: Westgate, 1931.

Borthwick, J. D. *Three Years in California, 1851–1854.* Edinburgh: Blackwood & Sons, 1857.

Buffum, Edward Gould. *Six Months in the Gold Mines.* Philadelphia: C. Sherman, 1850; repr., Ann Arbor: UMI Microfilms, 1966.

Chao Buwei. *Autobiography of a Chinese Woman.* Westport, Conn.: Greenwood Press, 1974.

Chun Ho. Interview in *Makers of America — Natives and Aliens, 1894–1903,* ed. Wayne Moquin, 115–20. New York: William Benton, 1971.

Clark, Walter Van Tilburg, ed. *The Journals of Alfred Doten, 1849–1903.* 3 vols. Reno: University of Nevada Press, 1973.

Cone, Mary. *Two Years in California.* Chicago: S. C. Griggs, 1876.

Dalls, Carolina H. *My First Holiday; or, Letters Home.* Boston: Roberts Bros., 1981.

Ellis, Henry Hiram. *From the Kennebec to California: Reminiscences of a California Pioneer,* ed. Laurence R. Cook. Los Angeles: Warren F. Louis, 1959.

Huie Kin. *Reminiscences.* Peiping: San Yu Press, 1909.

Kemble, John H. "Andrew Wilson's Jottings on Civil War in California." *California Historical Society Quarterly* 32, nos. 2 and 3 (September and December 1953): 209–24, 303–12.

Leslie, Myriam F. *California: A Pleasure Trip from Gotham to the Golden Gate.* New York: C. W. Carleton, 1877. Selection reprinted in *Let Them Speak for Themselves: Women in the American West, 1849–1900,* ed. Christiane Fischer. Hamden, Conn.: Archon Books, 1977.

MacGregor, William Laird. *San Francisco, California in 1876.* Edinburgh: T. Laurie, 1876.

Martin, William Alexander Parsons. *Cycle of Cathay; or China, South and North, with Personal Reminiscences.* New York: Fleming H. Revell, 1896.

Mother Teng [pseud.]. "Life History." In *The Sandalwood Mountains: Readings and Stories of the Early Chinese in Hawaii,* ed. Tin-Yuke Char, 247–53. Honolulu: University of Hawaii Press, 1975.

Ning Lao T'ai-t'ai. *A Daughter of Han: The Autobiography of a Chinese Working Woman,* ed. Ida Pruitt. Stanford: Stanford University Press, 1945.

Rose [pseud.]. "Experiences of 'Rose' — A Slave Girl." In Social Science Institute, *Orientals and Their Cultural Adjustment,* 36–38. Nashville: Fisk University, 1946.

Twain, Mark. *Mark Twain's San Francisco,* ed. Bernard Taper. New York: McGraw-Hill, 1963.

Williams, Harry T., ed. *Hayes: The Diary of a President, 1875–1881.* New York: D. McKay, 1964.

Wong Ah So. "Letter from Wong Ah So to Her Mother." In Social Science Institute, *Orientals and Their Cultural Adjustment,* 34–35. Nashville: Fisk University, 1946.

———. "Story of Wong Ah So — Experiences as a Prostitute." In Social Science Institute, *Orientals and Their Cultural Adjustment,* 31–33. Nashville: Fisk University, 1946.

Wong, Elizabeth. "Leaves from the Life History of a Chinese Immigrant." *Social Process in Hawaii* 2 (1936): 39–42.

Wu Ting-fang. *America Through the Spectacles of an Oriental Diplomat.* New York: Frederick A. Stokes, 1914.

Yan Phou Lee. *When I Was a Boy in China.* Boston: D. Lothrop, 1887.

Young, William Stewart. *William Stewart Young, 1859–1937: Builder of California Institutions: An Intimate Biography,* ed. Nellie Mary Young. Glendale, Calif.: Arthur H. Clark, 1967.

LITERARY WORKS

"The Bitter Society: *Kushehui,* a translation, Chapters 37–46." Translated by June Mei and Jean Pang Yip with Russell Leong. *Amerasia Journal* 8, no. 1 (1981): 33–67.

Dexter, Peter. *Deadwood.* New York: Random House, 1986.

Eaton, Edith [Sui Sin Far, pseud.]. *Mrs. Spring Fragrance.* Chicago: A. L. McClurg, 1912.

Hom, Marlon K., ed. and trans. "A *Muk-yu* from Gold Mountain." In *Chinese America: History and Perspectives 1989,* 15–41. San Francisco: Chinese Historical Society of America, 1989.

———, ed. and trans. *Songs of Gold Mountain: Cantonese Rhymes from San Francisco Chinatown.* Berkeley: University of California Press, 1987.

McCunn, Ruthanne Lum. *Thousand Pieces of Gold*. San Francisco: Design Enterprises, 1981.

Norris, Frank. "The Third Circle." In *The Third Circle, A Deal in Wheat, and Other Stories of the New and Old West*. Garden City, N.Y.: Doubleday, Doran, 1928.

Stephenson, Bertha M. *A New Life for Ling Wang*. Cincinnati: Woman's Home Missionary Society, n.d.

Van Etten, Ida M. "The House of Dragons." *Cosmopolitan* (March 1893): 615–25.

MISCELLANEOUS

"Chinese Classified Business Directory." In *D. M. Bishop Annual Directory of the City and County of San Francisco for 1877*, 1426–1431. San Francisco: B. C. Vandall, 1877.

Dressler, Albert, ed. *California Chinese Chatter*. San Francisco: Albert Dressler, 1927.

Humphery, William P. *San Francisco Map*. San Francisco: Britton & Ray, 1870.

Imperial Maritime Customs, Treaties, Conventions, etc., Between China and Foreign States. 3 vols. Shanghai: Statistical Department of the Inspectorate General of Customs, 1905.

Langley, H. G., comp. *The San Francisco Directory for the Year, 1852–1853*. San Francisco: James M. Parker, 1852.

————. *The San Francisco Directory for the Year* (1867–1881). 15 vols. San Francisco: H. G. Langley.

Pacific Union Express Company. *Address of Principal Chinese Merchants of San Francisco, in Chinese and English, for the Guidance of Our Agents in Addressing Letters, for 1868 and 1869*. Reprinted in Gladys C. Hansen, *The Chinese in California: A Brief Bibliographic History*, frontispiece. Portland, Oreg.: R. Abel, 1970.

Parker, J. M. *The San Francisco Directory for the Year 1852–1853, Embracing a General Directory of Citi-*

zens, a *Street Directory*. San Francisco: J. M. Parker, 1852.

Rasmussen, Louis J., comp. *San Francisco Ship Passenger Lists*. 5 vols. Colma, Calif.: San Francisco Historic Records, 1965.

"Sanborn Fire Insurance Maps of Phoenix, 1889." New York: Sanborn Map Publishing, 1890; repr., Palo Alto, Calif.: Vladshurkin, 1982.

"Sanborn Fire Insurance Maps of Tombstone, 1883." New York: Sanborn Map Publishing, 1890; repr., Palo Alto, Calif.: Vladshurkin, 1982.

Wells Fargo & Company's Express. *Directory of Chinese Business Houses*. San Francisco: Britton & Ray, 1878.

————. *Directory of Chinese Merchants in San Francisco and Sacramento*. San Francisco: Britton & Ray, 1873.

Wong Sam, and Assistants. *An English-Chinese Phrase Book*. San Francisco: Cubery, 1875.

NEWSPAPERS
Alta California, 1851–54, 1860–79.
California Police Gazette, 1858–59, 1866–69, 1874–75.
Daily Evening Bulletin, 1864–67, 1871–80.
Daily Morning Chronicle, 1868–69.
Evening Post, 1876–79.
Morning Call, 1869–71, 1877–79.
Occident, 1876–77.
The Oriental/Tung Ngai San Luk, 1855–56.
San Francisco Chronicle, 1868–73, 1878–79.
San Francisco Examiner, 1887–88.

Secondary Sources

DISSERTATIONS AND THESES
Barnhart, Jacqueline Baker. "Working Women: Prostitution in San Francisco from the Gold Rush to 1900."

Ph.D. diss., University of California, Santa Cruz, 1976.

Chen Chang-fang. "Barbarian Paradise: Chinese Views of the United States, 1784–1911." Ph.D. diss., Indiana University, 1985.

Chih, Ginger. "Immigration of Chinese Women to the United States, 1900–1940." M.A. thesis, Sarah Lawrence College, 1977.

Gardner, John Berdan. "The Image of the Chinese in the United States." Ph.D. diss., University of Pennsylvania, 1961.

Gonzales, Deena J. "The Spanish-Mexican Women of Santa Fe: Patterns of Their Resistance and Accommodation, 1820–1880." Ph.D. diss., University of California, Berkeley, 1985.

Locke, Mary Lou. "'Like a Machine or an Animal': Working Women of the Late Nineteenth-Century Urban Far West, in San Francisco, Portland, and Los Angeles." Ph.D. diss., University of California, San Diego, 1982.

Peffer, George Anthony. "Forbidden Families." M.A. thesis, San Francisco State University, 1981.

St. Laurence, Ronald A. "The Myth and the Reality: Prostitution in San Francisco, 1880–1913." M.A. thesis, California State University, Hayward, 1974.

Siu, Paul C. P. "The Chinese Laundryman: A Study of Social Isolation." Ph.D. diss., University of Chicago, 1953.

Wen Djang-chu. "The Background of the Chinese Immigration into the United States." M.A. thesis, University of Washington, 1949.

Wiley, James Hundley. "A Study of Chinese Prostitution." M.A. thesis, University of Chicago, 1928.

Woo, Wesley S. "Protestant Work Among the Chinese in San Francisco Bay Area, 1850–1920." Ph.D. diss., Graduate Theological Union, University of California, Berkeley, 1983.

Yip, Christopher Lee. "San Francisco's Chinatown: An

Architectural and Urban History." Ph.D. diss., University of California, Berkeley, 1985.

Zo Kil Young. "Chinese Immigration into the United States, 1850–1880." Ph.D. diss., Columbia University, 1971.

ARTICLES

Ahern, Emily. "The Power and Pollution of Chinese Women." In *Women in Chinese Society*, eds. Margery Wolf and Roxane Witke, 193–214. Stanford: Stanford University Press, 1975.

Anderson, Harry N. "Deadwood, South Dakota: An Effort at Stability." *Montana: The Magazine of Western History* 20 (January 1970): 40–47.

Armentrout-Ma, Eve L. "Big and Medium Businesses of Chinese Emigrants to the United States, 1850–1890: An Outline." *Bulletin of the Chinese Historical Society of America* 13 (September 1978): 1–5.

———. "Urban Chinese at the Sinetic Frontier: Social Organizations in United States' Chinatowns, 1849–1898." *Modern Asian Studies* 17, no. 1 (1983): 107–35.

Auerbach, Alvin. "San Francisco's South of Market District, 1850–1950: The Emergence of a Skid Row." *California Historical Quarterly* 52 (Fall 1973): 192–223.

Beesley, David. "From Chinese to Chinese American: Chinese Women and Families in a Sierra Nevada County." *California History* 67 (September 1988): 168–79.

Best, Joel. "Keeping the Peace in St. Paul: Crime, Vice, and Police Work, 1869–1874." *Minnesota History* 47 (Summer 1981): 240–48.

Blackburn, George M., and Sherman L. Ricards. "The Chinese of Virginia City, Nevada: 1870." *Amerasia Journal* 7, no. 1 (1980): 51–71.

———. "The Prostitutes and Gamblers of Virginia City, Nevada: 1870." *Pacific Historical Review* 38 (May 1979): 239–58.

Blackwelder, Julia Kirk. "Crime, Policing, and the Dangerous Classes." *Journal of Urban History* 10 (May 1984): 329–37.

Brown, Rev. Arthur J. "'Lo Mo' of San Francisco: Donaldina Cameron and Her Work for the Rescue of Chinese Girls." *Missionary Review* 55 (May 1932): 263–66.

Brown, Richard Maxwell. "Western Violence: Structure, Values, Myth." *Western Historical Quarterly* 24 (February 1993): 5–20.

Butler, Anne M. "Still in Chains: Black Women in Western Prisons, 1865–1910." *Western Historical Quarterly* 20 (February 1989): 18–35.

Caldwell, Dan. "The Negroization of the Chinese Stereotype in California." *Southern California Quarterly* 53 (June 1971): 123–31.

Carranco, Lynwood. "Chinese Expulsion from Humboldt County." *Pacific Historical Review* 30 (November 1961): 329–40.

Carter, Gregg Lee. "Social Demography of the Chinese in Nevada, 1870–1880." *Nevada Historical Society Quarterly* 18 (Summer 1975): 73–89.

Chan, Loren B. "The Chinese in Nevada: An Historical Survey, 1856–1970." *Nevada Historical Society Quarterly* 25 (Winter 1982): 266–314.

Chan, Sucheng. "The Exclusion of Chinese Women, 1870–1943." In *Entry Denied: Exclusion and the Chinese Community in America, 1882–1943*, ed. Sucheng Chan, 94–146. Philadelphia: Temple University Press, 1991.

Choy, Phillip. "Golden Mountain of Lead: The Chinese Experience in California." *California Historical Quarterly* 50 (June 1971): 267–76.

Conk, Margo Anderson. "Occupational Classification in the United States Census, 1870–1940." *Journal of Interdisciplinary History* 9 (Summer 1978): 111–30.

Conway, Jill. "Women Reformers and American Culture, 1870–1930." *Journal of Social History* 5 (Winter 1971/72): 164–77.

Corbett, P. Scott, and Nancy Parker Corbett. "The Chinese in Oregon, c. 1870–1880." *Oregon Historical Society* 78, no. 1 (1977): 73–85.

Cott, Nancy. "Passionlessness: An Interpretation of Victorian Sexual Ideology, 1790–1850." *Signs* 4 (Winter 1978): 219–36.

Davis, W. N. "Research Uses of County Court Records, 1850–1879: and Incidental Intimate Glimpses of California Life and Society, Part 1." *California Historical Quarterly* 52 (Fall 1973): 241–66.

Davis-Friedmann, Deborah. "Village Wives." In *Lives: Chinese Working Women*, eds. Mary E. Sheridan and Janet W. Salaff, 71–75. Bloomington: Indiana University Press, 1984.

de Graaf, Lawrence B. "Race, Sex, and Region: Black Women in in the American West, 1850–1920." *Pacific Historical Review* 49 (May 1980): 285–313.

Dong, Lorraine, and Marlon K. Hom. "Defiance or Perpetuation: An Analysis of Characters in *Mrs. Spring Fragrance*." In *Chinese America: History and Perspectives 1987*, 139–68. San Francisco: Chinese Historical Society of America, 1987.

Dufault, David. "The Chinese in the Mining Camps of California, 1848–1870." *Historical Society of Southern California Quarterly* 41 (June 1959): 155–70.

Elliott, J. F. "The Great Western: Sarah Bowman, Mother and Mistress to the U.S. Army." *Journal of Arizona History* 30 (Spring 1989): 1–26.

Eun Sik Yang. "Korean Women of America: From Subordination to Partnership, 1903–1930." *Amerasia Journal* 11, no. 2 (1984): 1–28.

Feldman, Egal. "Prostitution, the Alien Woman and the Progressive Imagination, 1910–1915." *American Quarterly* 19 (Summer 1967): 192–206.

Fischer, Christiane. "Women in California in the Early 1850s." *Southern California Quarterly* 60 (Fall 1978): 231–53.

Fong, Lawrence Michael. "Sojourners and Settlers: The

Chinese Experience in Arizona." *Journal of Arizona History* 21 (Autumn 1980): 227–56.

Frederick, Theodore N. "Politics, the Police, and Arresting Policies in Salem, Massachusetts, and the Civil War." *Social Problems* 19 (Spring 1972): 572–88.

Freedman, Maurice. "The Family in China, Past and Present." *Pacific Affairs* 34 (Winter 1961/62): 323–36.

Fritz, Christian G. "Bitter Strength (*k'u-1i*) and the Constitution: the Chinese Before the Federal Courts in California." *Historical Reporter* 1 (Autumn 1980): 2–3, 8–15.

————. "Due Process, Treaty Rights, and Chinese Exclusion, 1882–1891." In *Entry Denied: Exclusion and the Chinese Community in America, 1882–1943*, ed. Sucheng Chan, 25–56. Philadelphia: Temple University Press, 1991.

Gilfoyle, Timothy J. "The Urban Geography of Commercial Sex: Prostitution in New York City, 1790–1860." *Journal of Urban History* 13 (August 1987): 371–93.

Glenn, Evelyn Nakano. "Split Household, Small Producer, and Dual Wage Earner: An Analysis of Chinese-American Family Strategies." *Journal of Marriage and Family* 45 (February 1983): 35–46.

Goldman, Marion. "Prostitution and Virtue in Nevada." *Society* 10 (November 1972): 32–38.

Graff, Harvey J. "'Pauperism, Misery, and Vice': Illiteracy and Criminality in the Nineteenth Century." *Journal of Social History* 11 (Winter 1977): 245–68.

Graulich, Melody. "Violence Against Women: Power Dynamics in Literature of the Western Family." In *The Women's West*, eds. Susan Armitage and Elizabeth Jameson, 111–25. Norman: University of Oklahoma Press, 1987.

Haller, John S., and Robbin M. Haller. "Sex in Victorian America." In *The Social Fabric: American Life from the Civil War to the Present*, eds. John H. Cary, Julius Weinberg, and Thomas L. Hartshorne, 87–103. Glenview, Ill.: Scott, Foresman, 1987.

Hammack, David. "Problems of Power in the Historical Study of Cities, 1800–1960." *American Historical Review* 83 (April 1978): 323–49.

Hill, Patricia. "'Heathen Women's Friends': The Role of the Methodist Episcopal Women in the Women's Foreign Mission Movement, 1869–1915." *Methodist History* 19, no. 3 (1981): 146–54.

Hirata, Lucie Cheng. "Chinese Immigrant Women in Nineteenth-Century California." In *Women of America*, eds. Carol Ruth Berkins and Mary Beth Norton, 224–44. Boston: Houghton Mifflin, 1979.

————. "Free, Indentured, Enslaved: Chinese Prostitutes in Nineteenth-Century America." *Signs* 5 (Autumn 1979): 3–29.

Holmes, Kay A. "Reflections by Gaslight: Prostitution in Another Age." *Issues in Criminology* 7 (Winter 1972): 83–101.

Hom, Marlon K. "Chinatown High Life: A Literary Pride." In *Chinese America: History and Perspectives 1988*, 108–30. San Francisco: Chinese Historical Society of America, 1988.

Hori, Joan. "Japanese Prostitution in Hawaii During the Immigration Period." *Hawaiian Journal of History* 15 (1980): 113–24.

Howe, Daniel W. "American Victorianism as a Culture." *American Quarterly* 27 (December 1975): 507–32.

Hoy, William J. "Chinatown Devises Its Own Street Names." *California Folklore Quarterly* 2 (April 1943): 71–75.

Hune, Shirley. "Politics of Chinese Exclusion: Legislative-Executive Conflict, 1876–1882." *Amerasia Journal* 9, no. 1 (1982): 5–27.

Ichioka, Yuji. "*Ameyuki-san*: Japanese Prostitutes in Nineteenth-Century America." *Amerasia Journal* 4, no. 1 (1977): 1–21.

Jameson, Elizabeth. "Women as Workers, Women as Civilizers: True Womanhood in the American West." In *The Women's West*, eds. Susan Armitage and Elizabeth Jameson, 145–64. Norman: University of Oklahoma Press, 1987.

Johnston, Susan L. "Sharing Bed and Board: Cohabitation and Cultural Difference in Central Arizona Mining Towns, 1863–1873." In *The Women's West*, eds. Susan Armitage and Elizabeth Jameson, 77–91. Norman: University of Oklahoma Press, 1987.

Kushner, Howard I. "Nineteenth-Century Sexuality and the 'Sexual Revolution' of the Progressive Era." *Canadian Review of American Studies* 9 (Spring 1978): 34–45.

Lai, Him Mark. "The Guangdong Historical Background, with Emphasis on the Development of the Pearl River Delta Region." In *Chinese America: History and Perspectives, 1991*, 75–99. San Francisco: Chinese Historical Society of America, 1991.

———. "Historical Development of the Chinese Consolidated Benevolent Association/*Huiguan* System." In *Chinese America: History and Perspectives, 1987*, 13–51. San Francisco: Chinese Historical Society of America, 1987.

LeCompte, Janet. "La Tules and the Americans." *Arizona and the West* 20 (Autumn 1978): 215–30.

Lee, Douglas W. "Sacred Cows and Paper Tigers: Politics in Chinese America, 1880–1900." In *Annals of the Chinese Historical Society of the Pacific Northwest*, ed. Douglas W. Lee, 86–103. Seattle: Chinese Historical Society of the Pacific Northwest, 1983.

Lee, Robert G. "The Origins of Chinese Immigration to the United States, 1848–1882." In *The Life, Influence, and the Role of the Chinese in the United States, 1776–1960*, 183–93. San Francisco: Chinese Historical Society of America, 1976.

Lee, Rose Hum. "Social Institutions of a Rocky Mountain Chinatown." *Social Forces* 27 (October 1948): 1–11.

Light, Ivan. "The Ethnic Vice Industry, 1880–1944." *American Sociological Review* 38 (May 1979): 464–79.

————. "From Vice District to Tourist Attraction: The Moral Career of American Chinatowns, 1880–1940." *Pacific Historical Review* 43 (August 1974): 367–94.

Lomax, Elizabeth. "Infantile Syphilis as an Example of Nineteenth-Century Belief in the Inheritance of Acquired Characteristics." *Journal of the History of Medicine and Allied Sciences* 34 (January 1979): 23–39.

Lubove, Roy. "The Progressives and the Prostitute." *Historian* 24 (May 1962): 308–30.

Lyman, Stanford M. "The Chinese Diaspora in America, 1850–1943." In *The Life, Influence, and the Role of the Chinese in the United States, 1776–1960*, 128–46. San Francisco: Chinese Historical Society of America, 1976.

————. "Conflict and the Web of Group Affiliation in San Francisco's Chinatown, 1850–1910." *Pacific Historical Review* 43 (November 1974): 473–99.

————. "Marriage and the Family Among Chinese Immigrants to America, 1850–1960." *Phylon* 29 (Winter 1968): 321–30.

————. "Red Guard on Grant Avenue: The Rise of Youthful Rebellion in Chinatown." In *Asian Americans: Psychological Perspectives*, eds. Stanley Sue and Nathaniel N. Wagner, 20–44. Ben Lomond, Calif.: Science and Behavior Books, 1973.

McClain, Charles J., Jr. "The Chinese Struggle for Civil Rights in Nineteenth Century America: The First Phase, 1850–1870." *California Law Review* 72 (July 1974): 529–68.

McClain, Charles J., and Laurene Wu McClain. "The Chinese Contribution to the Development of American Law." In *Entry Denied: Exclusion and the Chinese Community in America, 1882–1943*, ed. Sucheng Chan, 3–24. Philadelphia: Temple University Press, 1991.

Magnaghi, Russell M. "Virginia City's Chinese Community, 1860–1880." *Nevada Historical Society Quarterly* 24 (Summer 1981): 130–57.

Mann, Ralph. "Frontier Opportunity and the New Social History." *Pacific Historical Review* 53 (November 1984): 463–91.

Mei, June. "Socioeconomic Origins of Emigration: Guangdong to California, 1850–1882." In *Labor Immigration Under Capitalism*, eds. Lucie Cheng and Edna Bonacich, 219–45. Berkeley: University of California Press, 1984.

Miller, Ronald D. "Hell's Belles." *Brandbook: Los Angeles Corral of Westerners* 12 (1965): 155–65.

Murphy, Mary. "The Private Lives of Public Women: Prostitution in Butte, Montana, 1878–1917." In *The Women's West*, eds. Susan Armitage and Elizabeth Jameson, 192–205. Norman: University of Oklahoma Press, 1987.

North, Hart H. "Chinese Highbinder Societies in California." *California Historical Society Quarterly* 27 (March 1948): 19–31.

"The Old Oriental Warehouse in San Francisco." *Bulletin of the Chinese Historical Society of America* 25 (November 1990): 1–3.

Ong, Paul M. "Chinese Labor in Early San Francisco: Racial Segmentation and Industrial Expansion." *Amerasia Journal* 8, no. 1 (1981): 69–92.

———. "An Ethnic Trade: The Chinese Laundries in Early California." *Journal of Ethnic Studies* 8, no. 4 (1981): 95–113.

Osumi, Megumi Dick. "Asians and California's Anti-Miscegenation Laws." In *Asian and Pacific American Experiences: Women's Perspectives*, ed. Nobuya Tsuchida, 1–37. Minneapolis: University of Minnesota Press, 1982.

Pascoe, Peggy. "Gender Systems in Conflict: The Marriages of Mission-Educated Chinese American Women, 1874–1939." *Journal of Social History* 22 (Summer 1989): 631–52.

Peffer, George Anthony. "Forbidden Families: Emigration Experiences of Chinese Women Under the Page Law, 1875–1882." *Journal of American Ethnic History* 6 (Fall 1986): 28–46.

————. "From Under the Sojourner's Shadow: A Historiographical Study of Chinese Female Immigration to America, 1852–1882." *Journal of American Ethnic History* 11 (Spring 1992): 41–67.

Penfield, Janet Harbison. "Women in the Presbyterian Church — An Historical Overview." *Journal of Presbyterian History* 55, no. 2 (1977): 107–23.

Peterson, David. "Wife Beating: An American Tradition." *Journal of Interdisciplinary History* 23 (Summer 1992): 97–118.

Petrik, Paula. "Capitalists with Rooms: Prostitution in Helena, Montana, 1865–1900." *Montana: The Magazine of Western History* 31 (Spring 1981): 28–41.

Riegel, Robert E. "Changing American Attitudes Toward Prostitution (1800–1920)." *Journal of the History of Ideas* 29 (July/September 1968): 437–52.

Richardson, James F. "The Police in the City: A History." In *The Urban Experience: Themes in American History*, eds. Raymond A. Mohl and James F. Richardson, 164–81. Belmont, Calif.: Wadsworth, 1973.

Riley, Glenda. "American Daughters: Black Women in the West." *Montana: The Magazine of Western History* 38 (Spring 1988): 14–27.

Rodecape, Lois. "Celestial Drama in the Golden Hills: The Chinese Theatre in California, 1849–1869." *California Historical Society Quarterly* 23 (June 1944): 97–116.

Rohe, Randall E. "After the Gold Rush: Chinese Mining in the Far West, 1850–1890." *Montana: The Magazine of Western History* 32 (Autumn 1980): 2–19.

Rosenberg, Caroll-Smith, and Charles Rosenberg. "The Female Animal: Medical and Biological Views of Woman and Her Role in Nineteenth-Century America." *Journal of American History* 60 (September 1973): 332–56.

Schneider, John C. "Public Order and the Geography of the City: Crime, Violence, and the Police in Detroit, 1845–1875." *Journal of Urban History* 4 (February 1978): 183–206.

Schwendinger, Robert J. "Chinese Sailors: America's Invisible Merchant Marine, 1876–1906." *California History* 57 (Spring 1978): 58–69.

———. "Investigating Chinese Immigrant Ships and Sailors." In *The Chinese American Experience*, ed. Genny Lim, 16–25. San Francisco: Chinese Historical Society of America and Chinese Culture Center, 1984.

Seager, Robert, II. "Some Denominational Reactions to Chinese Immigration to California, 1856–1892." *Pacific Historical Review* 28 (1959): 49–66.

Sheridan, Mary E. and Janet W. Salaff. "Introduction." In *Lives: Chinese Working Women*, eds. Mary E. Sheridan and Janet W. Salaff, 1–10. Bloomington: Indiana University Press, 1984.

Shumsky, Neil Larry. "Tacit Acceptance: Respectable Americans and Segregated Prostitution, 1870–1910." *Journal of Social History* 19 (Summer 1986): 665–79.

Shumsky, Neil Larry, and Larry M. Springer. "San Francisco's Zone of Prostitution, 1880–1934." *Journal of Historical Geography* 7, no. 1 (1981): 71–89.

Soong Ching-ling. "Women's Liberation." In *Women in China: Studies in Social Change and Feminism*, ed. Marilyn B. Young, 201–4. Ann Arbor: Center for Chinese Studies, University of Michigan, 1973.

Spoehr, Luther W. "Sambo and the Heathen Chinee: Californians' Racial Stereotypes in the Late 1870s." *Pacific Historical Review* 42 (May 1973): 185–204.

Stahler, Michael L. "William Speer: Champion of California's Chinese, 1852–1857." *Journal of Presbyterian History* 48 (Summer 1970): 113–29.

Stephens, John W. "A Quantitative History of Chinatown, San Francisco, 1870 and 1880." In *The Life, Influence, and the Role of the Chinese in the United States, 1776–1960*, 71–88. San Francisco: Chinese Historical Society of America, 1976.

Swartout, Robert R., Jr. "Kwangtung to Big Sky: The Chinese in Montana, 1864–1900." *Montana: The Magazine of Western History* 38 (Winter 1988): 42–53.

Tachibana, Judy M. "Outwitting the Whites: One Image of the Chinese in California Fiction and Poetry, 1849–1924." *Southern California Quarterly* 61 (Winter 1979): 379–89.

Tang, Vincente. "Chinese Women Immigrants and the Two-Edged Sword of Habeas Corpus." In *The Chinese American Experience*, ed. Genny Lim, 48–56. San Francisco: Chinese Historical Society of America and Chinese Culture Center, 1984.

Tilly, Charles. "Collective Violence in European Perspective." In *Violence in America*, eds. Hugh Davis Graham and Ted Robert Gurr, 4–45. Beverly Hills, Calif.: Sage, 1979.

Tipton, Gary P. "Men Out of China: Origins of the Chinese Colony in Phoenix." *Journal of Arizona History* 18 (Autumn 1977): 341–56.

Topley, Marjorie. "Marriage Resistance in Rural Kwangtung." In *Women in Chinese Society*, eds. Margery Wolf and Roxane Witke, 67–88. Stanford: Stanford University Press, 1975.

Tragen, Irving G. "Statutory Prohibitions Against Interracial Marriage." *California Law Review* 32 (1944): 269–80.

Trauner, Joan B. "The Chinese as Medical Scapegoats in San Francisco, 1870–1905." *California History* 57 (Spring 1978): 70–87.

Tylor, Peter L. "'Denied the Power to Choose the Good': Sexuality and Mental Defect in American Medical Practice, 1850–1920." *Journal of Social History* 10 (June 1977): 472–85.

Wade, Richard C. "Violence in the Cities: A Historical View." In *Cities in American History*, eds. Kenneth Jackson and Stanley K. Schultz, 475–91. New York: Knopf, 1972.

Weinstein, Robert A. "North from Panama, West to the Orient: The Pacific Mail Steamship Company." *California History* 57 (Spring 1978): 46–57.

Welter, Barbara. "The Cult of True Womanhood, 1820–1860." *American Quarterly* 18 (Summer 1966): 151–74.

West, Elliot. "Scarlet West: The Oldest Profession in the Trans-Mississippi West." *Montana: The Magazine of Western History* 31 (Spring 1981): 16–27.

Wolf, Margery. "Women and Suicide in China." In *Women in Chinese Society*, eds. Margery Wolf and Roxane Witke, 111–41. Stanford: Stanford University Press, 1975.

Yu, Connie Young. "A History of San Francisco Chinatown Housing." *Amerasia Journal* 8, no. 1 (1981): 93–110.

Yung, Judy. "The Social Awakening of Chinese American Women as Reported in *Chung Sai Yat Po*, 1900–1911." In *Chinese America: History and Perspectives 1988*, 80–102. San Francisco: Chinese Historical Society of America, 1988.

BOOKS

Anderson, Margo. *The American Census: A Social History*. New Haven: Yale University Press, 1988.

Armentrout-Ma, Eve L. *Revolutionaries, Monarchists, and Chinatowns: Chinese Politics in the Americas and the 1911 Revolution*. Honolulu: University of Hawaii Press, 1990.

Asbury, Herbert. *The Barbary Coast*. New York: Garden City Publishing, 1933.

Ayscough, Florence. *Chinese Women: Yesterday and Today*. Shanghai: Modern Books, 1930.

Barnhart, Jacqueline Baker. *The Fair but Frail: Prostitu-*

tion in San Francisco, 1849–1900. Reno: University of Nevada Press, 1986.

Barth, Gunther. *Bitter Strength: A History of the Chinese in the United States, 1850–1870*. Cambridge: Harvard University Press, 1964.

———. *Instant Cities: Urbanization and the Rise of San Francisco and Denver*. New York: Oxford University Press, 1975.

Becker, Jules. *The Course of Exclusion, 1882–1924: San Francisco Newspaper Coverage of the Chinese and Japanese in the United States*. San Francisco: Mellen Research University Press, 1991.

Boyer, Paul. *Urban Masses and Moral Order in America, 1820–1920*. Cambridge: Harvard University Press, 1978.

Butler, Anne M. *Daughters of Joy, Sisters of Misery: Prostitutes in the American West, 1865–1890*. Urbana: University of Illinois Press, 1985.

Cain, Ella. *The Story of Bodie*. San Francisco: Fearon Publishers, 1956.

Carter, Helen Virginia. *The History of San Francisco's Chinatown*. San Francisco: R & E Research Associates, 1974.

Chan, Anthony. *Gold Mountain: The Chinese in the New World*. Vancouver: New Star Books, 1983.

Chan, Sucheng. *Asian Americans: An Interpretive History*. Boston: Twayne Publishers, 1991.

———. *This Bittersweet Soil: The Chinese in California Agriculture, 1860–1910*. Berkeley: University of California Press, 1986.

Chinese Hospital, San Francisco. *Chinese Hospital Medica Staff Archives, 1978–1981*. San Francisco: Chinese Hospital, 1981.

Chinn, Thomas W., Him Mark Lai, and Phillip P. Choy, eds. *A History of the Chinese in California: A Syllabus*. San Francisco: Chinese Historical Society of America, 1969.

Connelly, Mark Thomas. *The Response to Prostitution*

in the Progressive Era. Chapel Hill: University of North Carolina Press, 1980.

Coolidge, Mary Roberts. *Chinese Immigration*. New York: Henry Holt, 1909.

Courtney, William J. *San Francisco's Anti-Chinese Ordinances, 1850–1900*. San Francisco: R & E Research Associates, 1974.

Croll, Elisabeth. *Wise Daughters from Foreign Lands: European Women Writers in China*. London: Pandora Press, 1989.

Daniels, Roger. *Asian America: Chinese and Japanese in the United States Since 1850*. Seattle: University of Washington Press, 1988.

Davis, Lawrence B. *Immigrants, Baptists, and the Protestant Mind in America*. Urbana: University of Illinois Press, 1973.

de Reincourt, Amaury. *Sex and Power in History*. New York: D. McKay, 1974.

Dillon, Richard H. *The Hatchet Men*. Sausalito, Calif.: Comstock, 1962.

Dobie, Charles Caldwell. *San Francisco: A Pageant*. New York: D. Appleton, 1933.

Dykstra, Robert R. *The Cattle Towns*. New York: Knopf, 1968.

Elsensohn, Sister M. Alfreda. *Idaho Chinese Lore*. Cottonwood: Idaho Corporation of Benedictine Sisters, 1971.

Friedman, Lawrence, and Robert V. Percival. *The Roots of Justice: Riots and Punishments in Alameda County, California, 1870–1910*. Chapel Hill: University of North Carolina Press, 1981.

Gamson, William A. *The Strategy of Social Protest*. Homewood, Ill.: Dorsey, 1975.

Gentry, Curt. *The Madams of San Francisco*. Garden City, N.Y.: Doubleday, 1954.

Gillenkirk, Jeff, and James Motlow. *Bitter Melon: Stories from the Last Rural Chinese Town in America*. Seattle: University of Washington Press, 1987.

Goldman, Eric. *Rendezvous with Destiny*. New York: Knopf, 1972.

Goldman, Marion. *Gold Diggers and Silver Miners: Prostitution and Social Life on the Comstock Lode*. Ann Arbor: University of Michigan Press, 1981.

Gordon, Linda. *U.S. Women's History*. New American History Series, ed. Eric Foner. Washington, D.C.: American Historical Association, 1990.

Grittner, Frederick K. *White Slavery: Myth, Ideology, and American Law*. New York: Garland Publishing, 1990.

Gronewold, Sue. *Beautiful Merchandise: Prostitution in China, 1860–1936*. New York: Haworth Press, 1982.

Harris, Henry. *California's Medical Story*. Springfield, Ill.: Grabhorn Press, 1932.

Henriques, Fernando. *Prostitution and Society: A Survey*. New York: Citadel Press, 1963.

Hill, Patricia R. *The World Their Household: The American Woman's Foreign Mission Movement and Cultural Transformation, 1870–1920*. Ann Arbor: University of Michigan Press, 1985.

Ho Ping-ti. *Studies on the Population of China, 1368–1953*. Cambridge: Harvard University Press, 1959.

Hollon, W. Eugene. *Frontier Violence: Another Look*. New York: Oxford University Press, 1974.

Hsu, Francis L. K. *The Challenge of the American Dream: The Chinese in the United States*. Belmont, Calif.: Wadsworth Publishing, 1971.

Hsu, Immanuel C. Y. *The Rise of Modern China*. New York: Oxford University Press, 1983.

Issel, William, and Robert I. Cherny. *San Francisco, 1865–932: Politics, Power, and Urban Development*. Berkeley: University of California Press, 1986.

Jacobs, Paul, Saul Landau, and Eve Pell. *To Serve the Devil: Colonials and Sojourners*. New York: Vintage Books, 1971.

Jaschok, Maria. *Concubines and Bondservants: The So-*

cial History of a Chinese Custom. London: Zed
Books, 1989.

Johnson, Kay Ann. *Women, the Family, and Peasant
Revolution in China.* Chicago: University of Chicago Press, 1983.

Jordan, Philip D. *Frontier Law and Order: Ten Essays.*
Lincoln: University of Nebraska Press, 1970.

Kasson, John F. *Rudeness and Civility: Manners in Nineteenth-Century Urban America.* New York: Hill &
Wang, 1990.

Kristeva, Julia. *About Chinese Women.* Translated by
Anita Barrows. London: Marion Boyars, 1974.

Lai, Him Mark, and Phillip P. Choy. *History of the Chinese in America.* San Francisco: H. M. Lai & P. P.
Choy, 1971.

Lai, Him Mark, Joe Huang, and Don Wong. *The Chinese
of America, 1785–1980.* San Francisco: Chinese Culture Center, 1980.

Lane, Roger. *Policing the City: Boston, 1822–1885.* New
York: Atheneum Books, 1977.

Larsen, Lawrence H. *The Urban West at the End of the
Frontier.* Lawrence: Regents Press of Kansas, 1978.

Lee, Moon L. *Cathay in Eldorado: The Chinese in California.* Weaverville: California Book Club, 1972.

Lee, Rose Hum. *The Growth and Decline of Chinese
Communities in the Rocky Mountain Region.* New
York: Arno Press, 1978.

Lerner, Gerda, ed. *The Female Experience: An American
Documentary.* Indianapolis: Bobbs-Merrill, 1977.

Limerick, Patricia Nelson. *The Legacy of Conquest: The
Unbroken Past of the American West.* New York: W.
W. Norton, 1987.

Ling, Amy. *Between Worlds: Women Writers of Chinese
Ancestry.* New York: Pergamon Press, 1990.

Lister, Florence C., and Robert H. Lister. *The Chinese of
Early Tucson: Historic Archaeology from the Tucson Urban Renewal Project.* Tucson: University of
Arizona Press, 1989.

Logan, Lorna E. *Ventures in Mission: The Cameron House Story*. Castro Valley, Calif.: Lorna E. Logan, 1976.

Longstreet, Stephen. *The Wilder Shore*. Garden City, N.Y.: Doubleday, 1968.

Lotchin, Roger W. *San Francisco, 1846–1856: From Hamlet to City*. New York: Oxford University Press, 1974.

Low, Victor. *The Unimpressible Race: A Century of Educational Struggle by the Chinese in San Francisco*. San Francisco: East/West 1982.

McDonald, Douglas. *The Legend of Julia Bulette and the Red Light Ladies of Nevada*. Las Vegas: Stanley Paher, 1983.

McGarth, Roger D. *Gunfighters, Highwaymen, and Vigilantes: Violence on the Frontier*. Berkeley: University of California Press, 1984.

Mark, Diane Mei Lin, and Ginger Chih. *A Place Called America*. San Francisco: Organization of Chinese Americans, 1982.

Martin, C. Y. *Whiskey and Wild Women*. New York: Hart Publishing, 1974.

Martin, Mildred Crowl. *Chinatown's Angry Angel: The Story of Donaldina Cameron*. Palo Alto, Calif.: Pacific Books, 1977.

Mau, Laurence Dicker. *The Chinese in San Francisco: A Pictorial History*. New York: Dover Publications, 1979.

Minke, Pauline. *Chinese in the Mother Lode*. San Francisco: R & E Research Associates, 1974.

Minnick, Sylvia Sun. *Sam Fow: The San Joaquin Chinese Legacy*. Fresno, Calif.: Panorama Publishing, 1988.

Monkkonen, Eric H. *Police in Urban America, 1860–1920*. Cambridge: Cambridge University Press, 1981.

Nee, Victor G., and Brett de Bary Nee. *Longtime Californ': A Documentary Study of an American Chinatown*. New York: Pantheon Books, 1972.

O'Hara, Albert Richard. *The Position of Woman in Early China*. Washington, D.C.: Catholic University of

America Press, 1945; repr., Westport, Conn.: Hyperion Press, 1981.

Ono Kazuko. *Chinese Women in a Century of Revolution, 1850–1950.* Translated by Joshua A. Fogel and others. Stanford: Stanford University Press, 1978.

Pascoe, Peggy. *Relations of Rescue: The Search for Female Moral Authority in the American West, 1874–1939.* New York: Oxford University Press, 1990.

Paul, Rodman Wilson. *Mining Frontiers of the Far West, 1848–1880.* New York: Holt, Rinehart & Winston, 1963.

Perrin, Linda. *Coming to America: Immigrants from the Far East.* New York: Delacorte Press, 1980.

Peterson, F. Ross. *Idaho: A Bicentennial History.* New York: W. W. Norton, 1976.

Prassel, Frank. *The Western Peace Officer: A Legacy of Law and Order.* Norman: University of Oklahoma Press, 1972.

Read, Jay Marion, and Mary E. Mathes. *The History of the San Francisco Medical Society, 1850–1900.* 2 vols. San Francisco: San Francisco Medical Society, 1958.

Reynolds, Helen. *The Economics of Prostitution.* Springfield, Ill.: Charles C. Thomas, 1986.

Richardson, James F. *Urban Police in the United States.* Port Washington, N.Y.: Kennikat Press, 1974.

Riddle, Ronald. *Flying Dragons, Flowing Streams: Music in the Life of San Francisco's Chinese.* Westport, Conn.: Greenwood Press, 1983.

Rosen, Ruth. *The Lost Sisterhood: Prostitution in America, 1900–1918.* Baltimore: Johns Hopkins University Press, 1982.

Rothman, Sheila A. *Woman's Proper Place.* New York: Basic Books, 1978.

Sandmeyer, Elmer C. *The Anti-Chinese Movement in California.* Berkeley: University of California Press, 1939.

Schwendinger, Robert J. *Ocean of Bitter Dreams: Maritime Relations Between China and the United States, 1850–1915.* Tucson: Westernlore Press, 1988.

Spence, Jonathan D. *The Search for Modern China.* New York: W. W. Norton, 1990.

Stacey, Judith. *Patriarchy and Socialist Revolution in China.* Berkeley: University of California Press, 1983.

Steiner, Stan. *Fushang: The Chinese Who Built America.* New York: Harper & Row, 1979.

Takaki, Ronald. *Strangers from a Different Shore.* Boston: Little, Brown, 1989; New York: Penguin Books, 1990.

Tannahill, Reay. *Sex in History.* New York: Stein & Day, 1980.

Tsai, Henry Shih-shan. *China and the Overseas Chinese in the United States, 1868–1911.* Fayetteville: University of Arkansas Press, 1983.

———. *The Chinese Experience in America.* Bloomington: Indiana University Press, 1986.

Wei Min She Labor Committee. *Chinese Working People in America: A Pictorial History.* San Francisco: United Front Press, 1974.

Weisberg, D. Kelly. *Children of the Night: A Study of Adolescent Prostitution.* Lexington, Mass.: D. C. Heath, 1985.

White, Richard. *It's Your Misfortune and None of My Own: A History of the American West.* Norman: University of Oklahoma Press, 1991.

Wilson, Carol Green. *Chinatown Quest: The Life Adventures of Donaldina Cameron.* Stanford: Stanford University Press, 1950.

Wolf, Arthur P., and Huang Chieh-shan. *Marriage and Adoption in China, 1845–1945.* Stanford: Stanford University Press, 1980.

Wong, H. K. *Gum Sahn Yun: Gold Mountain Men.* n.p.: for the author, 1987.

Wu Cheng-tsu, ed. *Chink! A Documentary History of Anti-Chinese Prejudice in America.* New York: World Publishing, 1972.

Wu, William F. *The Yellow Peril: Chinese Americans in American Fiction, 1850–1940.* Hamden, Conn.: Archon Books, 1984.

Young, Marilyn B., ed. *Women in China: Studies in Social Change and Feminism*. Ann Arbor: Center for Chinese Studies, University of Michigan, 1973.

Yung, Judy. *Chinese Women of America: A Pictorial History*. Seattle: University of Washington Press, 1986.

MISCELLANEOUS

California State Automobile Association. *A Map of San Francisco*. San Francisco: California State Automobile Association, 1979.

Loewenstein, Louis K. *Streets of San Francisco: The Origins of Street and Place Names*. San Francisco: Lexikos, 1984.

Index